Urban Principal:
Leadership Lessons

Bret Allan Anderson

BookLocker

Trenton, Georgia

Print ISBN: 978-1-958891-92-6
Ebook ISBN: 979-8-88531-668-2

Published by BookLocker.com, Inc., Trenton, Georgia.

BookLocker.com, Inc.
2024

First Edition

Library of Congress Cataloguing in Publication Data
Anderson, Bret Allan
Urban Principal: Leadership Lessons by Bret Allan Anderson
Library of Congress Control Number: 2023923371

DISCLAIMER

This book details the author's personal experiences with and opinions about health. The author is not a licensed medical professional.

The author and publisher are providing this book and its contents on an "as is" basis and make no representations or warranties of any kind with respect to this book or its contents. The author and publisher disclaim all such representations and warranties, including for example warranties of merchantability and medical advice for a particular purpose. In addition, the author and publisher do not represent or warrant that the information accessible via this book is accurate, complete or current.

The statements made about products and services have not been evaluated by the U.S. government. Please consult with your own legal, accounting, medical, or other licensed professional regarding the suggestions and recommendations made in this book.

Except as specifically stated in this book, neither the author or publisher, nor any authors, contributors, or other representatives will be liable for damages arising out of or in connection with the use of this book. This is a comprehensive limitation of liability that applies to all damages of any kind, including (without limitation) compensatory; direct, indirect or consequential damages; loss of data, income or profit; loss of or damage to property and claims of third parties.

You understand that this book is not intended as a substitute for consultation with a licensed medical, legal or accounting professional. Before you begin any change to your lifestyle in any way, you will consult a licensed professional to ensure that you are doing what's best for your situation.

This book provides content related to medical topics. As such, use of this book implies your acceptance of this disclaimer.

Testimonials and What People Are Saying About Bret Anderson

"I have known Bret for the three years I have been assigned to the Southeast Precinct. As the principal of Indian Hill School, he has had to deal with extraordinary problems relating to safety. He has dealt with neighborhood violence, shots fired near the school, trespassers, drug dealers, and graffiti. His influence has created a zone of safety not only in his assigned school, but in the neighborhood surrounding the school as well. Drug dealers have lined some streets that children had to walk on their way home. The drug dealers had been kicked out of the nearby public housing development and had to move to locations closer to school. Bret actually escorts his students past these areas until they are safely home. This is far beyond the requirements of his job, yet he does it anyway. Working with police, he reported up-to-date information that helped focus police efforts on eliminating the drug dealing…I've found Bret working long after one would think he should have gone home. During all this, he has maintained a positive, forward-thinking attitude. Bret opens Indian Hill School for neighborhood meetings and participates actively in the South Omaha Project Impact Working Team. This team is comprised of police, government, and community leaders, and develops strategies to improve the neighborhood. Bret helped conceive and lead initiatives such as Meet the Challenge - Know Your Neighbors and South Omaha Impact Walking the Talk. These initiatives allowed law-abiding residents to set the tone and helped to replace drug activity and violent crime with a much healthier neighborhood atmosphere. Bret's commitment to the Indian Hill neighborhood is well known and has been extremely effective."

Mark Sundermeier (2002)
Former Southeast Precinct Captain, Community & School Supporter
Omaha Police Department

"I have known Mr. Anderson personally and professionally for nearly 20 years. I met him while I was working for the Omaha Police Department, and he was principal at Indian Hill Elementary School. We were administering the Police Athletic League recreation program, and I could observe his commitment to his students' personal growth and development. He also had an excellent relationship with his staff, and he was active in the community.

Throughout his 20 years as a Principal, Mr. Anderson has distinguished himself as an administrator and leader, and he has been an exceptional representative of the Omaha Public Schools (OPS) District. He has led the Wilson Focus School since its inception, which has become a model program for the Douglas - Sarpy County Learning Community. He has earned the respect of his peers and colleagues, and he has coached and mentored several current OPS administrators."

Thomas H. Warren, Sr. (2017)
Chief of Staff for City of Omaha; Former President/CEO Urban
League of Nebraska; Omaha Chief of Police

"Bret's training was inspiring and really helped to set the positive tone for the year. It meshed perfectly with the philosophy that we are creating here at Walnut Hill. To hear Bret speak about his experiences and to learn how he applied strategies to real-life situations was not only helpful but left us wanting more. Thank you Bret for sharing your expertise and knowledge with us!"

Nikki Longlee (2022)
Principal, Walnut Hill Elementary; Former Assistant Principal,
Gateway and Saddlebrook Elementary Schools;
Teacher, Indian Hill, Omaha Public Schools

"As the counselor of the school, I have worked with Mr. Anderson closely and have found him to be the epitome of what a prominent leader is. His vision for the school has been embraced by the staff, parents and students. He is consistently affirming of staff, parents and students; yet can step in and effectively coach staff, parents and students when the situation necessitates it. He has an open door policy which is inviting and ensures that small problems are resolved before turning into larger ones. The staff, parents and students trust him and truly work as a team.

He is inspirational in the manner in which he manages the school functioning. He is always calm, positive, and organized. This creates a school culture that is safe and confident. His high expectations of appropriate behavior and academic success, backed by a solid foundation of research, have resulted in a respectful school climate and higher test scores each year. He effectively achieves short and long term goals for Wilson Focus School. His expertise is also exhibited in the many requests for his participation on Omaha Public Schools boards, district-wide school coaching opportunities, and mentoring involvement. He is a recognized outstanding leader in the district."

Pam Schiffbauer, Ed. D. (2019)
School Counselor, Wilson Focus School, Omaha Public Schools;
Former Principal in Parochial School

"Thank you for allowing your students from Wilson Focus Elementary School to be involved in the City of Omaha's MLK celebration. Events like this that bring the city together to celebrate our common American heritage are a great example of what makes Omaha a great place to live, work and play. I deeply appreciate your help in making MLK Day a huge success in our city.

As a civic leader who understands the value of a quality education for every child, I am very proud of the reputation for academic excellence that Wilson Focus Elementary School has earned under your leadership. In particular, I congratulate you and the rest of the Wilson Focus community for your technology program recently being recognized as an Apple Distinguished Program. Once again, thank you for joining us at Omaha's MLK celebration and for all the hard work that you do to make your school a leader in public education in our great city."

Jim Suttle (2013)
Mayor, City of Omaha

"I am elated to tell you that I will be the Principal at Lewis & Clark Elementary in Council Bluffs next year. It is a small building that will be going into Behavior Support Programs next year. When I look back on my educational journey, you were such a foundation for me. Your passion and desire to constantly improve gave me a solid model to follow. You were and continue to be a principal that guides with creativity, care and concern for all students. Thank you for being there for me when I began my teaching career. Thank you for believing in me to hire me on after I student taught under you. Thank you for giving me a chance at the counselor position when I had zero experience. Thank you for letting me in and allowing me to support the leadership team while I was at Indian Hill. Thank you for your support when I married Tim and started my life with him. Thank you for supporting me even when I no longer worked under you!!! Thank you. Thank you. Thank you!"

Teresa Hamilton (2017)
Principal, Carter Lake and Lewis & Clark Elementary Schools,
Council Bluffs Community Schools; Former Assistant Principal,
Former Counselor; Teacher; Student Teacher, Indian Hill
Elementary School, Omaha Public Schools

"Bret Anderson is one of the finest principals I have had the pleasure of working with in my career. He genuinely cares about students and staff. He is highly visible and interacts with both students and staff each day. He knows the students by name and interests. He is always there for staff. It is a joy to work in an environment like Wilson Focus School. He is fantastic!"

Teacher Comment from District Climate Survey (2017)

"You have made such an empowering positive influence on so many people through creating a one-of-a-kind school. I am one of those who are grateful for all that you have taught me. You are the best, hands down."

Scott Hilger (2019)
Assistant Principal, Highland Elementary School;
Former Teacher, Wilson Focus School, Omaha Public Schools

"Hi Bret! You have been instrumental in my development and approach to being a principal. The Gordon book you gifted me was a great resource for me to refer to as I developed my why regarding the principalship. I've never forgotten it! You will be missed but never forgotten!"

Glenn Mitchell (2019)
Principal, Harrison Elementary School;
Former Principal, Jesuit Academy; Assistant Principal, Creighton
Preparatory School; Teacher, Wilson Focus School,
Omaha Public Schools

"Mr. Anderson, I would like to thank you for being willing to come to Belvedere (referring to subbing for a principal). Although I know the school is challenging, you have come in ready to take the bull by the horn. Greatly appreciated! If I can assist in anyway, please let me know."

Salema Stewart-Hunter (2019)
Provisionally Licensed Mental Health Practitioner, Behavioral
Health Advocate
Belvedere Elementary School, Omaha Public Schools

"You have grown and mentored so many leaders in this district! You are so knowledgeable, levelheaded, and can see the bigger picture. You have always known how to work collaboratively with all building staff, district, and community members. You get things done and don't rely on what has always been done before. I remember the time at Indian Hill, from the beginning, and watched you turn that place around and build back the trust of the teachers, students and neighborhood."

Melissa Schroeder (2014)
Instructional Research Administrator, Former Elementary
Curriculum Consultant; Instructional Facilitator; Teacher,
Indian Hill Elementary School, Omaha Public Schools

"Wilson is such an impressive school, and I am happy that we can be a part of your success…by speaking out and educating the community, we can work to make a stronger majority. Thank you for taking the lead and showing all of us how to create a No Place for Hate school."

Jessica Gall (2012)
Senior Associate Regional Director of the Anti-Defamation League
(ADL) of Midwest, Former ADL/Community Relations Committee
(CRC) Plains States Education Director

"…Wilson has featured strong leadership, high performing teachers, extensive enrichment opportunities, and an intense focus on technology and leadership, including laptops for every student and a student-run television studio. Most encouragingly, the students have achieved great results in reading, math and science…."

"…On behalf of the Empowerment Network and our community partners, we want to thank you for your outstanding presentations this past Saturday at our monthly community meeting. The insights you provided were encouraging, inspiring and challenging. Hopefully, you could sense how well the audience received your comments. We all took extensive notes that we will report back to our various organizations and partners. Our goal is to see the pace of innovation accelerated throughout OPS. We appreciate all of you dedicating your Saturday morning to helping us gain more insights on your models for success. We look forward to working with each of you. And thank you for the work you do every single day to EMPOWER students, families, teachers and the entire community."

Willie Barney (2015-2016)
CEO, Empowerment Network, Former Focus School Parent,
President & Co-Publisher Revive Magazine, Civic
Leader/Community Advocate

"I have had the privilege to call Mr. Anderson my colleague for the past 13 years. During this time, I have served on various committees with Mr. Anderson. He is always a leader, offering suggestions and new ideas. I am aware of the great work he has done as Principal of Indian Hill Elementary and in his position as the Principal of Wilson Focus School. In his tenure at Wilson Focus, he has "broken the mold" extending both the school day and school year along with partnering with a large number of agencies and adapting new ideas to engage students. In each venue, Mr. Anderson shares his passion and continuously takes on new challenges. He advocates for both students and staff and is the type of administrator colleagues seek out. Mr. Anderson is a hardworking individual who always puts students first. He reflects a true instructional leader. He leads professional development and seeks out best practices to increase academic excellence in each school he has led. He is a visionary leader who is not afraid to think outside the box. Mr. Anderson's tenacity to achieve academic success for each student, along with innovation, are areas that make him well respected by many colleagues. "

Susan M. Aguilera-Robles (2017)
Associate Director of Program Development at Buffett Early
Childhood Institute; Former Community Relations, Outreach
Coordinator, City of Omaha; Principal, Spring Lake Magnet Center,
Omaha Public Schools

"Bret Anderson is a high-quality administrator and educator. He has an incredible working relationship with his impressive teaching staff and is one of the best conflict resolution experts I have seen. We had a particular issue with one of the teachers and he helped resolve it very quickly."

Parent Comment from District Climate Survey (2017)

"Experience is the hardest kind of teacher. It gives you the test first and the lesson afterward."

— *Oscar Wilde*

Dedication

I dedicate this book to all the administrators, especially principals, leaders and staff who are working so hard daily, staying the course in the trenches, to provide the best education possible for our children. Finally, I dedicate this book to my wife, Ingra Winkler Anderson, a talented writer, editor, graphic artist, marketer, and public relations expert. We have completed many projects together! She's been my supporter and partner in life and has advocated for me throughout my career.

Acknowledgements

I would like to thank everyone who has helped to make me the person I am. There are many people—too many to mention—who have shaped me and affected my life. I included some in this book, but there are many more people who played a role and may not be listed. I am grateful to all those who have affected my life and career trajectory. I appreciate all the support, kindness, love, friendship, mentoring and growth that people have given me. Let's continue to pass this on to future generations. If you have been one of those people, Thank You!

Putting This Book to Use

This book provides lessons I have learned in more than 31 years as an educator and administrator. I do not profess to be an outstanding writer, but I *have* been recognized as an excellent leader, and have a desire to pass this knowledge on to others in the field. I want to help improve education. Many would have created multiple books, whereas I compiled a great deal of information into one edition. I have documented my journey, including stories and experiences that shaped my ability as I became an effective leader. I have a strong passion for leadership and developing other effective leaders, and know every new leader is hungry for tips to be successful. Everyone has their own style in how they process and learn from a book. I like to highlight books as I read, especially points of interest or things I can use. I often use index cards, Post-its, or tab markers for certain pages to which I may want to refer in the future. For example, there is a section on Sharing Lessons Learned (Chapter 22), that can be a quick reference of useful tips. Staff members can use the positive behavior intervention support chapters to talk about behavior and working with children. Many of the chapters encourage discussion and contain self-reflection tools. At the very end is a list of useful resources. Being a principal is a multi-faceted, challenging job. This book's leadership practices apply to all leaders, regardless of their field. Wherever you are on your journey, my hope is this book will start you thinking, questioning, and moving you forward toward positive growth.

Contents

"Do not go where the path may lead, go instead where there is no path and leave a trail."

— Ralph Waldo Emerson

Introduction

There will always be a need for excellent school leaders. The role of the principal, specifically, is demanding and encompasses a wide range of skills. We need more support for those serving in this role. Building leadership capacity is where my heart lies and why I wrote this book. I have 31 years of experience as an educator and administrator--21 of which were as a principal. I can offer support to other leaders based on this experience.

The Omaha Public School System (OPS) has over 51,000 students and is a diverse urban district, with almost 40,000 in poverty--the highest percentage in the state. Over 9,000 students make up the average special education population. There are over 11,000 English Language Learners, including 2,200 refugees. The district also serves students of 107 different languages. The urban population in this midwest state faces many challenges that people don't realize.

Anyone in a leadership position can learn effective practices from this book, although it is largely aimed at education leaders. After retiring as a principal from an innovative school, I offer practical tools to principals through consulting. There is an ever-increasing need for principal support and the development of leadership capacity. As a principal, I became a problem-solver and coach, a mentor developing leaders along the way. This is my genuine passion, and an area in which most districts could do a much better job. The principal's role is critical in the success of a building or organization, and effective

1

leadership is key. Many consultants don't have enough experience as principals before going to central office roles. People listen better to those who have experience in their role and have a lot of knowledge.

As a new administrator, my first role was in a large facility with mostly low-income students (89%), ranging from pre-K to 6th grade, and an enrollment of 675. We reduced the school's mobility rate from 59% to 39%. The academics were low, and this was an area we would change as well. This became my home for 10 years—one year as an assistant principal and the rest as the principal. This experience was a perfect way to hone my skills and develop successful leadership techniques. That introductory quote by Ralph Waldo Emerson eventually became one of my mantras, and found its way onto the wall in the Focus School I later helped create. Experience truly matters, and it is the number one ingredient in shaping effective leadership.

I started my career as an art teacher at McMillan Middle School and King Science Center at Mann (fourth through eighth grade). I taught eight periods a day: four to fourth through sixth graders and four to seventh through eighth graders. It was a grueling day with little plan time as the travel consumed much of it. Luckily, I only had to do it for my first year because I accepted a full-time position at King Science Center the following year and worked there for 10 years. I learned the art of teaching a diverse population of students with many needs. I always looked for ways to do things better and use my strengths. Achiever is one of my top themes of talent in StrengthsFinder (rebranded as the Clifton Strengths Assessment) and a driving force in many of the things I do.

My achiever again kicked in when I began working on my master's degree in administration and supervision. I searched for opportunities to grow and develop leadership skills while teaching. I started devouring leadership books and studied effective leaders. I loved studying what makes people tick and how to lead and motivate them effectively. This became and is still a passion of mine—even a hobby, my wife, Ingra, would say. She has spent the better part of our over 30 years of marriage watching me begin and end most days reading leadership books.

While teaching, I looked for opportunities to grow. I developed a weight-training program for at-risk students, wrote grants and looked for ways to gain experience. My responsibilities included lunch supervision, school committee chairing, district committee membership, and curriculum/test writing. I was a typical, excited, and highly involved teacher. I designed a logo for Positive Peer Culture and led one of these groups, geared at helping students navigate the challenges of middle school.

I created a sculpture for the school at which I taught. The sculpture endeavor was a valuable experience which allowed me to be creative, and lead a project from inception to completion. The sculpture journey began when I heard the Parent Teacher Association (PTA) wanted to purchase a sculpture for the courtyard. I jumped right in with a design, created a set of drawings with specs, and presented my idea to the principal, who approved it. To follow up, I presented to the PTA board to explain my concept, and the proposal was well-accepted. They thought it was a great idea to use an existing teacher in the design of this art element representing the school. They funded the materials, and I received the experience of managing a project—no pay involved, but it helped our school, and I gained experience. My design ended up being a 14-foot modern symbolic rocket going through the clouds, promoting our school's science magnet theme. I crafted the rocket from large metal heavy gauge sheets. I worked with a local welding company—Ace Welding—as we created the sculpture from large templates I made from brown craft paper. They painted it a dark blue, and it is still there today, symbolizing a science theme in the school courtyard. We completed it in 1990 and you can see it at King Science Center at Mann.

Once your principal knows you are interested in developing as a leader, they often assign duties to help you gain experience and growth. This is especially true if he or she is an active developer of leaders, secure in their own leadership and willing to mentor and support your advancement. Some people are insecure or controlling, which is not helpful. Abraham Lincoln reinforces this point by saying, "All men can stand adversity, but if you want to test a man's character, give him power."

I continued to develop from a variety of opportunities. I took part in two college practicum sessions, shadowing excellent principals. Through these experiences, I gained insight into the reality of urban education. I sought principals who excelled in overseeing finances, managing behavior, and showing strong leadership. Their schools were my classrooms. My goal was to learn the most effective leadership skills I could from them. When I graduated with my advanced degree, I had a master's degree in administration and supervision with a K-12 endorsement. This double-practicum gave me extra experiences and made me more marketable.

I had been in the classroom for three years. I had also taught in a unique summer school program called Creative Connections and was seeking other leadership experiences. Creative Connections was an excellent multi-cultural program focused on a certain culture each summer. It honored me to have worked with a group of very creative educators in this highly effective, well-attended program.

It would still take time before I finally tested my ability as a leader. I applied with our district to become a summer school principal. This role allows an individual with an administrative degree to practice being a principal of a building. While still teaching, I became a summer school principal several times. I improved my leadership skills by problem-solving with staff and small groups of students during summer school. Less staff also meant I had to do most of the work on my own. One of the summer buildings I led ended up having a large hearing-impaired population with it. It was a great experience, and it gave me some wonderful insight that children are children, no matter what abilities they have. They had all the same challenges that simply come with growing up. I learned to work with varying demographics during summer principalships across the city. These experiences gave me solid leadership skills and prepared me for different socio-economic groups.

The principal and assistant principal nominated me for The Leadership Institute. This also put attendees in a pool of potential future school leaders. The assistant principal who nominated me saw my potential, took me under her wing, and encouraged me to continue. When I was a principal, I helped change The Leadership Institute into The Principal Pipeline, which prepares and selects future leaders.

I realize real leadership is difficult. Many people don't want to do what they need to excel and eventually get burned out too soon. It is a pace that never ends, with days that vary and require extreme flexibility, plus emotional intelligence to work with many people. There are far too many individuals addicted to the status quo of just getting by, uninterested in innovation or growth. This is not me (perhaps because of my inner achiever). However, I am not an advocate of change for the sake of change. Show the logic and demonstrate improvement through the data! I have always had a drive to be better, to use my strengths, to shoot for the top—my wife, Ingra, also has the Achiever theme of talent and a similar drive. According to Gallup, people are happiest using their strengths and talents. Therefore, finding the strengths of your staff and looking for ways they can work within these areas will ensure a positive workplace.

They frustrated me when I didn't get interviewed for principal positions, despite my experience as a summer school principal. This can often happen since your plan may not match up with the district plan! I followed the district's typical path to principalship, but I saw others who didn't follow it getting promoted ahead of me. There are often superintendent and human resource changes that can set back knowledge and history. There are politics in every organization, especially large ones, so you must strive to be diligent without getting frustrated.

At Ingra's suggestion, I finally created a portfolio of experience and scheduled a meeting with the superintendent. I remember sitting across from him, showing my resume and portfolio of work, and explaining my target goal of being in a leadership position. I was eager and ready to meet any challenge and eager to make a difference with the children of our district. One question he asked was, "If I gave you the opportunity to turn around a building, would you take it?"

After being an assistant principal for one year, I said I would welcome the challenge and the opportunity to become the principal a year later. Not realizing at this point it usually takes three to five years to make any significant change, I soon found out I had my work cut out for me.

After 10 years and a successful track record, I was honored to be selected from a citywide pool of 36 individuals to start the first focus school of Douglas and Sarpy Counties, where I served 11 years. I had the joy and challenge of creating a school from the ground up. This is something not everyone gets a chance to do, so I realize this was a blessing and a great opportunity.

The focus school was like a magnet concept, with a longer calendar and longer school day. We incorporated many successful practices from my first school into the focus school. I am a firm believer in learning from others and using what really works. As one of my old college professors, Dr. Gary Hartzell, used to say, "The best educators are intellectual thieves!"

We need to continue to find ways of replicating the ideas and concepts that are working well. People often push aside ideas to maintain the status quo because they find it inconvenient to change the current narrative. Outside of technology, we are in an educational system that has hardly changed throughout history. I appreciate the educators who are embracing positive change and making a difference. It is important we continue to strengthen an educational system which encourages and challenges students.

This book is based upon my experiences as a leader and the ways I have found to excel as a principal. I am an avid reader on leadership and have amassed a broad collection of relevant books throughout my career. I'm fascinated with what motivates people, and how to cultivate positivity, creativity and innovation.

I usually have more than one leadership book going. I had someone question me once, asking, "Why are you reading that book—you've already got the job!" My response was, "I want to get better."

The learning and studying never ends if you want to continue to grow effective leadership skills. As a principal, you can't just read educational books. Learn from effective leaders in all fields to improve yourself. Find role models—people who are masters at their craft—and learn from them.

My goal is to help people become better, more effective leaders. As I share from my personal journey, my hope is you will find nuggets of wisdom and helpful tips on which you can expand. While much of this applies to a variety of leadership positions, I truly hope it can help build more effective principals at all school levels. The higher the competence in our school leaders, the better our educational system will become. The principal is key to a school's success. As one of my favorite leadership authors—John Maxwell—says, "Everything rises and falls on leadership."

It's clear I enjoy looking at what effective leaders do, and what their role is in making things better. We cling to familiar methods in education, rather than seeking better options.

Creativity needs to be at the heart of what educators do. There is a quote I have on my computer as a reminder to keep. The quote reads: "Creativity is bound to stir up controversy, because its ultimate impact always is to change the status quo." (O.A. Battista).

People are often uncomfortable if you are changing what has always been done. If you are reading this book, my assumption is you are planning on being an effective leader, which involves embracing worthwhile changes. I wish you brilliant success as you challenge the status quo, make improvements, and get meaningful results in a positive direction. Be a difference maker!

"Leadership is not about being in charge. Leadership is taking care of those in your charge."

— *Simon Sinek*

Chapter 1:
Taking the Reigns as Principal

The role of the principal is crucial, and positive leadership is instrumental to success. It is also important to have powerful teachers for sound engaging instruction, and all staff members moving forward in a cohesive manner. Proper leadership allows teachers and staff members to function at their peak level professionally. We need strong principals who will remain in the role for a significant period in order to make a difference. Unfortunately, it is rare to find someone who has been a principal for even 10 years.

One study done by Fuller and Young from 1995 to 2008 of over 16,500 public school principals showed some interesting—but not surprising—results. The average tenure for elementary school principals was 4.96 years, for middle school principals, 4.48 years, and for high school principals, 3.38 years. Many principals leave the role because of the increased complexity of the job, or because they are using it as a steppingstone to move up the ladder. These roles are challenging and demand long hours to create conditions for student success.

I have always believed in putting in the time to be an expert at what you do. If the 10,000-hour rule (Gladwell, 2008) shows it takes 10 years or 10,000 hours to do so, most principals will never get there. Wanting to move up the ladder is okay, but we should do it for the right reasons, which vary from person to person. I applied for a few roles after serving as a principal for many years but was very selective in finding the right fit to use my strengths and talents. I learned through debriefings that my recognition as a strong principal made it difficult for higher ups to replace me in that position.

According to a 2008 study by the National Center for Education Statistics, the average public school principal has 7.5 years of experience. The average years a district kept a principal in the same school was 4.2. The study said 34.1 percent had less than two years at their current school as a principal; 13.4 percent had two years; 10.8 percent had three years; 29.9 percent had four to nine years; and 11.9 percent had 10 years or more. While districts have their reasons for moving principals, I believe it is difficult for a leader to succeed with such mobility.

Consistent leadership in schools remains difficult, as per the 2016-2017 Principal Follow-Up Survey by The National Center for Education Statistics. The sample had 5,700 public schools and discovered that about 82% of public school principals stayed at their school for the following year. Also, 2% of principals were from schools where the principal had left, but the school didn't know if the principal was working elsewhere.

(Rebecca Goldring, Soheyla Tale, Isaiah O'Rear, 2018) This study also shows principals continue to leave, no matter what the demographics of the school may be. Among schools where less than 35% of students received free or reduced-price lunches, 85% of principals stayed, 5% moved, and 8% left. The study found that in schools with over 75% of students approved for free or reduced-price lunches, 79% of principals stayed, 7% moved and 11% left. There is a higher percentage leaving with a tougher population or higher poverty, but there are many leaving no matter what the demographics.

There is a need for consistent training, mentoring, and giving principals the skills and tools to be excellent at their jobs. Educational organizations must look for successful ways to manage talent and keep outstanding leaders. We don't need people leaving due to lack of support or inadequate leadership development programs. While a principal in high-needs and specialty program buildings, I supported and mentored emerging leaders. I knew developing principal leadership capacity in a positive framework would be key to their success.

Many successful principals find it helpful to develop a network of support. As I started my career, it was sink or swim, trial by fire, and I was very grateful to have the camaraderie, knowledge, and experience base of a principals' group. After retiring as a principal, I started consulting to give tools that make the job of principals easier. I created the Urban Principal: Leadership Lessons podcast to teach people how to be better leaders. I speak from experience, read, research, and share tried-and-true practices and solutions. Too many people don't stay a principal long enough to develop the strategies they need. These happen through experience and life in the field. Developing better leaders and leadership capacity are goals for which I have a passion and have worked toward my entire career as a principal. As Kenneth Blanchard has said, "The key to successful leadership is influence, not authority."

When I became an assistant principal, one of our parents, Ms. Smith, said, "You have a good temperament. You are a good assistant principal and would make an excellent principal." I knew then I was up for the challenge of leading a school effectively. I like to think she was right, and I'm sure her confidence in me influenced the trajectory of my life.

"The only person you are destined to become is the
person you decide to be."

— *Ralph Waldo Emerson*

Chapter 2:
Getting the Job: Marketing Yourself

It is important to market yourself and go for your dreams. You have one life and need to do what you can to make the most of it. I learned this lesson the hard way after being passed over for a dream job following a change of superintendents. The superintendent's plan had a section for "evidence of success," so I created a portfolio with letters, certificates, surveys, and data. It looked professional, organized with binder covers I learned from Ingra.

I made social media accounts on different platforms like LinkedIn, Facebook, Twitter, and Instagram. You can show off your skills and have fun with them. We are in an unprecedented time of communication, where an online presence is important to remain at the top of your field. This becomes a digital resume of sorts. Although I have a paper resume that I use for certain job applications, LinkedIn is often the primary source for employers in this digital age. I also have a vitae or "CV", which is a short-written summary of my career, qualifications, awards and education. It proves useful for the university when they require a bio or for consulting purposes.

I have noticed many who are trying to get into an administrative role often give up too easily. It takes time. You must network, put in the effort, and make the most of the chances to prove yourself. Being persistent is key and sticking to your goals. My podcast (Urban Principal: Leadership Lessons) is one example of how I have built an online presence to market my consulting business. It is based upon my years of experience as a principal and what has worked for me. It also gives me a chance to talk about educational issues, share research and assist in my goal of creating more effective leaders.

Taking part in committees and volunteer boards and giving back to the community can strengthen your reputation. It took me seven years of applying for administrative positions before finally landing one. I had my share of disappointing letters, but also had the tenacity and motivation to continue to pursue my goal. Think of all the people throughout history who never gave up. Many of the inventions and big discoveries of today would not have happened if those people had failed and just said, "Oh well, I'll give up and do something else." If you want to do it and it's important to you, be resilient and go for it.

Then you must work hard, develop a solid reputation for success, and stay the course. Again, I must reiterate, stay the course. Develop an inner drive like I did, and it will keep you going when others are just giving up. Take every opportunity to show your abilities and talents. I had my share of "Dear John" letters--in fact, quite a stack! Be persistent! Then you can show what you can do. It seems like every role I have ever taken; I have always had to prove myself. People often underestimate me, but I usually end up on top. It doesn't hurt to be the underdog!

"People with goals succeed because they
know where they are going."

— Earl Nightingale

Chapter 3:
Developing a Mission and Vision

I was first selected as an assistant principal for Indian Hill Elementary
School and over that first year; I grew in ways unimaginable. I spoke
earlier of the old sink-or-swim scenario. This high-needs building had
a new principal who was experiencing challenges with the role. She
would get upset, resign, tell me I'm in charge, and then leave. It was a
surprise the first time she did this. Then she would return a week or
two later. You can call this unpredictability an opportunity to learn, but
it was more like being shoved off a cliff. However, in the times she
was away, I could learn much as the temporary principal, and I learned
FAST! I led a busy high-needs building while also coordinating an
open house, fundraiser kick-off, and school picture day.

The building experienced a decline in its track record of stability
despite having successful leadership in the previous years. I found
through this experience you can actually learn a great deal from an
ineffective leadership style—about what not to do. After
approximately three months of this principal's exit/re-entry pattern and
erratic behavior, an interim principal—Joan McCrea—was assigned.

Joan was a solid, excellent principal who had retired and then returned
to the district. She had taken an assistant principal position at another
high-needs building and was happy in that role. Then she moved to
Indian Hill to cover the principal position for the rest of the year. I
appreciated her mentorship and continued to learn about the job.

I've noticed interesting things seem to happen around the holidays, and this year was no different. The staff felt stressed because of various personal activities going on outside of work/school. Joan was an excellent leader who helped calm the waters and become a role model for me. I learned a great deal from her knowledge and expertise. She was a master at working with people and showed the key relationship-building skills of an effective leader. I saw her communicate kindly and respectfully with people on the phone and in person while achieving tasks and acknowledging their strengths. She completed the rest of the year with me, and together we became a team, friends and colleagues. At first, she took charge of completing the budget and other important areas that had been neglected while I continued with my work. Together, we brought that building back on track. By the end of the year, Joan was really ready to stay retired, which officially opened the principal position for this building.

I watched for the posting, and I quietly applied for the placement. Joan recommended me for the position but could not make any guarantees. We worked together, and she recognized my talents. (A strong mentor is helpful, but schools need to make transitions easier.). We met with different groups, including district personnel, teachers' union, community representatives, and staff. They all wanted stability in the building. They selected me for an interview after I applied, and they instructed me not to disclose it to anyone, including the current staff. It is not always normal to move up assistant principals into a principal role at the same building (at least it wasn't in our district).

I remember going to a district office meeting and coming back to the building that same evening for a panel interview with selected staff. This was definitely not a done deal. I wasn't sure at the time they even wanted me, even though I had developed relationships with the staff. This was different. I would be their overall principal and leader. It had burned them having inconsistent leadership. They liked Mrs. McCrea, but they knew she was a temporary fix. They seemed to like what I had done so far in building relationships, but I didn't know if I was even in the running for the job before that point.

I was nervous, and they were apprehensive as we moved into a large format interview session. They had one staff member ask questions, and a panel observed and took notes. The teachers' union was present, and they did not want a repeat of experiences in the past. They asked pointed questions of what I would do to build trust and empower the staff, and wanted to know how certain situations I would handle. The others watched and took notes—giving looks of what I perceived as *I wonder if he can do it.* It was not an easy interview, and I definitely did not feel like I had an ace in the hole. They asked specific questions and wanted genuine answers. It was their right at this point. The wounds were deep, and everyone was ready to be done with the past. They invested all these stakeholders in the building and wanted to make sure their leader would be as well.

After a few excruciatingly long days of waiting, the superintendent ended up calling me in to his office and offered me the job as principal. I felt this was a pretty quick decision in the scheme of things, as many human resource departments take weeks for an application process.

Mrs. McCrea said she was glad to hand me the keys. Though she had recommended me, she knew she couldn't guarantee the outcome of the process.

I returned to the superintendent's question about turning a high poverty building into a successful environment. It was time to put up or shut up, as the kids say. My goal was to build trust and make improvements in a school of 675 pre-k to sixth grade students and 112 staff members.

Time to get to work! Responsibility for the staff, students, facility, instruction, achievement, and community is required when holding the keys and becoming a leader. The pressure is immediate. If you are a principal or leader of an organization, you understand.

My task as a new leader was to develop trust, stability, and provide direction, consistency, and attention to this urban elementary school. Right away, I worked with staff on reviewing what was present, what was working, and where we stood as a building. Our baseline data became the starting point for a needs assessment. One of the first tasks was redefining a vision and mission for our school. We needed to get everyone on the same page. Having been there a year as an assistant principal, I was already aware of the history and the elements that were important to the staff. Change is hard, and it needs to be done carefully, not haphazardly. There needed to be a revival of purpose and building of staff, as well as a change in philosophy for how we work with students. The mission already in place was typical of most school missions, but after reviewing it with our new goals in mind, we landed on:

We will provide a caring, educational environment that develops students with strong foundations for success as lifelong learners and responsible citizens. We believe: All students have the right to an education that will enable them to reach their highest potential; Education requires sustained systematic efforts by students, staff, parents and community; Students should be educated in a climate that fosters self-worth and respect for others.

All schools develop both mission and vision statements, and I found creating the vision statement the most powerful of the two. We met as a staff to discuss our vision and goals for the school's future. The planning sessions were productive. We had collaborative meetings with large staff groups, smaller grade levels, and teams. I did a lot of listening and guiding of discussions, and together, we grew. Our vision had meaning and purpose. I can still recite the vision from memory today:

Our vision sets high achievement as a priority with positive expectations for staff, students and the community. We want Indian Hill to be a safe place where students see a future for themselves.

It had to be something everyone could remember, and it worked for me—I can't forget it. Achieving success was crucial due to the high percentage of students from low-income housing and free/reduced lunch. The statement: "positive expectations for staff, students and community" was a goal, and where most of our work was going to take place—a great deal of work. We wanted the school to be a safe positive environment where students could succeed—another enormous area of work. We needed an attitude of positivity and success, with a belief that all students will succeed.

"A place where students see a future for themselves" came out of the need to break the poverty cycle, develop hope, and create career awareness. We encouraged career development and understanding of occupations through college visits, career fairs, and guest speakers. We wanted to break the cycle of poverty and guide students towards self-sufficiency and positive societal impact. The meticulous word selection of our vision paid off with agreement and support from all.

Another step was concentrating on the staff members themselves, helping them learn about their strengths. They went on a self-reflection journey and found their strengths and talents with Gallup's StrengthsFinder. Originally, I could take them to actual training at Gallup. Then later, I would just use the resources of *How Full is Your*

Bucket and *StrengthsFinder* materials and resources with staff. I also could go through the training on "Leading with Strengths" through our district. We soon understood each other. Gradually, a change took place. We worked hard at getting our staff together and on being productive, collaborative staff members.

The vision became our catalyst for making change. Visions are powerful and can create momentum while being a dramatic change agent. The leader must promote this vision, steer the ship and keep it on track. I created large posters with an improved image of our bear mascot and the vision. Branding around the school became extremely important to add to the climate and promote the vision. Luckily Ingra (my wife) was a marketing and public relations director with a great deal of talent in graphic art and design, as well as promotion. She helped with the branding and professional look we needed. I have used her talents throughout my career many times in this capacity. They were large posters, produced on colored card stock and laminated with some being framed and posted throughout the building.

I also used the vision on staff agendas, in PowerPoints, and put it in front of the staff at every opportunity. This was a visual reference for us to use and say, "How are we doing? Are we moving toward our vision?" We could also use the vision as a talking point. It's easier to work with staff and discuss things by asking, "does this fit our vision?" This way, strategic planning and school improvement can be based on the vision. Strategies developed to target key elements in making this vision a reality. The key, as with any initiative, is getting support and ownership. You can't create a vision and just drop it on a shelf somewhere. There has to be self-reflection and checks on progress. The staff had created this vision together based on what we needed as a building and community. If you practice shared leadership, with collaboration and team building, this ownership and support will happen.

When I started the focus school, it was very similar. Once I had staff selected, we met to craft our mission and vision. I started by giving them all the StrengthsFinder tool to identify their top five strengths or talents. I used this at my previous school. We worked with a rep from Gallup to administer and talk about the results. This is a tool I still use to this day to identify the unique individual qualities of the staff. As I add staff, I have them take StrengthsFinder and we add their strengths to a spreadsheet that I make available to all staff. At Indian Hill with over a hundred staff, I created a book called "The Strengths of Indian Hill" and everyone had this document.

At the Focus School, I had our assistant create a spreadsheet with our Staff Strengths and it was available to all staff. Our assistant updated the spreadsheet each year and added new staff to it. This became a useful tool for working with staff. You can purchase most of the excellent Gallup books and they come with a code to allow access to the StrengthsFinder tool. Each year, staff would get a copy of this grid of strengths to use as we collaborate. The more they understand each other, the better the collaboration will be.

Why am I spending so much time on staff strengths and talents? Well, if you are working toward a vision, there are many pieces that need to be in place. Everyone should develop self-awareness about their unique qualities, including the staff. The ability to understand one another helps to develop productive relationships. Everyone comes with their own background and lenss of perception. Communication is still at the core of everything, including relationships and--done well--it can keep focus on the goals at hand. This also develops culture, and culture is everything!

At the focus school, once we identified our strengths and talents, we worked on our mission and vision for the school. I started the discussion by looking at original examples and models from schools and businesses. Then we started brainstorming key characteristics of the school we wanted. Those key descriptors are to define us. Early on, I pulled the staff together, and we spent two days developing the mission and vision. It went pretty fast--I think because we were creating a new concept for an innovative school from scratch, and everyone was excited to set the course. We selected the staff based on their various qualities, which differed from inheriting a staff as I had in the past. I provided examples from different institutions, and we swiftly agreed on the qualities that we want our students to possess.

The staff had some great input and even got into some heated discussions with differing opinions. This is actually a good thing. At a certain point, I told them let's table it and come back fresh the next day, since we had started spinning our wheels. Sure enough, they came back the next day when we all had some rest and time to think, and we knocked out that final draft in a short time with consensus.

I had faith in the staff. The mission ended up as: *It is the mission of Wilson Focus School to help all children embrace diversity and cultivate learning using leadership, technology and communication. By broadening the vision of students, families, educators and community, we will create leaders who contribute to the global society.*

The vision just seemed to flow after we completed the mission and the tweaking around our theme helped this to be:

Our vision promotes leadership through technology and communication as a pathway to achieve academic excellence.

To achieve academic excellence, we believe:

In the value of diversity.

In the development of individual talents.

In the partnerships between families, school, and community.

In the importance of relationships.

In using effective and innovative instructional strategies.

These beliefs will ensure that the students at Wilson Focus School become positive leaders reflective of the global society.

This vision encompassed what we wanted all our students coming from any of the 11 surrounding districts to learn. It was about opportunities for all, no matter what culture you came from and what your background was.

This sounds similar to many, I am sure, but the vision can be the driving force for your school and can be the difference in making sustainable change. The agreement, support and ownership of staff make the difference. The school improvement plan ties to the mission and vision of the school and addresses the strategies you are using to make this change happen. Keeping the staff excited and motivated towards the vision is a challenge, but if they are involved in all aspects, it becomes easier. As you add new staff, it is important to bring them into the mission and vision, periodically review it and see if it needs tweaking. Building ongoing ownership and commitment is important.

If you, as a leader, are moving forward and exemplifying the vision, your staff will want to move with you. Developing trust amongst staff is crucial to making and sustaining any actual change. The best way you can do this is through modeling the vision and following through with what you say you are going to do. This sounds simple, but many leaders do not do this simple thing and lose critical credibility. Your actions must match your words.

If staff knows they can share with you, as well as problem-solve, you have won part of the battle. Their input matters! Listen and collaborate. Most schools want to reach their vision and make progress, which is why I use the word "change" frequently. School improvement is never ending. Reaching for the ideal positive vision is an ongoing process. Progress never ends.

People are talking about "elevator speeches" that can quickly promote their business or building during a brief interaction. This can be an effective tool to sell your school. The elevator speech I had for Wilson Focus was:

"I enjoy being a leader of an innovative school that focuses on leadership, technology and communication. My position allows me to motivate staff to improve instruction and achievement. I coach teachers to use effective instructional strategies, review data, and look for ways to increase success. Bringing out the best in people and developing a positive environment is a priority for my leadership."

I made this one while working with Kathy Kennedy, a consultant and former assistant superintendent who coached our district. This elevator speech gives people a quick synopsis of what I do, and it also framed many of my leadership duties as a principal to help people understand our role. I have often found people don't really know what a principal does, so my statement helps to enlighten people with a broad perspective on the duties of the job. Staff members could use this in many public situations. I could change my speech depending on how the audience views education and our school. This helps me give them a better understanding of job duties.

The school staff should be able to recite and give a version of the mission and vision while being close to the original and still holding the core principles. You want this mantra to be part of their internal drive. I have seen some fantastic, short and sweet mission and visions. When I talk about the schools I was in, I get excited, and my enthusiasm comes out and it becomes part of the speech. Your passion and excitement help drive the impression of your organization.

Keeping the vision in front of people and alive is important. This is where leadership comes in. As John Maxwell has said, "People buy into the leader before they buy into the vision." The vision becomes part of your culture. This is another reason to make posters and use them on agendas, putting it out there so the common knowledge and language becomes the reality you want. Having it in front of you reminds you where your journey is headed. There are so many things you as a leader can intentionally do to keep a school or business improving, I will hit upon many of these within this book. You must start with a clear mission and vision. A strong vision guides your purpose!

"Most people are as happy as they make up their minds to be."

— *Abraham Lincoln*

Chapter 4:
Creating a Culture of Success

Mr. Lincoln was right about attitudes making a big difference. To create a positive environment, acknowledge people's strengths and help them achieve their best. It is about allowing them to be themselves. It is about being a builder! This is all a part of culture. Creating an atmosphere of success creates success. A true, positive culture is contagious.

Part of my journey of developing trust was to be consistent and mean what I say--following through and modeling what I expected. Here it is again: your actions *must* follow your words. I said this in the last chapter, but it's worth repeating. It sounds simple, but very few leaders do this and undermine their own success.

Some leaders can also fall into the trap of misusing their power or position. Like it or not, some people change when they reach leadership roles. I am sure you have heard the famous saying by a 19th century British politician, Lord Acton, who said "Absolute power corrupts absolutely." Implying that as a person's power increases, their moral sense diminishes. This has obviously been true throughout history and many people have misused power. Leadership has a powerful effect on people, and not everyone can handle it. It can intensify your personality, good or bad. Leadership does not always bring out the best in some people. Work on becoming a caring, positive leader with integrity. These characteristics are important to develop.

The leader has a definite impact on the culture. The culture is everything about a school building or organization. Culture is sometimes hard to describe. When it is a warm, inviting culture, you know it and feel it. When it is not, you also know it and feel it. You can walk into any school building and within a matter of minutes have a pretty good idea of what kind of environment you are in. You just feel the culture.

There are many factors and variables that combine to make a culture positive. The culture is the way things are done; the climate can change in a minute. If you say it is a jeans day tomorrow, you have immediately changed the climate. Everyone is glad. The culture develops over time and is at the core of an organization. There are values and norms built into the fabric that bring the culture to life. The culture is powerful and is the driving force at the center.

I am convinced that culture can play a major role in setting up the right circumstances for student success and achievement. The culture can trump strategy any day. I am not the first person to say this for sure, but it is so true! I have proven it in the buildings I have led and successfully moved forward. The culture is a change factor.

When I first became an assistant principal, I remember riding up to the back of this highly urban school located two blocks from the projects. I was riding a Honda CB550-four (I have a fondness for motorcycles and still maintain one). I remember taking off my helmet and a teacher walking by said, "Can I help you?" and I explained I was the new assistant principal. She approached me and we exchanged introductions. My first impression of the building was cautious, as the friendly staff member checked my reason for being there. I could tell going in that this was not a place that immediately welcomed you. It didn't have the feel of a warm, positive environment. It was like a mouse stopping to check out a noise or smell something and then scurrying on. Notice I said "feel" since there are intangibles you can't always put your finger on, but they are there.

Then I got a real feel for the culture. I started the year suspending students' right and left, since this was the endorsed practice. I soon realized this system was not working. This was a practice of the current culture of pushing students out and away. We were sending home the very students we were trying to increase academic achievement and test scores with.

This was the era of "No Child Left Behind" and with NCLB being promoted federally, you had to always make that bar that was increasing every year. I expected the students to make the prescribed level of proficiency. The penalty was, of course, fewer resources for assisting the same students you were trying to help. Somewhat of a contradiction to developing support. We had an assembly line system that was pushing students out and did not have a focus on reteaching.

The environment was punitive and negative--what research calls a toxic environment. The culture was not one of success or positivity. Teachers would often hurry about, stick to their jobs, go to meetings and then scurry back to their rooms. There were pockets of support amongst themselves, and silos existed. Silos in themselves can destroy an organization. In an environment like this, staff do what they must to survive. As stated earlier, they had some solid principals in the past, but that was not the current state. The current mode was survival. The sad part is they believed in the students and wanted to help them, but the current status quo did not fully support this course of action.

When I took over as principal, I started developing the climate to change the culture. In fact, it was a priority. Having a background in art and knowing the impact aesthetics can make on your surroundings, we improved the overall environment. One of the first things I did at Indian Hill Elementary was to have the exterior painted. They had built it in 1957 and still had many of the trappings of an old building. I had them paint the trim dark brown and all the panels within the brick tan. They were bright orange, which dated the building.

The grounds were also rough, so my wife and I started trimming bushes and doing plantings. This caught on and soon the custodial staff realized how we wanted the grounds to look and started doing more to the exterior. Butch Mort, the head engineer, was a good worker. He started helping and soon we were cutting down trees, planting and doing all kinds of work together. We remain friends to this day, even though I moved on to other challenges and he retired. Mike Shuput, the night custodian, was another hard worker who assisted us in making the place presentable. Others assisted from the custodial staff, but Butch and Mike were the constants.

This is a good tip of leadership don't be afraid to do anything that you would want your staff to do. Leading by example and modeling the behavior you would like to see. Many have documented the benefits of being a servant leader and consider it an excellent practice. The staff developed respect around seeing how much I cared for the school/community and what we could do as a team to improve it. The culture I promoted was doing whatever it takes to help our students succeed.

Staff observed I wasn't against doing what needed to be done and it was clear in my actions. Soon, everyone got on board, and we started making changes. They assisted with a school garden area where we added a cobblestone path, a fence and many plantings of perennial plants. There was also a large acorn tree in the middle area that kindergarten rooms would often use. We spent some Saturdays making a concrete path and completing this outdoor classroom area around this tree.

During the weekend grounds renovation, I had a student assist me in planting roses, edging, and mulching a highly visible area. We gave positive opportunities to the student who needed extra attention for their behavior difficulties. He met me at the school and was eager to help. The plantings added instant color and improved the look of the building. His reward ended up being the biggest hamburger he could get from a fast-food restaurant, which highly satisfied him. He ate more than I thought he could.

Students love to help if you give them the chance and opportunity to make a difference. They can easily take ownership and develop pride in their school and surroundings if given the right tools. As he improved in behavior, I eventually went to his apartment in the projects and helped him fix his bike tire that was flat. Some of the help he needed was understanding the process of how to fix things and what tools to use.

Improving the school's aesthetics wasn't easy. It helped that I had an art degree and Ingra was artistically talented. She had excellent skills and ideas! We painted some murals around the school of bears, learning and giving directions to subjects, since the mascot was a bear. Some students enjoyed watching me (their principal) paint some of these during the day. It was a good example of using your talents. Students would watch me on the ladder painting in the hallway, make positive comments and show that they had pride in our school. They saw that I too had pride in the school. They loved observing the process!

Another project involved working with an artist in residence to create student artwork and permanently mount the works in the hallway. I had the district carpenters build frames and installed Plexiglas over the artwork to protect it. It was student artwork of colorful handmade paper collages. It is important to consider how to protect and install visuals to help the artwork last.

The district carpenters became my friends. We established a history line of staff photographs by mounting nice plaques on long oak strips which held the photos. They displayed the principal, staff, and a nameplate with the year. Scholastic Photography was great at making these plaques and did so as a bonus for those of us using them. This timeline was important. These photographs helped to establish a history with the neighborhood, so we posted all the years of the building from its opening. It helped to connect our community. Everyone loved seeing their families and related school staff posted. The more people can connect with their school, the more they will interact with it. This was in a main hallway and today still has room for many more years. History is important, and it ties people to locations and communities. Connections matter.

The front office became better by adding an aquarium, painting, hanging pictures, and putting up motivational posters. We also added new office furniture which added color and style. With improvements to the front office counter, it created a welcoming environment. The staff lounge received a fresh coat of paint. The interior was looking good and inviting!

The exterior still needed some work! The school yearned for a marquee out front--like the newer buildings of the district. We worked at adding a lighted sign out front. I got estimates on school signs until I found the right design (it also had to meet city codes and size requirements). We had the district electrician run a line to it. I had the concrete crew put in a slab with bolts for the sign and ordered the sign through an outside company. There are many companies out there. To install it, you might have to learn the district's process, become a contractor, and use contracted services from outside. The sign ended up being a multi-colored lighted sign with room for messages on each side. It had our mascot on it as well. Digital and LCD signs were not the norm and were very expensive.

I also found a company I liked called Descon for interior signage. They make vinyl signs that hang down to designate rooms in a hallway. I used a double-sided sign that helped to direct and label rooms and areas. You can also select colors, fonts and customize them for your building, which gave a professional look. I have done these signs in all three of the buildings I have set up. As rooms change or the program grows, you can easily reuse and move them around. They look professional and can easily guide people through your building. These exterior and interior touches helped to establish the culture and develop a warm and inviting atmosphere. Culture, as stated earlier, is one of those things that is hard to put a finger on, but you know it. It is more than just stuff set up to look nice. You can feel the culture of a school or business building when you enter it. It can be inviting, warm, and successful, or the opposite, cold, sterile, and fear based. Building the right environment and culture is important to success.

My first building project taught me that aesthetics is important, but building trust in the culture takes time and is vital. Remember, as a leader, your actions must match your words. Staff views this and it can make or break your credibility. This also becomes part of the culture.

When I started the focus school, it was the same. We added new furniture where we could, added a 55-gallon aquarium in the front office (donated to me from my mother and father-in-law) and a 30-gallon aquarium in the library. We also had a vinyl wall decal made for the front office--thanks to Ingra--of a quote that established what we were trying to do as a school, and the quote became our philosophy. It is the saying by Ralph Waldo Emerson and became the motto for our school: "Do not go where the path may lead, go instead where there is no path and make a trail." This was done in large font and placed in a prominent location as you enter the building. This sign establishes right away that this is no ordinary place. There are many sign companies that will enlarge a quote for you and most of these are stick or rub-on when completed. I have seen positive quotes or signs in many buildings, and they help to enhance the culture and tell what you are about.

Using color can make a difference. We painted the office a nice warm, inviting dusty teal color. We added a small couch and four nice chairs and a large, seated lion statue, since our mascot was a lion. A lion graphic was added to every set of glass doors, using a type of vunyl that gives a classy etched glass look. This idea came from my wife, who had done this at her previous business building, and was aware of this frosted glass effect. This can really improve the character of a building. It sends a professional image.

To reinforce our mascot, we placed other lion statues throughout the hallways. I spray-painted many of them the same metallic looking bronze to tie them together. All this added to the feel of the building. I even employed my art degree and painted a large oil painting of a lion's face for the library. Then I airbrushed, in large scale, our lion's head branding on two different gym walls—the first, when I started the building, and the second, when we moved to a new location. All of this helped to build pride in the school.

Ingra helped with details and decorating, including a lion fountain and a "Lions Rule" large creative sign in a common area. I definitely used her strong decorating skills. She found many pieces to help our school look its best. We placed a small couch and nice chairs in the office lobby. These elements contributed to our positive culture.

First impressions count, and our administrative assistant, Ms. Carole Yanovich, was an excellent representative who made everyone feel welcome at our school. Even when she was tired, she would still light up when people visited us. It was a wonderful first impression. The sad part is most places are not like this. She was often saying, "Welcome to Wilson Focus. Is this your first time at our school?" when anyone walked through the door. She would say "Welcome" and she meant it. Her energy was contagious. She lit up with a sparkle in her eye. She was genuine, and it came across. I always got comments--she was such a great greeter and first impression! She developed her own elevator speech and could rattle off the concept of our unique school. She fit well and was a part of our positive environment that set up our warm, inviting culture.

At Underwood Hills Focus School, the district grounds crew cut down a dead tree outside, leaving a five-foot stump. One of my teachers, Garret Higginbotham (Garret is now a principal in the Westside District) had the great idea of having someone carve it into a lion. We ended up finding a guy that carved tree trunks into sculptures and had him create our seated lion mascot. The result was a really nice-looking wooden lion statue. We then varnished heavily the lion with many coats. I think Garret did it for the first years and then I ended up taking on this responsibility as time passed.

When we had to find another location, parents and staff asked us if we were going to take the lion, our mascot. I hadn't really thought of moving him, but of course I said, "Yes, it's our mascot," so we employed a tree company to cut it from the ground and move it to our new location. Then the lion found its home right in front of our main door at the new Wilson Focus School site. I think it ended up being a symbol of the unity of the school and everyone loved the transition to a new location. The parents at the time wanted--no needed--to see that lion out in front of our school. It was important to them. It vested them in the school and the success. The school community can be powerful.

The people and staff within a building become a good indicator of the culture/climate. In fact, the style of leadership is often clear in the staff and surroundings. Don't underestimate the power of creating a positive culture. People can be happy and effective or put down and micromanaged--often a sign of an insecure leader. Peter Drucker suggested stating the desired outcome rather than dictating directions. Developing a professional staff who feels ownership of the school's development is important for a positive culture. The culture encompasses everyone.

Creating an inviting school is important. In the first school in which I served as principal, for example, the former principal had a practice of keeping community out and stakeholders out. This affected the culture of this inner-city school. My first year as principal, we had many issues to deal with. Most of the 89 percent free and reduced population needed more supports to achieve and develop any kind of academic success.

In our first year, we had 256 suspensions--not a good sign of stability--and as I grew as an experienced principal, I soon realized the number of suspensions you give is not a badge of success or honor. It is quite the opposite. It means you don't have any supports set up to help those students to be successful. New principals often lack training in creating

Positive Behavioral Interventions and Supports. It is much harder to work with students and find that connection that sets them up for a positive school experience. The students must be there and present in order to improve academic achievement. We can do this through developing a sense of belonging and strong connections.

Early on, it was like an assembly line, and we were pushing kids out that needed to be in school. This was the current culture. Something was wrong with this setup, and it needed to stop. The very students we wanted to assist were being setup for failure. Now, we are doing something wrong as a school if we have to send a student home. What could we do better to help make that connection and success within the school? There are cases where you need to suspend or expel students, but many strategies need to be in place to ensure student success. Policies alone aren't enough. We must implement restorative practices and reteaching to prevent issues from continuing. How can we ensure students are successful?

To promote positive behavior, our school psychologist, Janet Benton-Gaillard, advised us to join a grant program in Nebraska. The program trains schools to build strong teams. It was called the Nebraska State Improvement Grant (NSIG) and focused on Positive Behavioral Interventions and Supports (PBIS). We applied through her help and were one of the selected schools. Schools throughout the state and a few other schools within our district became involved in the grant at the time as well. This was the beginning of building a pyramid of Positive Behavioral Interventions and Supports for our students. It was also the beginning of us turning into a model safe school and turning this building around.

Being a part of the Nebraska State Improvement Grant was where I developed a passion for PBIS. Our focus was on promoting student success, and we looked at research by George Sugai, Jeff Sprague, Tim Lewis, Randy Sprick, and other researchers for a system of supports to make sure students are being set on the correct path. I saw that you can truly set students up for success and give positive outlets, connections and hope.

Positive Behavioral Interventions and Supports and Multi-Tiered System of Supports for Behavior (MTSS-B), as it is often being called now, are crucial to a school's success. I ended up using PBIS throughout most of my career as a principal. Now, as a consultant, I teach others how to use these systems of support. I will address more on these systems in a following chapter.

I have many stories from my work in developing this culture within an inner-city high poverty area. A good indicator of things changing, or-- I should say--an excellent compliment was from a student who told his mother at a family night., "Mr. Anderson treats us like students, not animals." Wow! The statement told us about their treatment in the past, or how they perceived things, and it was hurtful.

I even remember early on as a new principal messing up on the intercom and laughing, a teacher said, "we haven't heard laughter around here in a while." This was another immediate insight into the past. This was not an acceptable cultural behavior in the past. I guess it wasn't okay to enjoy your work and be happy, have joy in what you are doing. It brings to mind the image of the stuffy educator, the stereotype. Movies and television often portray us in a certain way. This is often not an accurate portrayal of most educators, especially principals. Someone often portrays them as buffoons or seriously hard. To be fair, I guess there have been some positive media impressions. In some respect, we must be models for society, but there is no reason you can't have fun and enjoy what you are doing. I am not trying to make blanket statements. Most of the educators I know are happy, positive people. They have a deep care for staff, students and community. It's all about personality and culture.

Finding the right people matters. I worked very hard at finding the right people, but learned unfortunately, sometimes you do and sometimes you don't find the best fit for a role. You will pay in the long run if you don't have the right people. The students need positive, well-adjusted role models with the right demeanor.

A mother called me and complimented my approach of talking *with* kids instead of *at* them, which reflects cultural change. The atmosphere can be so constructive with the right attitude. I remember having leadership team meetings and turning something that was said into a positive. "We have more work to do" or "What are we going to do to change that?" and "We are off to a good start!" My counselor would say, "That is why you are the principal--always seeing that glass half full--looking for the positive!" We all know this, but why is it so hard sometimes?

My first year as an assistant principal, I walked out of the building one night to find three of the four tires on my SUV with knife cuts in them. Not fun. Especially after a long, hard day. Also, there were knife cuts on the driver's side door. Not a good sign of a positive culture. The culture around the school was not the most positive. Now, looking at the bright side, they were not totally flat, but had to be replaced to prevent failure. I wasn't sure who did it but had a pretty good idea about a student who was frequently being suspended. I was working closely with this family and had many visits to their apartment to work with the mother and her two boys. I later learned that they sentenced the same boy for an armed robbery in his twenties and he even committed a homicide. We worked hard with him, but he still was making many poor choices. We tried to help him and reverse his direction. This time, it didn't happen.

The work of an educator is to help all students succeed, but they may feel disappointed when some don't progress as desired. I have plenty of success stories and you don't always see the impact you are making in the lives of young people, but as an educator, it is there. All we can do is help them on their path, give them opportunities, and help make connections while influencing positive character along the way.

Hopefully, you will be the one that turns them around. The right connection they need at the right time. The overall goal is always helping all students to get better and succeed. Most educators are saints for all the work they do to help children. I have witnessed this time and time again. There is a great deal of dedication. There are many miracle stories of success. These are the ones we need to remember to define our purpose.

Helping students succeed became one of many stances as I worked in this area. As a teacher, I can remember working closely on many students to help them grow. There were many days where I worked on making connections with students to help them succeed. Creating positive relationships and mentoring can lead to a more stable classroom and engaged students. Mentors make a difference in a student's life, and there are never enough mentors to go around. Mentoring programs have had a positive impact, such as Teammates, Mentoring, Avenue Scholars, and Midlands Mentoring. We tried as a building to get each teacher to connect or match up to a student in the building. This can also help to change your culture as it becomes a culture of care.

As a principal, the experiences started adding up through the years, and I have many stories or memories. One day, two teens that could have benefitted from mentoring had stolen a car and were being chased by police. They hit a pole near the school and knocked it and the transformer out. Guess what, we lost power; it was close to lunchtime, and they did not repair it for about six hours. It forced us to make it work, finish lunch while keeping heat within the food warmers, and get through the day without electricity.

These kinds of things happen, are unpredictable and keep you thinking and problem-solving constantly. As a leader, you must be flexible! I have learned to expect anything. The staff also learns we can handle anything, and we will address it as it comes along. Embracing the "I can do" attitude can foster a positive team spirit. It becomes a part of your culture.

At my retirement, my last counselor, Dr. Pam, summed up a nice sentiment on a card. "The other day I was discussing you with someone and I said, I always feel safe with Bret. After I reflected on this, I realized it was because I knew you gave everyone the benefit of the doubt and always reacted in positive, productive ways (I was going to say calming, but let's stick with the alliteration!). You are the best administrator I've ever worked with and though I will miss you a lot, I'm very happy about the paths your energy bus will be going on now. My very best wishes for all of your endeavors and Godspeed. Fondly Pam." Her comments had strength since she was a past Catholic school principal and was a current counselor in the Omaha Public Schools District. She had worked on the principal frontlines. I respected and valued her. I let staff be themselves, but also worked to bring out the best in them. This became part of the culture. The leader continually makes a positive impact on the pulse of an organization.

Every day, we had safety patrols that crossed students into the projects. This stop was two blocks from school, stretching what we were supposed to be covering, but we knew it helped our students to get home safely. After school, we had teachers with the patrols and administration. In the morning, it was just patrols and a teacher rotating and checking posts.

One morning, the patrols had a man threaten them and show them he had a gun. They reported it and we shared this immediately with the police, who gave us support. I had a great relationship with law enforcement and, in fact, got to know every precinct captain for that area very well within the ten years I led at this location.

This relationship enabled me to make direct calls without always calling 911, and why was this important? I was in a high need, top action area. You run the risk or danger of calls being picked up by a reporter's scanner or others searching for a story. I needed to have a hotline for the police and the ability to take action before the story was being covered. It seems they were always ready for a negative story. Even if the situation was under control, taken care of or over, they were still looking for a story. I lost track of how many news stories I did, for incidents in this area.

My goal was to let news hounds know what we did to make the students safe and what positive things we have in place. We always aired on the side of safety of the students and families. I valued the fact that our Public Information Representative, Luanne Nelson, was highly supportive and trusted me as a professional. She reached a point where she would refer journalists to me for upbeat South Omaha stories. She would also assist when needed and was open to conversations about issues. She had confidence in principals and was there to support us. This is the way it should be. The culture within the district was "you are the professionals and the CEOs of your buildings."

There was always something happening. One time I had a mother come in to pick up her child, totally drunk. The security guard walked her to me, and I walked her into my office to talk, away from everyone. It is always good to study the situation and—in her case--get her out of the busy hallway and into a more private office situation (out of the public flow). The mother explained she was there to pick up her child. I said, "It appears you have had a little to drink?" (really, a lot).

She said, "Only a few, possibly more."

Then I said it would be best if she walked home with her daughter. She did her best to explain she only had a few drinks. I told her we were concerned about her daughter's safety. The police were called from another room, and when they arrived, she was assisted home. We kept the encounter positive and then monitored her closely thereafter.

Another day, while on the playground at lunch recess, I heard a screeching of tires and turned to look off the playground and down the side street from our school. To my surprise, there was a man running away, down the street towards the apartments/projects. This was looking down a small hill with a six-foot fence around part of our playground, and the street went by our playground and turned out away from us. The fence was open many feet between the playground and the building. He was running away, but the car had done a quick screeching of tires and whipped around to chase the man who had run in another direction. After turning around to evade the car, he was running up the street toward the playground. The noise caught my attention.

Then I heard bang-bang-bang--men within the car were shooting at the running man. Immediately, instincts took hold. I blew my whistle for the students to line up. It was sixth grade recess. I used my phone's quick key command to call 911 while watching their location. I brought the students into the building, and we went into lock down while waiting for the police.

The interesting thing is the students responded extremely well. The minute they heard shots, they looked to see where they had come from and almost automatically ducked down and went low to the ground— a skill picked up from living in the area and being accustomed to issues. The students were very resilient, and this was a good example of such self-preservation. They saw the school as a safe place.

Even our school district wanted to send out extra student community service people and counselors. I called the police captain after entering and created a letter that was sent home to parents that evening. They also had extra police visibly on hand at dismissal to help develop a secure, safe feeling throughout dismissal. Thereafter, they provided extra police presence around the neighborhood.

Communication is so important. A simple letter and even an automated call can go a long way in getting the correct information out to your families. I have written many of these letters for various reasons, as well as sent automated updates. Most of the time, they were for something that happened near us. They helped squash rumors and send a coherent message of safety being a priority.

The quick moving pace of social media makes things happen even faster now. In my last few years as principal, I would tweet, post on Facebook, update our website, etc. Times have changed. To reach everyone, send a printed letter and or an automated call to all families in the language they speak.

The letter always comes across as an official communication. Districts' Public Information Departments and community support systems can assist in communication. You have the choice to activate different routines, automated calls, and message distribution systems. The simple fact is schools need to be prepared for a crisis. It is a fact of life in schools. I have adopted the phrase author Lee Child has given to Jack Reacher since I needed to think this way. I always hope for the best, but plan for the worst. The letter I wrote said:

February 23, 2000

Dear Parents,

An incident occurred at the noon hour today. I feel it is important that you have the facts as we know them.

At approximately 12:10 P.M. shots could be heard in the neighborhood along 31st and V Streets, near our school. Calls were placed immediately to the police, and the incident is being investigated. As a precautionary measure, the students on the playground were taken in and we canceled noon recess for the rest of the school. Also, the primary students in classrooms facing 31st street were moved temporarily to the hallway.

While the incident did not involve our school, or put our students in imminent danger, we feel it's important that you know we took, and will continue to take, precautions anytime safety is in question.

We have made our Indian Hill family aware of the situation and feel confident that students are not frightened. However, if you, after talking to your child, feel that talking with a counselor would be helpful, simply let us know to arrange a visit.

I have contacted the south area police captain, and he will provide the police on duty at dismissal time for the rest of the week. We expect continued police patrols in our area and appreciate the support of the Omaha Police Department in this matter.

Thank you for your continued support and interest in our school. Together we can make our South Omaha community better!

Sincerely,

Bret A. Anderson

Principal

This became one of many letters that were sent to inform families of incidents that occurred close to school. Families want to know the school is taking action and the safety of students is a priority, and it needs to be. After an incident, we would hold a staff meeting to provide more details and reassure them that everything was under control. I also did this by an earlier email. Communication is so important during any crisis and my staff knew I would keep them informed as needed. This was part of our developed trust.

Schools and workplaces regularly practice drills for lockdowns, evacuations, fires, and disasters. Pandemic protocols have become part of the routine. Everyone needs to practice and know what to do in a crisis. This can make it second nature and avoid confusion. It is good practice to have crisis plans in place and well thought out intervention plans, since we need them so we can take swift action.

Another time, we had an officer chase a man through our playground. We ended up doing a lock down as they continued after the man. I was close enough to see him with a revolver in his waistband. It was important to have your finger on the pulse of the neighborhood to support your families. Being close to the projects brought many challenges, but we served many families and students in need. Our school became a center of community support.

There were also many instances of parents that had to be banned and barred from the building for having such an aggressive stance towards the school. My goal was to change these parents and help them develop a more positive attitude toward school. This doesn't always happen, and some are so entrenched in the negative aspects of their life that they take it out on you. This becomes a safety concern if they are unstable.

One evening, as I was working in my office, a man stormed in and threw his glasses on my conference table. He started going off shouting all kinds of things about the school and me. He was saying "C'mon" and wanted to fight. I did not know who this was, since I had never seen him at a parent or family night. I remained calm and asked who he was and remained seated, which probably, now that I think of it, helped to lessen the aggression. This is an actual calm down technique. It is also important if standing up to turn sideways, so you are less of a target if needed. Yes, these are things to consider and keep in mind even though a principal should not have to be this mindful. He said he was [name of student's] father, that I had sent his daughter to the nurse, and that I had not done enough for this (minor) cut she had gotten on the playground. He said I was treating her differently since she was African American.

I remained calm and told him, as a school, we can only do certain things. She received the same treatment we give all students, cleaning the wound and applying a bandage while notifying home through a note or phone. He said I would have done more for a white girl. His tone was highly aggressive, loud, and confrontational. I tried to re-explain what we did, including calling mother and sending a nurse's notice home. He was unimpressed, turned and then stormed out and on the way out screamed "I am going to kill you, you f**kin' white boy!" You can fill in the blanks since it was not very complimentary. As a principal, you get some of these intense phrases and threats thrown at you. It is important you develop a thick skin and the ability to withstand a substantial amount of abuse. It is a reality of the position. I am relational and try to make parents happy, but not all want to work things out.

Some teachers that were working heard this threat and came to see if everything was okay. Ms. Wills, a very experienced African American teacher, heard the shouting and documented what they said. She lightened up the moment and said, "You know (looking at my arm), you're not really that white (because of my olive skin tone)!" She was right, and we both laughed. Having good staff is a plus! She changed the mood and lightened the moment as she made me laugh. It is important to support one another. I then called the police captain to report the incident and just inform him and he said we need to put a warrant out on the guy for threatening your life. I told him I had never seen him before this incident. He said we can't have people coming in and threatening the life of another, especially the school principal. It is unacceptable. He looked him up and guess what? The father was from another area of town, a known gang member, and already had multiple warrants for an arrest. The one I had just called in added to the list. He was a wanted man. They kept an eye out on patrols and, let's say, I was always aware of my surroundings. Luckily, I never heard or saw from him again. These are the things they don't tell you when becoming a principal. They did not cover this in my administrative courses. Welcome to the world of being a principal!

Child Abuse was another common issue in this area as we worked on systems to improve processes and support students. Over the years, I've had great counselors who worked with the principal and assistant principal to help families. Many of those stories are heartbreaking and you realize how resilient children really are and what they have to endure. The culture around the school became one of protecting our children and providing what they needed to succeed. Parents needed a positive connection to the school. The staff needed to move into trust and collaboration. This needed to be the norm of the culture.

Through family nights and support, we changed the perception of the school. We became the place to go for help, providing help and a positive influence in the neighborhood. I added a Family Room with resources available for families. Spanish-speaking parents had access to a liaison and resources, like training and materials they could borrow.

I was open to programs and ideas. We even started weekly parent classes to teach English and help with everyday needs. These weekly training sessions grew, and parents started bringing food and making it a social learning time. They were learning English and having fun. It was a place of learning for adults and children. It was a wonderful support for our families.

We also offered financial classes and tax help, including evening GED classes for those needing to complete their High School diplomas. We became a hub of activity for the neighborhood and community. Parents asked us for help and where to find services and we made those available. Volunteers assisted in classrooms and the library.

We became a haven for the community. Parents would come in while in crisis mode and say the boyfriend was beating up on them. It scared them to go home. I would counsel and connect them to resources that could help, including law enforcement or agencies. Often, families bring their problems to school and direct them towards the school. Being patient and a good listener goes a long way, as well as helping to seek solutions that truly help the family. Our team increased the ability to assist families. Our school was about families and our community.

A teacher believed a family's children were alone after school and needed daycare, so my assistant reported them. This is well and good and fits the procedure and protocol, but it did not consider that a police officer went to their house to do a wellness check. The mother spoke Spanish and had little English. It scared them when the police came by unannounced. She thought it was immigration. The mother came to school crying and upset, worried they were going to take her children away (this was an excellent mother).

Using a translator, I informed her that was not the case; we just wanted to make sure the children were not alone for a long period until she returns from work. Then she worked out a plan for a distinct drop off for the bus and could use a nearby daycare. I then discussed with the staff how we could have just called the mother and expressed our concerns and asked how we could help. The way we did it caused a great deal of fear and confusion and I said, "What if the mother couldn't afford daycare, and we needed to find other resources for her?" The family may not have been able to do it any other way. We need to use common sense and weigh what is best for the family. You can't always look through the lenses of policy and procedure. Many situations need to be contemplated.

These kinds of stories are part of many urban school principals' experiences and just when you think you have had it, something comes up you didn't expect. I had another parent who was walking her child to and from school with a steak knife in her pocket. One teacher saw this and told me, so guess what? It was my job to take care of this and ensure our students' safety on the school grounds. Security was elsewhere directing traffic and time was a factor here. They had seen it sticking out of her pocket. I approached her as we walked down the hill toward the projects and said "Ms. [name of parent], I heard you have a knife. Can I get that from you? We don't want anyone to get hurt." Only because I had developed a relationship and had the trust of this mother, did she hand it over, and I thanked her. The situation was de-escalated. She told me she was carrying it for protection, and we discussed the situation and options.

I had another incident where two former students who had presented challenges in the past, had parked outside on the side street of the school to pick up a sibling. Someone came in and reported that they had seen a revolver in the car. These guys were in high school now. They had arrested the father in the past for dog fighting while they attended our school, and we had many conferences. I asked if they had a gun, told them it was against the law and could scare kids. They denied having one and said they wouldn't do that. I took the license plate and quietly reported it. I used the relationship with the students to prevent a tense situation from getting worse. This showed them the culture of the school and surrounding area will not tolerate crime and this kind of behavior.

You want to develop the culture that has a positive reputation around your community. You want teachers and staff wanting to teach and work within your school building. Even in tough areas, teachers and staff will work if we provide them support, resources, respect and empowerment. You want families to want to attend and send their children to you. It is important they know they are safe and under good care. An ideal culture and climate do this and more.

A school can become the center of the neighborhood and an agent of change. There are some excellent resources on culture and relationships. I enjoyed reading *School Culture Rewired: How To Define, Assess, and Transform It (2015)* by Steve Gruenert and Todd Whitaker and *Leading Change in Your School: How To Conquer Myths, Build Commitment, and Get Results (2009)* by Doug Reeves. Another excellent resource on culture is *The Power of Positive Leadership: How and Why Positive Leaders Transform Teams and Organizations and Change the World (2017)* by Jon Gordon. It is important to continue to grow as a leader and help your staff grow.

As a leader, promoting positivity and encouraging all stakeholders takes intentional effort every day. It is non-stop and an effective leader must carry that positive torch. As I say, create a positive culture, value staff, build trust and the organization will be prepared to conquer obstacles along any path.

"There is no power for change greater than a community discovering what it cares about."

— *Margaret J. Wheatley*

Chapter 5:
Cultivating Community Partnerships

The development of an effective school depends heavily on cultivating partnerships with external stakeholders and fostering internal relationships and collaboration. Education is easier when we all come together to help our children grow.

Having the right people is a key to developing a successful school. Most administrators inherit some of their staff and this creates a challenge. People have lives, have baggage, different backgrounds and even the different lenses with which they view the world. This is where our challenge lies, getting the most out of all staff and bringing out the positive and the talent within everyone. A leader must deal with this and so much more! True leadership encourages people and brings out the best in their character. Developing a collaborative mission and vision is just the beginning; a leader needs to invest time in getting staff on board with the building philosophy and developing trust. Jim Collins was exactly right saying businesses and organizations that do well get the right people on the bus.

Moving a school is much easier with the right people—true in any organization. Over the years, I have learned many lessons in interviewing and finding the right people. The ability to build relationships and foster teamwork is essential for the success of an organization. I have learned people are not always what they seem.

You can find people that have strong resumes and come from the best schools/colleges but may not always be the best choice. They may have no skills in working with children or adults-- what we would term relationship skills. Occasionally you find some people with the full package.

Research tells us the best teachers have a strong rapport and ability to develop relationships with students. I have also found your intuition and feeling about a person is usually right. If relationships do not come easily to someone, there may be a long road ahead, trying to change a developed pattern of behavior or attitude. This is not a simple task! I learned that the most important qualities for teachers and staff are relationship skills. They must also be able to self-reflect. Coaching can help attain and teach the rest of the skills.

My overall goal with teachers and staff has always been empowering them to use their strengths and talents. Over the years, I have developed an interest in positivity. Morale is an important factor and can help establish an effective environment or culture, as previously discussed. As the leader, you need to always exhibit the behavior you want others to emulate. You may have days when you don't feel that positive or want to focus on relationships, but guess what? Your role as a leader defines your goal of keeping morale up. One of your major roles is being a cheerleader for the staff and school. If you don't like the word cheerleader, then it is a motivator, but you get my point. You are the advocate that keeps pumping up the positive!

There are ways you can promote the good things happening. At one school, we gave *Teacher Tags,* acknowledging the positives taking place with teachers. They could write compliments to each other that were read at staff meetings, which became a fun process. You can give prizes, a jeans day or whatever can work for your organization. I have done drawings at staff meetings, staff shout outs and other clever ways of acknowledging staff. Having staff involved in the process is another way to get buy-in and make it fun.

Collaboration and teamwork make a building and school effective. Building community support is extremely important. The school building itself can become the center of a community and be a positive reflection of the area. In my experience, as the culture became more positive and the grounds more respectable, people started cleaning up around the area. It inspired the neighborhood to improve their surroundings.

At my first building as principal, I met some of the most amazing people around the community. Throughout my 10 years there, we supported each other and worked together. Parents did not always have positive experiences at school, so this was a culture shift we needed to make. We started each year doing large BBQ events to get the community out to the school. We called these events "Meet the Teachers", and we held these in the back parking lot.

I purchased a large grill, and we would make over 600+ hotdogs, get chips, cookies and refreshments--many donated. We would get school T-shirts created through a grant and would pass these out for free to develop pride in the school and neighborhood. We also had raffles throughout the night. The parents and students loved these giveaways. I had Little Joe--a local DJ we found—play music, and we used him frequently. He would play fun music really loud and get the entire neighborhood up to our back parking lot. Everyone wanted to be at the party! Occasionally, I would step in on the microphone to talk about maintaining school attendance. We gave messages to our captive audience, making inroads into changing the generational poverty that existed. These were positive reminders about why we were there. It didn't hurt to have fun either! The staff came in our school spirit wear and would dance together and with the students. It was a big block party while the students viewed the posters of what classroom they were in.

We also had booths all around with all kinds of agencies and support services. Everything from: South Omaha Probation, Omaha Housing Authority, Omaha Police Department, Gang Unit, Omaha Fire Department, Boys and Girls Club, etc. There were often representatives from the mayor's office and sometimes city council members. They all would hand out information and give freebies. It was an excellent time to develop relationships and change attitudes about the school and community.

The parent group or past PTO (Parent Teacher Organization) had a hard time and there was little trust built previously. The past principal and parent group did not get along. There was a strong Neighborhood Association, and I worked at moving our Neighborhood Association to take the place of our PTO. They were getting established, and this group would soon be a major change agent for us and the community. They met in the library at my school. I was open to providing a common space, and we were the center of our community. We met monthly and our goal was acting and getting things done. They were collaborative action meetings. Many groups talk and very little gets done. Our goal was creating action plans and carrying them out. There was strength in numbers, and this group grew to represent the community around the school.

Belinda Malone was one of the first parents I met in the neighborhood. She was the Neighborhood Association President and had two children at the school, a boy and a girl. We hit it off immediately and had many discussions about the neighborhood and making changes. She was a strong community advocate. She had the pulse of the neighborhood and their respect. We planned and carried out many events together.

When violence and drugs increased in the area, Project Impact/Weed and Seed and our Neighborhood Association would plan an event and act on it. Our goal was taking action and making a difference. We did large rallies on the weekends, usually Saturdays like "Walk the Talk" and "Meet the Challenge." We met in a large parking lot across from the projects, had a BBQ, and did the same thing we did at the school, with all kinds of supports and agencies available. There we could take turns spreading our positive message of hope and success.

At one point, when the neighborhood was having issues, we marched through the projects, making a stand against drugs. Pastor John Williams and I marched through the projects, telling the area that we would not tolerate any more drugs and violence. Our message was clear and strong. It was all the sponsors, families and kids making a statement about what was acceptable. These school and community gatherings were highly effective and brought people together to start a change.

Another person I met was a small, gray-haired African American woman named Laverne Harris. She knew most kids in the neighborhood and was a dear friend of Belinda, the Neighborhood Association president. Her role was to help students, who were aware they shouldn't be disrespectful towards her. Her mighty voice only enhanced her small stature. I have seen her step up to gang members and confront them with no fear. She would say I know your parents and most people in the neighborhood. She would also confront anyone who talked negatively about me. She would say, "Don't you talk about my son!" She was and is still a loyal supporter!

Ms. Harris was in the Foster Grandparent Program and assisted in the school, working in the library with students. She also lived in the neighborhood, near Ms. Malone, and to say they were a dynamic team was an understatement for sure. Ms. Harris became a grandmother to the school and to this day, I still call her Grandma Harris. I surprised her years later as I wrote a tribute to her and sent it into the Public Pulse Section of our city newspaper. You can never praise those working with you enough. Here is what it said:

Grandma Harris - Tribute to a Community Hero

When we celebrate Martin Luther King, Jr., it is a perfect time to recognize one of the many African American Heroes in our community. I had the honor of celebrating the 80th birthday this past week of one of these people. Her name is Laverne Harris and I and many know her as "Grandma Harris". While I was principal at Indian Hill for over 10 years, she was a foster grandparent and community advocate, and we worked side by side through marches and rallies to improve the community and stop drugs and violence. She worked daily, mentoring children and working with agencies through the neighborhood association. Her passion and commitment to the neighborhood is contagious. She is still involved in creating a better community and continues to do so. Her never-ending faith and expectations for all children are admirable. As one who no longer has a grandmother, she became my grandmother, and she continues to make a positive impact on those around her. We developed a bond wrapped around a common vision for the community. To Grandma Harris and all those that are working to improve our community, thank you!

Another person I had in the Foster Grandparent Program was Joe Mattox. Joe, also known as "Papa," had a career as a firefighter and was one of the first African Americans to serve in the Omaha Fire Department. Prior to this, he had been in the Air Force. He was with me for about 16 of my 21 years as principal. Our running joke is that he was following me. He always said, "Mr. Anderson knew I was so good, he had to take me with him!"

He began working with me at Indian Hill when I was the principal. Later, when I started the Underwood Hills Focus School, he offered to become a foster grandparent since he was nearby. Then we moved the Focus program to Wilson Focus, and he came along, so he has followed me around to three schools. He played the role of a good grandpa figure to the students, offering his help with reading and classroom activities. In addition, he supervised recess, aided Kids Club, and assisted Boy Scouts. He loved telling visitors or subs to our building that he was in charge when I was gone or how long he had worked alongside me.

I am a firm believer in thanking everyone and acknowledging all they do, keeping that positivity going! As we started building community and school supports, we continued to add more partners to our goal of supporting the school. I met the South Omaha Police Precinct captain, Mark Sundermeier. He joined our neighborhood group and soon we were involved in a Federal/city program connected to the mayor's office called Project Impact. Ray Fidone worked for the police and helped start this grant against drugs and violence in the area. We had a partnership with law enforcement, and I got to know all the captains that came through this acute needs area while I was principal there.

Many organizations and agencies came forward to help us when we invited them to assist. There was Reverend John Williams from Bethel Baptist Church, a few blocks from school. Girls Inc. was at the bottom of the hill from us, and we also had representation from the local

YMCA. I worked closely with the Omaha Housing Authority (OHA) since many of our families came from South Terrace Apartments. Sal Issaka worked with us to make sure our students were making it to school and could do home checks for us at OHA.

Communication with others was instrumental in our success. Another person I met and soon admired as well was Alberto Gonzalez. "Beto," as we called him, was a Hispanic man who had been involved in gangs when he was younger. After he had sorted out his own life, his focus was on aiding young individuals, particularly boys, in avoiding gang activity, drug use, and violence. He was working for the Chicano Awareness Center and then moved to the Boys and Girls Club for many years. We met and hit it off and I had him coming into the school weekly to work with at-risk youth within small groups. Beto later became part of the Omaha Police Department as a gang specialist for the South Omaha area and has been an asset to the department. He has great relationships and connections to the families of the area.

Paco Fuentes, who ran the South Boys and Girls Club, was active with the group and many of our projects. His club was a national award winner. He has provided programs to assist boys and girls, especially during those critical hours after school and throughout the evening. He has touched the lives of many as well and was a superb partner.

Another individual I met was Angelo Desanto. Angelo and his team oversaw the south area probation at the time, and we also worked well together. He could come over and help keep the neighborhood safe from drug activity and harassment of students. His team always assisted our rallies and provided help and support.

Dave Cisar ran the Eagles Football league in the neighborhood and would have students earning shoes and gear. He would also check with me on behavior and academics and see how the students were doing in our school. He would often stop by while I was at playground lunch recess and get some feedback. This helped the students to have some accountability and aimed at teaching responsibility.

Two of the most kind-hearted people I met while at this south inner-city school were Virgil and Angie Armendariz. This married couple was great at helping me with school events by getting donations and providing support. They were making a difference by assisting multiple groups in the community. The South Omaha area benefited from their involvement. They had a pickup, and a large trailer and Angie could charm donations out of anyone--super giving people! They had connections that helped us and others to run many community events.

Another giving and caring pair was Virgil and Rebecca Patlan. Virgil was with the Latino Peace Officers and with the Omaha Police department. I would work with Rebecca in various neighborhood and city groups throughout my time there. Both were advocates for positive change and community improvement.

Our school library hosted The Neighborhood Association Meetings and Project Impact. Throughout my 10 years as principal of this school, my network grew, and the school became a command center for getting things done. When the Project Impact funds ran out, we sought and received Weed and Seed Funds. The Weed and Seed grant involved many of us in the area, including the mayor's office. The goal of Weed and Seed was to stop drugs and violence and seed new productive positive programs in the area. We met mainly at school and sometimes the Weed and Seed group met at the LaFern Williams Center--a community recreation center who was also a partner right down the street. The grant included money for more public policing and neighborhood groups to improve the community. There were efforts to develop strong community partnerships and relationships. We worked hard at cleaning up the area and keeping it safe.

Our goal became finding productive things for children to do after school and by finding ways of extending the day. We started a Community Learning Center (CLC). The program provided after-school physical and academic activities. This federal funding came through based on the needs of the area. This program provided classes and an after-school meal.

We had a before and after school Kids Club (run through the Omaha Schools Foundation). Parents can drop off and pick up their kids at this program, which runs before and after school hours.

I became a member of the Girls Inc. board since it directly worked with the students, girls of my school and area. Roberta Wilhelm ran the organization well, helping girls to be strong, smart and bold. It is a game changer for many girls and was another needed assist for the girls in our area. They are now focusing on STEM and getting girls started on a positive career path.

Over the years, I kept working with the different precinct captains. These included Captains Sundermeier, Peppin, Friend, and Martinez. Sundermeier became involved in our early efforts to get violence and drugs under control. Martinez became a school board member and was a good advocate for the needs of schools. I can remember working late and he would come into the school and say, "I figured you'd be here" and then he would sit down and chat for a bit.

We would discuss the area and latest developments. He was especially good at getting around the neighborhood and checking how things were going. The Weed and Seed grant increased patrols and community policing to better connect with the community. These were positive individuals working to improve the community.

When Thomas Warren took over as police chief, we saw some excellent programs that were proactive in assisting the youth of the city. He started the Police Athletic Program, or what we called PAL (Police Athletic League). PAL was a program that had our school open a few nights a week until about 9:00 PM and was open gym for the community. We invited all ages. Extra funds were available to pay teachers and police officers to assist. They coached and played basketball with the students. Tom Gamble, Duane Chism and Mike Peitzmeier were the teachers who consistently coached in this program. It was an excellent program.

I got to know Tom Warren, and he is still a good friend today. Tom is a standup guy and has been a solid friend for over 20 years. I don't say that lightly. I am in a breakfast group with him and Duane Chism--one of my old teachers from Indian Hill--that tries to meet once a quarter as we can. Our careers have all changed, but our friendship has not. Tom Warren is now retired from the police department and moved into the CEO of the Urban League and then the Chief of Staff for the city of Omaha. Dwayne Chism went from teacher to principal, then became an Executive Director of Schools. Now, he's a university professor who runs his own consulting business, Shifting Perspectives, LLC and writes books.

Tom Warren is a mentor of mine and continues to mentor many others throughout the community. I trust his judgement and guidance. He has never failed to support me, and I know he does this for others. It honored me to receive a community award with him from the Empowerment Network at a community event. I was proud to be among the many people making a difference in the lives of children.

As a leader, I sought opportunities to get involved in the community, and was especially interested in community efforts that assisted our goal of strengthening our school. Bright Futures Omaha, Early Childhood Committee, Mental Health Task Force, and Strengthening Neighborhoods and Communities Task Force were among the groups included. I was also involved with the state in developing a definition of bullying and strategies for educators to respond to this growing trend in behavior. The point is, I was getting connected to resources and contacts that could collaborate with us and benefit the school and community. This provided information and involvement for us with resources and connections for our families.

I mentioned the family room earlier as one of our supports. We even offered tax classes and other classes periodically from the police and financial industry. Our family room liaison started a support group that offered English classes and ways to support your children's education. The parents ended up bringing food each week and spent much of the day working and assisting each other. It became a place of growth for many of our immigrant families. A school can become a connector for many of the families that attend, and a hub of productivity and growth.

One way I could get families to come to conferences at this high poverty school was to provide incentives. There was not a lot of trust early in this acute needs building, and a big goal was getting families to understand that the school was on their side. I had to win them over and develop a partnership. I had to show them we were collaborating for their child's success. We, as a school, offered resources and help in many areas.

We bought bicycles from a discount store and displayed them outside the office before conferences. The deal was for every teacher students met with at conferences, they received a ticket that was placed in a raffle box. The more teachers they saw, the more chances the students had at winning the bikes. We would do a small bike for primary and a larger bike for intermediate, and even offered helmets with the bikes. We needed incentives to get attendance up. We also provided food and access to services. This was a priority, and we did that by allowing agencies to have booths at unique events to reach our families. Sometimes we even had special guest speakers on various topics of interest.

Health care is a priority, especially in a high needs area. We used a vision truck that would come to high-poverty areas and do eye checks on the spot and set students up with glasses for no charge. We even would assist with dental services, and now there are dental trucks that come around doing check-ups and even assisting with dental care on the spot. These were important, because if the children were not in good health, they couldn't learn. We worked at getting any help we could to provide them needed services.

I once spoke for an organization called Voices with Children at a school press conference. We talked about bills that would help fund the health needs of impoverished students. It was important for these to pass again. It is so important that student needs are being met, so they are in the best state of health to learn. Once we had to push to help one student get to the dentist who had some serious tooth issues that were not being cared for. It is hard to concentrate on your academics with a sore tooth! Making connections with families and assisting them in getting connected to the services they need were important. Eventually, this school would have a school-based health center, which was highly needed. Other organizations have come together to assist the children of Omaha. These include: The Sherwood Foundation (Susie Buffett), Collective for Youth, Midlands Mentoring, Avenue Scholars, Partnership 4 Kids, and Building Healthy Futures (the last two sponsored through Mike and Gale Yanney). The philanthropists in Omaha are amazing and support the success of public education and our children!

As I mentioned before, a simple way I connected families to the school was making sure I posted all the history. I had the district carpenters make long wooden picture holders in a main hallway that ran for over 25 feet. I was able then to slide staff photos on plaques in this wooden track, creating a chronological history of the school. It had the 10 years I was principal (one as an assistant), as well as the previous years when another building combined into this building. Then it continued with the years after I left, keeping the history. Each plaque had a year and families could easily reflect on when generations of their family had attended there. This is important stuff for building community--history matters!

We dedicated the gym to the first African American quarterback in the American Football League (after being drafted by the Denver Broncos in 1968). Marlin Briscoe had attended the school in his elementary years, and we brought him back as someone who had worked and succeeded. We contacted him and invited him back, had a special assembly, and presented a plaque that would be on display outside of the gym in his honor.

The more you can connect with the community, the better. We invited a diverse group of people to speak at our school, including career influencers. All students need exposure to people and organizations within our society. Building a career focus was important for the success of our students. It still is and should be in many areas!

Anytime someone visited, we made sure they left with a school pen, school flashlight pen, pen stylus or some small symbol of thanks for giving us their time. Time, of course, is one of the most precious commodities there is, and it is a gift to give. Schools are community assets that can benefit from the support of outside agencies, businesses, and groups to improve areas in need.

I worked with the University of Nebraska at Omaha as a resource mentor for classes that helped upcoming administrators. The International Language University of Nebraska at Omaha student group (ILUNO) visited our third graders and discussed cultures while also learning about our school. My former ESL teacher joined UNO and helped teach the ILUNO group, creating a lasting partnership. We coordinated college visits and career awareness.

I invited other universities to visit our school and learn. They appreciated the diverse group of students in our building. The first building gave a chance to nearby universities to provide experience to future educators in a low-income city area. Many would visit us as a class for observations, to hear about the school, and join student teaching experiences.

We partnered with the Midwest Dairy Council and did the Fuel Up to Play Program for years. This is where the students track their nutrition and exercise daily. We did so well that they asked our school team to speak to the Dairy Council of Nebraska in Lincoln. We also beat other schools in the area and won a visit from an NFL professional football player from the Chicago Bears. The school and the Center for Nutrition partnered to train professionals on monitoring student physical activity.

We were open to partnerships, and that added to the success of the school and experiences for students. I had a pilot study from the university, a group that used Bricklayer, a type of coding system, who wanted to prove its efficacy for students. We implemented the strategy as an enrichment course. The goal of the study was to show how student coding could improve math scores. We had already been using different coding and knew it was helping our students, especially with math. We agreed to have some teachers trained and to supplement our math through enrichment courses. It is often extra work to open your doors but can be well worth it!

You can't underestimate the power of student families. I had parents join the focus school initiative because of its push for equity and to provide innovative experiences for all students. The way schools should be throughout every city. One of these families was the Barneys. Willie Barney was one of these advocating parents. I got to know him early on at the focus school since we had his son. The Empowerment Network, which he led, aimed to improve opportunities for African American students and families in Omaha. We discussed the initiative often. He is actively involved in the revitalization of North Omaha's *Village Zone* and works with the city and mayor's office with his wife, Yolanda.

Willie and Yolanda Barney are a powerhouse team. They publish Revive Magazine and work on community projects to better the city, such as Omaha 360, Cradle to Career, Step Up Omaha, and the Revive Center. Willie hosts monthly summits, forums and conferences. These are some initiatives they are involved in. He played a key role in obtaining Village Zone Federal Grants to upgrade the region along 24th street in North Omaha. His background in marketing, writing, and data research has influenced his holistic approach. He also hosts large African American leadership conferences in Omaha.

Willie Barney led a group to help change the law so districts could have focus school collaborations. He liked our success, after having observed three years at the Underwood Hills Focus School. He organized a group to attend the legislature and testified to get the legislation changed. The Byrds, Browns, Vollmers, and students organized and went to the state capital by bus to give testimony for new legislation. The parents and students testified to the success of the focus school and the merits of it being an excellent model. It worked and soon, even with two of the districts bailing, we could move back to my home district and continue the vision. I continued to be a part of his Cradle to Career Advisory for over 10 years, as principal of a school model succeeding with all populations. There is power in community support.

Another time, I had a grad student working on her degree in conflict resolution. I had her attend our opening meeting to get a feel for the philosophy and design of our building. Then she had some focus groups with teachers to study how they deal with conflict. The event ended with teacher interviews, a final presentation to staff, and her sharing results with the administrative team. It was excellent stuff! Most of what we found out we already knew, since we work hard with building a problem-solving environment. There are always things you can do to get better, and it is great to have more useful culture data to reflect on!

Keep partnering with universities to develop student teachers and cultivate educational leaders. Look for additional chances to do more. Look to join groups that are affecting education positively. Julie Sigmon was another of these influencers, becoming the director of Omaha STEM. The Omaha STEM Ecosystem was a group that started out of a desire to increase STEM opportunities for students across the Omaha area. I joined as a school representative to find out more of what is out there and to be a part of the design process in crafting these connections. Many groups, including schools, museums, and businesses, joined in the efforts. We were all coming together for a significant cause.

Pete Mott, our cafeteria manager, spearheaded the building of our school garden beds at the focus school, and the staff helped construct them. We built 13 raised garden beds on a weekend. It became a service project for our students as they helped move dirt, gravel and mulch. They also learned how to plant and grow vegetables. We eventually gained some support and help from the Omaha Garden Club, Boy Scouts and Burke and Bryan High School partners.

The Omaha School Foundation was a powerful partner and eventually, at the focus school, I got to know Toba Cohen-Dunning, the executive director. I also had two of her children go through the focus program. The foundation funded Kids Club in two of my schools, which included special speakers, field trips and experiences for students. The Sherwood Foundation played a key role in giving grants and support to our students, which is mentioned in different chapters of this book. Most districts have foundations and avenues for support, but these two are pretty incredible!

One of the biggest partnerships you can never overlook is your parents and families that make up your school community. This is what it is all about, partnering for the success of the students. A parent organization can help create a sense of ownership in the school. Relationships with your families are at the top of the list.

At all the schools I have led, I've used a teacher, student and parent compact (agreement). The first school I was at was a Title 1 building. This required you had a family compact. At the focus schools, we developed our own version of the family compact as a way of solidifying our partnership. We wanted everyone to be aware of our expectations for success. Staff crafted the first compact I had, printed it with our school logo, and worded it like this:

Indian Hill Academy - Teacher, Student, and Parent Compact

As a School, we will...
- provide quality instruction.
- frequently communicate student progress to families.
- provide guidance to help parents with homework.
- provide a safe and secure learning environment.

As a Student, I will...
- complete assignments and ask questions if I have a problem.
- resolve conflicts in a positive, non-violent way.
- talk to my family about what I am learning in school.
- come to school with a positive attitude ready to learn.

As a Family, we will...
- attend school events and parent-teacher conferences.
- ensure regular attendance and expect proper behavior.
- monitor homework completion and encourage daily reading.
- provide a safe home.

Teacher Signature_____
Date_____

Student Signature_____
Date_____

Parent Signature_____
Date_____

Gold copy to school; pink copy to parent.

I did this on No Carbon Required (NCR) paper to make it easier. We'd go over this with families at our BBQs and get them to sign the opening packets stuff. If that didn't happen, we could get it signed at Open House. Did it set everything in stone? No, but it gave our expectations. The compacts set the tone of what is important. The compacts we created for the focus schools were similar:

Teacher, Student, and Parent Compact

As a School, we will…
- provide quality instruction.
- frequently communicate student progress to families.
- provide guidance to help parents with homework.
- provide a safe and secure learning environment.
- develop and teach good character and positive leadership.
- respect and value diversity.

As a Student, I will…
- complete assignments and ask questions if I have a problem.
- resolve conflicts in a positive, non-violent way.
- talk to my family about what I am learning in school.
- come to school with a positive attitude, ready to learn.
- support good character and positive leadership.
- respect and value diversity.

As a Family, we will…
- attend school events and parent-teacher conferences.
- ensure regular attendance and expect proper behavior.
- monitor homework completion and encourage daily reading.
- provide a safe home.
- support and model good character and positive leadership.
- respect and value diversity.

Teacher Signature_____

Date_____

Student Signature_____

Date_____

Parent Signature_____

Date_____

White copy to school; yellow copy to parent.

We listed and talked about more partners in the focus school sections because we wanted to build a community and bring people together. Using the talents and strengths of partners is just as important as developing talents and strengths within your staff. Education is easier when people work together and realize we are all on the same team.

"Everybody has a story to tell; just listen to the story."

— Norman Cousins

Chapter 6:
Fostering Strong Relationships

Relationships are the one key that makes everything possible. This topic plays a role in many aspects of other chapters in this book, but the importance cannot be overstated. It deserves its own chapter! As you progress in leadership, it is so important to develop relationships. Everything becomes possible with strong relationships. Relationships end up being the keystone to making everything meld together. We need relationships to become an effective leader, working with staff and working with all internal and external groups.

As a leader, you must become a chameleon and understand the importance of emotional intelligence and getting along with many people. As a principal, you need to be a good listener, because everyone wants to share their problems with you. You become a counselor, a problem-solver, a motivator, an encourager…I could go on and on. The multi-faceted job takes on a life of its own and relationships are so important to making everything work.

I had this wonderful 3rd grader, Ania, who always gave me hugs on the playground and always maintained a smile. She told me her mom puts notes in her lunch almost every day and she never knows what they will say. One day she showed me one, and it said, "You are smart and beautiful!" What a nice thing for a parent to do. She was giving her positives all the time. She was so excited to get these notes every day. It was a small thing that meant a lot to her. Many of our students don't come with this luxury, so we must be the ones to increase that positive to negative ratio. I told her that is neat and suggested maybe my wife could write me notes or I could write notes to her too. She thought that was a great idea and the next day, of course, handed me a note she wrote for me that said, "Have a good day your asome." She had some punctuation and spelling issues, but you get the idea--the intent was there--great positive stuff! As a third grader, she was passing it forward. I loved it!

One thing I liked to do is give birthday cards to all the staff. You can buy them in bulk and keep them on hand. I would mark in my calendar the dates of staff birthdays and then, when appropriate, just grab a card and fill it out and put it in their mailbox. I also ordered some stickers that said, "We love our teachers and staff" and I started putting those on the seal at my third building. I also started taping a pencil (birthday or specialty that was on hand). This is a slight gesture that can make someone's day. The card and just remembering the day is the most important.

During the holidays, I'd also give a card, especially during the winter break around Christmas. I selected a card general for the holiday, since not all celebrate Christmas. I would hand write a message with something like, "I appreciate your strength on our team." It was always positive and promoted our collaboration and teamwork. The staff is a part of your work/school family and needs to be treated well. Then I would get a tin of shortbread cookies from a local box warehouse store for each staff member. It cost me some, but it was an investment in my team. Many looked forward to these shortbread cookies.

For staff and teacher appreciation, we did a card from the office team with a positive message and found something to buy that all could use. Most of the time, it was something with our school logo or something about the impact they were making with students. We actually liked to spread it out over the week with special treats, PTO lunch and partner treats provided on different days.

Another easy way to assist staff is by giving them a packet of Emergen-C when they are getting rundown or ill. This is something I kept on hand for myself at work and I would buy it by the case. There are 30 packets to a box, and I would buy it from warehouse stores, so you usually get three boxes. Anytime someone seemed to feel ill, I would put one packet in their box, sometimes with a pick me up note or sometimes just the packet. They knew it came from me and someone was thinking about their health. A small thing that shows you do care and want them to be 100%. Being positive is contagious and can influence the entire staff!

It is always good to acknowledge all the things people do throughout your staff. I would constantly thank people in my *Friday Focus* and publicly during a staff meeting or on the morning news. Acknowledging the accomplishments of others helps connect people to the vision.

As people retired or left, moving up to other positions, we recognized their transition. At Wilson, for example, we purchased small glass paperweights that had a lion head (mascot) done with laser on the inside. They came in a delicate case and were a nice remembrance of their time with us. Something with your mascot on it can make a friendly gesture. We would give these out at our end of the year luncheon and make it a fun time. At the first building I was at, we had small bells engraved for people retiring or leaving.

Celebrations are an important part of the culture. The staff may also want to do a quick get together in the library or gym or a special night. It depends upon your staff and the circumstance. We also had holiday parties and potlucks. The courtesy committee acknowledged staff difficulties and successes, and also addressed needs as they presented themselves.

To build good relationships, it's important to be a good listener. Staff, students, and parents need to feel heard and supported. Do I get drained? Yes, and that is why I have a chapter on balance. Working with people and bringing out the best in them is tiring and requires rejuvenation. As the leader, you address and deal with it all. It is important to understand the pulse of your building. True leadership is about helping people be their best.

Outstanding teachers and administrators are excellent at relationships. Teachers in the high poverty building taught parents how to help their children learn at home while they volunteered in class. Smart! Modeling and then giving a gradual release to parents, so they had the tools to support their student at home and in the classroom.

One day, one of the teacher's students was walking home and had a backpack that was full and heavy. He was dragging it down the hill to the projects where he lived. The counselor stopped him, and I was there also wondering what was going on. Why was the bag so heavy? He appeared not to care what damage the dragging was doing to his bag. Guess what? The bag ended up being filled with can goods and food for the family for the weekend. His teacher was making sure his needs were being met and he would come to school ready to learn. This was even before there was such a thing as backpack programs, which we later had, to provide food for students in need during a weekend. Amazing! Great educators know the value of relationships and consistently use it to bring out the best in their students while supporting families.

As a principal, you get to know your staff, and it develops into a family of sorts. If you are a relational leader, which to me is the best kind to be, you have an extended family. They have their difficulties, and you end up going through many life changes with them. I could joke with them and say, "We are one big dysfunctional family!" We would laugh and that is because we had positive relationships and went through difficulties together. We were a strong team! I have been through marriages, divorces and deaths with staff, other life events as well. As a leader, you end up attending many ceremonies and occasions.

I had a really delightful surprise once--an indicator that we had become a real team--when my staff on spirit day came to school full of spirit. I saw two teachers in the hallway on my way to the bus unloading area. One was leaning on the wall and the other was facing me. One had an image on her neck and the other on her face. It looked like a tattoo. As I approached, I asked what that was, and one told me they went out last night and got a little wild and got these tattoos. I tried to not act surprised or worried as I am thinking, "What in the world is that?" What I saw amazed me when I looked closer! I then exclaimed, "Hey, that's me!"

One teacher had found some special tattoo paper and created an image of an elf body with my face on it. It was close to the holidays, so they thought they would really liven things up on our spirit day. This continued throughout the morning as I continued to spot these mini tattoos on staff. Then I saw another teacher with one on her face. Another teacher had put it on his biceps and was flexing and trying to be sly by showing it. I continued to discover myself throughout the day. It was fun and showed how much I had empowered our staff. We support each other. It is not very often people will put their bosses' picture on themselves, since we practice shared and collaborative leadership, we are a team. It was so funny. What a fun moment! What an elite group!

One of our staff members at the Focus School was *highly* Irish, and every St. Patrick's Day, it was a big deal to meet friends at a local Irish Pub and enjoy Irish music. One year, I called her early in the evening and asked her if she had her lesson plans completed, knowing she was at the pub. She was with her educator friends and said, "My principal just called to check on my lesson plans!" She got a kick out of it, especially since she knew I did coaching visits and relied on classroom visits to tell the story. I usually wouldn't bother anyone in their personal time. It caught her off guard and we actually had a good laugh about that instance. She was also a top teacher anyway, so really, this was irrelevant. It all comes down to the relationship, or this would not have been funny or appropriate.

The one thing you will notice about this book is that about every one of my chapters has a story or situation that had something to do with relationships. This common thread is in everything that makes us successful. It is the cornerstone of success. You must be a builder of relationships. I could have an entire book and one page with "relationships" written on it and it would be enough to summarize leadership, so true. If you want to grow your leadership, grow your relationships! You cannot overlook this one important factor. Relationships are the glue that makes all things possible. If you don't have great people skills, you are working with a deficit and need to improve. Relating matters! This affects everything!

I had one of my teachers write me a note during appreciation week that said, "You believe in all students and teachers. I love that you put love and fun into your leadership and that you allow kids to be kids. You are an exceptional leader!" This was a wonderful note and identified the importance of care and fun too! More leaders should receive notes like this. It is okay to have fun and be happy and productive. People want to be cared for and know that you care as a leader. A team is exactly that, everyone working and experiencing together.

Every year I served as a principal, Ingra and I opened our house and had an annual big backyard BBQ to kick-off the new year with staff. It was a potluck, and we provided pulled pork and buns. It was a fantastic way to get new people introduced and start building those positive relationships. This was another gesture that went a long way in building our staff team. I did this at all three of the buildings I led. It was an excellent kick-off to the start of the year. A way to say I believe in you and support you as we begin a new year. It also helped to break the ice with new staff.

As a leader, building a community of care is important in developing a positive culture and team. It is so important to encourage and recognize staff and do it regularly. The Q 12 from Gallup's *Questions that Matter*, states: "My supervisor, or someone at work, seems to care about me as a person." If your staff cannot support this statement, you have some work to do with your culture. If your staff feels included and part of the team, you're moving in the right direction! If more leaders would build people up, there would be no stopping the success of an organization.

"If you don't teach it, don't punish kids for not being good at it."

— *Eric Jensen*

Chapter 7:
Introducing Positive Behavioral
Interventions and Supports

As a teacher, I learned the importance of relationships and motivating students within a classroom. Kids need to know they are safe and there are expectations with respect. As a new teacher, it takes a while to learn the skills necessary to work well with students.

Right out of college you get some strategies, but really little training with true classroom management. It seems as if the textbook suggestions of just using proximity control and a stern look don't always do the trick. As a new teacher, I had to learn how to create strong procedures and routines while developing a rapport. Building a classroom culture with high expectations and positive relationships is something you have to learn. When setting expectations, it's important to have proper procedures and routines in place.

I remember one of my early years as a green teacher at the middle school. We were having an afternoon dance and things got strange really fast. These were the days where school shootings were far and few between--at least mass shootings. We had practiced lockdowns, but nothing too serious. Gang members entered the building during the seventh and eighth-grade dance and went directly to the gym where we were. All of us supervising thought no big deal. I bet this is the opposing team coming for the wrestling meet we were going to have right after school. They weren't. Their goal was to get one of our students. They felt extremely comfortable just walking right in during our activity. They walked in as a group and immediately started looking for the student, who they went after once they spotted him. Our security guard at the time grabbed the one trying to get our student, and we all headed over toward them. The group then ran out into the hall with the principal and other adults chasing them out of the gym. As a new teacher, thinking I was smart, I ran the other direction and thought I could head them off before they got to the back door to exit the building. The principal all along was thinking, let's just chase them off and get them off the premises so no one will get hurt. I cut them off and jumped out in front of them. It was four guys, maybe more. I just remember a group. When I think back, I don't know what I was thinking I would do by myself, anyway. They did not care that I was a teacher in the building. The one immediately said, "We'll just kill you!" The principal and the group of teachers were close behind and were yelling, "Just let them go, Anderson!"

After receiving the threat, encouragement to move, and realizing they meant it, I moved so they could run out the back door by the dock and get away. This appeared to be the same door they came in through. These guys were wearing coats, covered up, and it was hard to tell if they were carrying any weapons. I would venture to say yes, they were carrying something. This could have gone worse.

I wish I could say that no one ever threatened my life again, but unfortunately, it would happen later as a principal. I was still in teacher mode. The principal was thinking of the safety of the school. I was not. I would soon think more globally and in a big picture way. Lesson learned!

This is also why you end up practicing lockdowns, tornado drills, fire drills, evacuations, pandemics, and other scenarios. You never know what will happen and it pays to have procedures and routines built in for whatever comes your way. Practice and conversation make it easier and allow you to take action with less thought. Your action becomes built in and almost reflex like. Safety, and especially the safety of all, becomes more important as a leader.

As I taught, traveling between two buildings, I developed my repertoire of teaching skills that would keep students engaged. Engaged students do not have time to misbehave and solid teaching can assist this. It took a while as I struggled like most first-year and new teachers do. Time, experience and training assist you in developing your toolbox of proven techniques and strategies. Learning to develop strong procedures and routines and looking ahead to how I wanted things to work made a difference. I learned how to develop a positive rapport with students and still could maintain high expectations.

I did my share of learning from master teachers, studying and researching and closely observing those who were successful. Many of those used positive behavior supports without realizing it. This was a time before that language was common, at least where I was. These were the days of building management plans, and they varied depending on the principal you were under. I never imagined I would train my staff and help others with positive behavior interventions.

Being at the acute needs, high poverty inner city elementary school led me into a Safe Schools Grant through the state. Our school psychologist, Janet Benton Gaillard, helped write and became a prominent member of the grant team. She had a positive philosophy for working with students, including those with special needs, to help them succeed in school.

As a new principal, I attended a statewide administrators conference in Kearny, NE and heard George Sugai present his research on using positive behavior support and assessment in schools. Timothy J. Lewis, from the University of Missouri, was another working on Positive Behavioral Interventions and Supports (PBIS). There were, of course, others, and many are still active in this area of study. They intrigued me with the challenges of educating students with severe behavior problems, how this area is increasing, and how we can set students up for success through various support systems.

At school, I suggested we needed to find alternatives to suspension so students can continue learning. We eventually became one of the five model safe schools for the district, but this didn't happen overnight. We had a lot of work to do in the meantime to develop our capacity to work with students. Keeping students in school needed to be a priority, and developing supports to meet their needs to keep academics flowing was the goal. We put together a team of teachers, administrators and key staff who could be the core team--a cross section of the school. We had done our mission and vision as a school and were now looking for ways to support it.

Discipline and behavior management was a problem. We needed to bring down behavior and increase academic success. Discipline means "to teach" and this was an area that needed further reflection. The philosophy of blaming the children was an area that had to change, and the new philosophy of working with students emerged. The focus was on teaching behaviors we wanted to observe. We reviewed George Sugai's research on tracking data and creating more of a data-driven decision-making system. We used William Sprague and Randy Sprick materials, and looked to best practices to set up our tiered system of supports.

We developed our positive philosophy around helping students to be successful. We developed what we called our "Instructional Discipline Leadership Team." Besides having a mission and vision for the school, we had a mission statement for this team as well. It read:

In collaboration with students, staff, parents and community, the Instructional Discipline Leadership Team provides for the development, implementation, and monitoring of procedures that promote responsible student behavior and a positive, safe learning environment in our school.

Having the time as a team--and as a staff--made this process possible through the state grant. The original team spent time over the summer learning about positive behavior supports. We learned productive ways of working with children. This safe school team met every Friday morning before school. Yes, early Friday mornings, and it turned out to be a fun, problem-solving group. We didn't always agree, but we had some great discussions. Each week, our leadership rotated, and we followed a template for our agenda. We set it up so whoever led started with a story, a joke, a quote, or something entertaining, then went through the agenda. This helped keep a consistent format for each meeting. Items were then on a cycle of rotating back to the larger staff meeting for discussion or vote, and there was a good back and forth. It was a good cross-section team of our school--about 8-10 people. We would review data, staff concerns, hot spots, trends and ways to be preventative. It was an action-driven team.

This core team made it easy to monitor what we needed. I practiced shared leadership with this team and could make sure we were moving toward our vision. After a school-wide philosophy was firmly in place, we were ready to move on. Then we dove into what supports we needed as a building. As a school, we developed building wide guidelines for success, settling on the three B's: Be respectful, Be Responsible, and Be Safe. The staff voted and selected these as our main building-wide guidelines. We reviewed examples from other schools and studied the research. Around these guidelines, we did what Sugai, Sprague and other researchers suggest. We developed rubrics of the behavior we want to see in different locations of the building. These expectations could then teach the correct behavior that we wanted to see happen.

We could promote this through our morning news, assemblies, and showing and modeling what we wanted to see. We used an instrument at the time called the Safe Schools Evaluation Rubric (SSER) from Ron Nelson and Barbara Ohlund, Arizona State University). The SSER had four components: Leadership Team to guide the strategic process, School-wide Organizational System, Non-Classroom Organizational System and Classroom Organizational System. Each area was setup to give what they called a service gap analysis. For each section, you would look at the current status of the system and decide if you were beginning, developing, or exemplary following a rubric guide.

The system used checkboxes to track progress and display strengths and weaknesses for key attributes. There was a descriptive summary of areas to improve. Then, the last area was the development of an action plan and timeline. We used this rubric under our first state grant a few times a year to gauge where we were. The rubric provided detailed characteristics for each system's beginning, developing, and exemplary phases. If you didn't have the characteristics in place as defined, the instrument decided where you currently stand. We completed this through discussion at a large staff meeting and set the pace for what still needed to be done.

The instrument assisted in discussions about behavior and helped articulate excellent talking points. By using intervention and prevention procedures, you can continue to help students with a high risk of failing.

As our district improved in positive behavior supports, they made a department for Safe, Secure and Disciplined Schools. The goal of this department was to teach and train principals, administrators, teachers and staff on effective positive behavior supports. It was effective. We were ahead of the curve and realized the importance of Positive Behavioral Interventions and Supports.

My counselor, James Cunningham, was a big part of our safe school's team and helped start this district department. James played an important role in bringing in programs that helped us identify child abuse cases and supported our students. This was a priority in our area since we had many incidents of abuse. We developed a sound reporting system that helped to keep tabs on the safety and welfare of our students. At the writing of this book, James is now serving as an assistant principal.

Teresa Hamilton was another strong counselor who followed in his footsteps. She became a principal. Eventually, I also had Brenda Martin as a part-time counselor who was a Jim Fay certified trainer. We could later use her skills in reinforcing Love and Logic with students, and offering parenting classes on Love and Logic. They all added to our excellent staff, providing needed supports! I had Brenda at two of my schools.

At one point, our district created its own rubric instrument called the OPS SET. It had five components: Beliefs, Foundation and Leadership, Common Area, Classroom, Individual Student Success, and Family and Community partnerships. OPS created this instrument similar to the SSER described earlier. Each component had 16 to 18 defining statements, and you marked whether it was: In Place, Partially In Place, Not in Place, or a Priority. These rubrics were excellent tools for gauging progress and setting the pace for what needed to be accomplished. Positive Behavioral Interventions and Supports (PBIS) have various ways to monitor progress and gather useful information. These versions define areas and have similar rubrics. The important piece is you have to have supports set up for all areas. Use your data, reflect, reassess, and change processes, procedures and supports around your needs. It is a constant situational assessment, allowing for a change of supports as needed.

There has been a larger national push recently to define the tiers of support that have been around since Sugai's work. Now, there is more of a focus in this area. The school had a pyramid system of support for students. It had three levels: Universal, Selected/Targeted, and Intensive. The education system now uses tiers to classify students based on their needs. Tier 1 is for everyone, Tier II is for targeted middle students, and Tier III is for high-needs students. The concept is constant: support needs to be personalized as we go up.

Those students at the top of the pyramid (Tier III) need more supports to succeed. George Sugai calls these students the "wolf pack." I remember that well from first hearing him at the principal conference in August 1999, when I first started getting interested more in PBIS. The pyramid of supports works the same for academics, and I often use a visual in presentations to staff that has academics on one side and behavior on another. These are the two extensive areas you look at for intervention and support. We must teach both academic and behavior areas.

At the high poverty building, we used no fancy data. Our data was based on our students' daily activity. It was what we were living every day and every hour. It was obvious the areas that needed our attention and support. This guided our team. The team analyzed various factors to identify areas that required help. We found through the data that when behavior goes down, achievement goes up! To track progress, we used an evaluation rubric and reflection sheets for the building and classroom regularly.

The school emphasized restorative practices in its Positive Behavioral Interventions and Supports. This staff handbook section has developed over time with input from staff and includes ways to support students:

STAFF HANDBOOK - DISCIPLINE, PBIS, MTSS-B:

The purpose of PBIS is to teach and reinforce rules, procedures, routines, and expectations to create a positive climate of success. All of us create this atmosphere of success. Teaching behavior is part of our curriculum and is as important as any other subject. Teachers handle routine discipline problems, and working directly with the parent is essential. Developing positive relationships will go a long way in making your work easier. Make frequent calls and keep them informed of their child's progress (positive and negative).

Go over the student handbook for the first two weeks of school and practice procedures.

Home visits can be made and should be arranged in advance. Notify the office when planning a visit and we will try to assist you. Please team up on home visits or Mr. Anderson, [name of assistant principal], or [name of counselor] can attend with you.

Make sure you have tried different intervention and problem solving before sending students to the office. **<u>Work with the student and call home/make contact on the day you have a problem.</u>**

If we send a student to the office, a student referral form must accompany him/her, stating the problem. We need referrals for proper documentation. State the facts of what happened; do not state your opinion or the recommended consequence. Make sure you sign and date all referrals, and spelling/grammar must be correct. Remember, our handbook gives guidelines for consequences. Our goal is problem-solving with students and keeping them on track with academics and behavior.

If the student used inappropriate language, write exactly what they said. Disrespect, fighting and serious offenses are to be referred to the office. **<u>Please do not use physical force of any nature in handling student situations unless it is for your safety or the safety of other students; call the office for an administrator.</u>**

The school management plan requires you to work with students positively, trying to find what works based on the individual needs of that student. Set up buddy rooms and time out areas. **Do not get into power struggles. Take care of problems without taking it personally. Practice and use "Fast Five" to gain attention. Develop those procedures and routines!**

It is extremely important that you pass out our handbook. Review expectations and consequences with your students and have them all sign the signature sheet. They are all to sign this document upon receipt of the handbook. We will then turn this signature sheet into

Mr. Anderson within the first two weeks of school. By this time, we expect that enrollment would have stabilized.

We will continue to collaborate on our Safe Schools Initiative to improve our positive approach to school management through PBIS. This continues to be an ongoing process.

Our Pyramid of Positive Behavioral Interventions and Supports

Conscious Classroom Management: Use Rick Smith's strategies from his Conscious Classroom Management book for effective classroom management. This is a great reference tool full of useable techniques and reminders. Teach all logical procedures and routines. Stay consistent. There are no punishments--just consequences. Teach two procedure routines per lesson. Constant reteaching is important. Assume the best, make positive connections, give choices and set them up for success (see other recommendations in our Professional Development section or the district PD 360).

Four Universal Skills: Positive Relationships, Preventative Teaching, High Staff Visibility, and Frequent Feedback

1-Positive Relationships: Establishing high-quality relationships between adults and students can influence student behavior.

2-Preventative Teaching: Systematic teaching and re-teaching of behavioral expectations using the same methods as used for teaching academics-direct instruction, practice, modeling and feedback.

3-High Staff Visibility: All staff is involved with the supervision of students based on agreed upon expectations for common areas.

4-Frequent Feedback: A teaching approach that reinforces responsible behavior and corrects irresponsible behavior through natural opportunities.

Fast Five: Building-wide attention getter. Eyes on the speaker, ears listening, mouths silent, hands folded, feet still. Signals 5, 3, 1 - Fast Five for attention, 3 for whisper voice, 1 for One-on-one conversations.

Positive Relationships: Don't underestimate the power of relationships and your students knowing you care. You can have high expectations and still be caring. All the research on discipline and PBIS always goes back to the power of the relationship.

Think Time: *Think Time* (Ron Nelson creator) is a non-confrontational way of controlling minor behaviors (procedures to be discussed and training provided). Send home the *Think Time* materials.

Review Think Time with Your Students and Model Expectations. This year, you are being assigned buddy rooms (see sheet). *Think Time* gives back classroom time, allows problem-solving and avoids power struggles.

Positive Action Center (PAC): Teachers may send students to the PAC room as a proactive reteaching/problem-solving intervention. Use classroom intervention first, then use *Think Time* and then send to PAC if needed. It is also best if the first call home is not from PAC. Use the Pac form, circle area, add comments, time and details. Students will use a script to call home from PAC and explain what happened.

Student Assistance Team (SAT): There will be an SAT coordinator. The SAT coordinator will manage behavior or academic SATs that are scheduled to assist our students as needed. It is helpful to have an informal grade level SAT or meeting to share ideas. Remember to document any interventions tried and bring those to the actual SAT (we will share more information on SATs at a faculty meeting).

Love and Logic: The simple use of love and logic can diffuse situations and assist you in working with our students. The easiest way is to create logical consequences for behavior and use comments that diffuse student remarks. Responses like: "I know," "Nice Try," "Bummer," "I like you too much to argue," or sometimes saying nothing at all can help diffuse a situation. Another option is to use "I've noticed" statements.

I Messages: Let students know what we expect by using I messages. For example, say "John, I need you to put the book in your tray." Handle situations calmly without using threats. We will do more training on de-escalation techniques.

Referrals: Explained earlier. Fill out fully. Our form gives us a student behavior analysis, which only works if we have all the data.

Suspensions: We will use short and long-term suspensions when appropriate. The administrators will follow the elementary student behavior guidelines listed in the student handbook and impose consequences at their discretion. Our goal is to re-teach through options like in-school suspension, moving to another classroom for a certain time, or restorative practices.

Emergency Exclusion: Used if a student has a communicable disease transmissible through normal contact or poses a threat to the health and safety of the school or if the student's conduct presents a clear threat to the physical safety of him/her or others, or is so extremely disruptive as to make temporary removal necessary to preserve the rights of other students in getting their education.

The best system uses a series of positive reinforcers that balance out the negatives. Praise and encouragement go a long way in

supporting our students. As a school, we are striving for a 4:1 positive to negative ratio.

Lion Pledge: Have the students say and learn the lion pledge daily. They can learn the meaning and make a promise each day to make positive choices. Developing School Pride builds our positive culture! We start with the *Pledge of Allegiance*, followed by the *Lion Pledge: "I pledge to do my best every day in every way, to be respectful, responsible and safe, to make our school no place for hate, showing true Lion Pride. Roar!"*

Teach the Three B's: Be Respectful, Be Responsible and Be Safe (building guidelines for success). All students will know this.

Character Counts: Teach and refer to the pillars of character regularly. Our Lions are trustworthy, respectful, responsible, fair, caring and display good citizenship. Teach the social skills needed.

No Place for Hate: We are a partner with the Anti-Defamation League, and we will provide activities throughout the year to reinforce accepting diversity and anti-bullying as well as staff students and community taking the *No Place for Hate Pledge*.

Reminder Sessions/School Meetings: Reminder sessions/school meetings happen once a month at the gym from 2:45-3:10 PM, led by the principal or assistant principal, with students grouped by bus lines.

Bus Groups: Since almost all our students arrive on buses, it is extremely important that we work with the students and develop positive relationships with your bus students and the buses you work with. Go over bus guidelines and the procedures the students will need to be successful.

Waging Peace: All classrooms will use the Waging Peace resource book and will do a lesson once a week (following the lesson schedule). You can use the time that works best for your classroom.

Steps to Respect: This is a bullying prevention program that all OPS has been implementing. There is a student bullying report form, prevention measures and response and coaching follow-up. [name of assistant principal] and [name of counselor] will coordinate these efforts.

Bus Incentives: Each day, the bus drivers will report to Mr. Anderson and [name of assistant principal] the success of the ride, and if the students receive a star. We post the stars on the board in the hall for students to see and, upon filling the chart, the bus receives an incentive.

Bus Compliments: Students can give bus compliments to their classmates using the bus compliment form, which we will read during our Friday Pride Power on air. They use the bus compliment form – a yellow half sheet.

Pride Power Coupons: Any adult in the building can give out Pride Power Coupons. Checking the exhibited character trait, we can add a

description. Take the top portion home and put the bottom part in the selection can for the corresponding grade level at the office. On Fridays, we will post them on the news, and about five students from each grade level will tell why they received it on air and choose a book/prize. It is important to ramp up the giving of these closer to breaks and before holidays. It should be a goal to give at least a few each day. Look for positives!

40 Developmental Assets: The Search Institute has identified 40 developmental assets as the things that must be present for a student to succeed in school. The target is 31 of the 40, but the average is usually 18.6. Keep this 40 in mind as we work with our students. The book *What Kids Need to Succeed* which has been provided to everyone is a good reference. *See 40 assets at the end of handbook

Check-In, Check-Out: We will setup processes for students in need to check-in in the AM and to check-out in the PM. These Check-In and Check-Out partners are important in making solid relationships and connections to help students be successful.

HeartMath: Teaching our students how to identify and control their behavior is important. The Emwave (with ear or finger sensor) is a tool for teaching students how to control their breathing and heart rate. Through using the computer program, they learn how to monitor and maintain self-control. We may use it as a calm down tool for certain students. Teach deep breathing skills to calm down.

De-Escalation: It is important that we work with students in a way that is respectful and that does not humiliate or stir them up more. The key is to calm them down and get them to a constructive state where reteaching can occur. Do not take things personally and escalate any situation in front of peers.

Lanyards for Hall Passes: Orange - Office, Green - Restroom, Yellow - Think Time, Purple - Messenger.

Morning News: In the live streamed news with principal and student anchors, we give reminders of: Three B's, Raising Hands, Fast Five, Think Time, Energy Bus Concepts, Character Reminders and then ending with our *Pride Pledge*. This reinforces a positive culture daily!

This ended the section of our staff handbook on student behavior.

There was also a section on child abuse, notifying parents and keeping our communication flowing. Other interventions not mentioned here were counseling sessions, mental health services, safety checks, and other types of support. The procedures and routines for lunch, recess, and enrichment were fully explained, and we had documents and schedules to support the processes.

The more routines and procedures with schedules in place there are, the smoother transitions will run. I originally had a hard copy handbook and eventually went to digital, but we reviewed it every year--especially our pyramid of supports for behavior. I always did a digital slide presentation with training that taught our PBIS as well as reviewed our handbook. It was updated each year as our behavior team made adjustments as needed. The handbook gives you a good idea of what was covered.

I would spend at least two-three hours on behavior, reviewing this section in our handbook, each process in more detail and giving de-escalation techniques. We'd talk about building a background of understanding around cultural proficiency, working with students in poverty, and our current demographics. The training helped to set our staff up for success. It was a must every year!

For the state grant, we had to track all kinds of data, and our early data was ugly. There is no other way to put it. I explored positive behavior supports because the data showed that kicking students out wasn't effective. As stated earlier, we had 256 suspensions, 2 expulsions, and this was during my first year as a principal! We had over 900 referrals. Our system--or lack of a system--was at capacity. Our workload overwhelmed us, and we couldn't keep up. We were in an unsuccessful mode of operation.

We had 40 students in special education with some verified behavior disorder, and our mobility rate (student turnover) was 45.4%. This even went up the next year to 54.2% until we developed strategies, eventually bringing mobility down to 32.9% within four years. This trend continued in a positive direction over the 10 years I was there. We also brought suspensions down to 40 within a few years, and those ended up being our repeat offenders for whom we had special action plans. We were making tremendous progress.

I am a firm believer in what Ruby Payne, Eric Jensen, and others say: it's important not to expect students to know what they haven't been taught or what they don't know. They come from many backgrounds and--if one of those is poverty--they have a unique set of survival skills that may not be the same as yours or mine. The students need to be taught the behaviors that are expected. and learn the acceptable social queues that are needed in various settings. They need to know how to survive in different environments. Many times, we must teach these, and since the real meaning of discipline is teaching, this is what we must do. I have always stressed to my staff we are always reteaching and reinforcing what we want to see. Teaching is our job, academics and behavior work together.

Jensen's research, in his 2009 book *Teaching with Poverty in Mind,* addressed the ability of the brain to change within all students. He shows how students in poverty can change. This is amazing. He states: "Those in poverty typically have dysregulated stress response systems. You must give kids appropriately increasing amounts of control over their lives at school and teach coping skills." There it is again: teach those skills that you want them to know. This also shows us that there really are no excuses. The brain can change, and we can, too. Teaching learning structures and specific strategies can help students, especially those with more needs. Learning and behavior connect.

I spent a large amount of time training staff about students in poverty and effective behavior practices to get the most out of students. It is extremely important that the staff know the demographics of the building. They must develop cultural proficiency in the school population. The staff needed to understand who we were working with and what that means in teaching and working with the students effectively. They needed training about our students and what they were going through, and the cultural norms they were following to survive. They learned to teach what they needed to succeed in our environment and society.

This also meant self-reflection for staff members, and coming to grips with the current lens through which they viewed students. It is especially important with a diverse mix of students and your community demographics. This requires the leader to help start self-reflection and self-discovery. Together, we looked at what skills and supports students needed to succeed.

This brought us to the research on 40 Developmental Assets. These are the building blocks of healthy development that help young people grow up healthy, caring, and responsible (Search Institute, 1997). The target for children is 31 of the *40 Developmental Assets* and the average number a "normal" student comes with is about 19. This means that higher need students or students in poverty are going to come with many of these assets not being met. This is where we come in--it is important for schools to fill the gaps and help make connections to address this need. We must patch the holes, so to speak. Schools have had to work at recovering missing assets over the years.

These assets, or what we call connections, are what make children well rounded, closing what I call growth gaps. Many of these are things that make students want to attend school and be a part of the school community.

Increasing attendance and helping students to connect to school is extremely important. At Indian Hill, we started a program through a federal grant called a Community Learning Center (CLO). The after-school classes met after dismissal and provided the students with a hot meal to ensure our students received a dinner. I had a CLC coordinator, and we ran 12-13 classes a night from Monday to Thursday. The classes went from the end of regular school until 5:30 PM. They helped our students stay engaged in that critical after-school time. The classes offered included homework help, martial arts, dance, tutoring for different grades, chess club, and more.

We also had evening programs like Fast Families (with provided meals and training), Ponca Tribe Karate, and Basketball that went from 5:00-7:30 PM and ended with open basketball PAL (Police Athletic Union) from 6:00-9:00 PM. This means our acute needs students might be at our school most of the day and evening. Keeping them busy and off the streets in constructive ways was great for our population. It was about providing opportunities for growth and success in school, as well as a safe place to be.

Besides understanding our population, we were working with all aspects of supporting our demographics. We spent time on de-escalation and how to work effectively with students. Every year, I trained in this area. Believe it or not, we can make as many problems as the students! How teachers react, address and work with students can build a partnership or create a war. The tone a teacher uses makes a big difference with a student. They can also see right through your demeanor and can tell if you are being sincere.

I have always believed in the power of *Love and Logic* (Jim Fay, 1994) as a technique in our toolbox. I continued to remind the staff to use Fay's "I've noticed" statements with hard students. This works particularly well with teachers that just don't have a natural talent for developing those relationships. The way it works is you pick out one of your most challenging students. Then make daily comments, like "I notice you like the Chicago Bulls" or whatever you notice about them. If you maintain the ability to keep conversations going around a subject that interests them, this can help your relationship. Students notice when you take notice of them and their lives. They can also tell if it is a show, or insincere. Try it and the results will surprise you.

If you are patient and deliver logical consequences, the students will respond well, especially if done properly. Students also must learn that being fair is not always equal. I always tried to be fair with students as much as possible and help them understand my logic, especially if there were variations. As with most practices, it is really based around relationships. In my training, I teach people an important point: we dislike the behavior, not the student. It is also important that the student knows and understands this.

I had a new teacher once who was struggling with relationships, and she was absent. We had a sub, which can often have a tough time, but on that day, we received fewer student problems from the class and no referrals. This started me checking out what was happening. We were already working with the actual teacher of the room, who was struggling. I was curious, so had to check it out. I always stop to greet subs anyway, let them know I am the principal, welcome them and let them know if they need anything, I am here, as is our supportive staff.

On this day, I stopped in more than once to see the dynamics and why the classroom was working so well. The sub ended up being a retired principal from another district, but the fact he was a former principal was not the key. He was a jovial, cheerful guy with a great positive attitude. His demeanor made them want to please him. This was a tough sixth grade class, but he was doing extremely well. While the students were at one of their special area classes and he was alone, I asked if he had any problems. He had Tonya (using this name for an actual student). She was a tough girl who was a natural leader and could be positive, but could also be a negative influence on the whole grade level--especially if she does not know you. He said right away she came in with an attitude and did not want to listen. When he said "Tonya" as he was giving her instructions, she refused to comply. She finally said, "My name is Kiki!" He did not miss a beat and said, "Okay Kiki, can you get out your assignment and…" He just did what I told our staff to do: choose your battles. It doesn't matter if she wanted to be called Kiki. He went right along with it--which showed respect--and she respected him back, and he immediately won her over. It is important not to go down that road of getting into power struggles. Why is it so many educators cannot stay out of power struggles? It is easy to escalate a situation. He did not escalate the situation and tactfully avoided a potential conflict. He was a smart educator!

When I first started teaching and was inexperienced, I became frustrated with a middle school class. I knew they were going to interrupt my lesson and one day I was ready. As a tough student interrupted me disrespectfully, I made myself angry (I am naturally patient, so yes, made myself angry). I hit the yardstick on a table, stopped and said, "Who runs this classroom?" I was fully aware of how she would respond. Boom she responded with a resounding "Me", and I said, "Get Out. Here is your referral" Not one of my proudest moments. I set her up and knew she would not answer that I was in charge. This would not have happened if I had better engagement, a relationship or other tools to use. I did not de-escalate the situation. I had to learn strategies beyond what they were teaching in college. I became skilled in positive behavior support and learned the significance of relationships. I would also learn to work with all kinds of students and understand them.

Culture is a big part of positive behavior supports and the *feel* of a building is always clear upon entering. Taking care of students and meeting their needs can often be clear. I was attending a meeting one day and was absent from bus duty at the focus school in the morning and received this text from our library media specialist. She said as the students were getting off the bus, one student said to another, "Why would you think I would have a lighter? I learned my lesson when I burned my house down." While this sounded absurd, it actually was true. The student was a third grader and played with fire and burned down the family's house. Not funny! The teacher checked on him just to be safe. We worked with the student, and they had counseling involved, so he was doing well at this point. I guess we are glad the sessions were working, at least by his response to the other student. It seemed like we were doing something right. We also had a relationship and were working closely with the family, who had four students going through our school.

It is interesting that positive behavior supports have been around for a long time, but I was unaware of them after becoming a new principal. George Sugai's seminar had a significant impact on my practice by introducing me to an alternative approach to behavior. We started with Positive Behavioral Interventions and Supports (PBIS) through the state grant in 2000 with a small cohort of schools from our district. This was even before my district was on board. In time, they started what were to be called Safe, Secure and Disciplined Schools. At the time of writing this, they have brought back Multi-Tiered System of Supports for Behavior (MTSS-B)--a different name, but still a pyramid of supports for students. These interventions are based on research by George Sugai, William Sprague, Randy Sprick, and Tim Lewis. Additional experts like Rick Smith, Allan and Brian Mendler, Jim Fay, Doug Fisher, and Nancy Fey have also contributed to the research.

I needed to do something better to keep students in school and used PBIS for most of my years as a principal. The district's behavior staff development system changed because of a change in superintendents. Incoming school staff had no consistent training or foundation for four years because of the lack of a Safe Schools Department. I cautioned the temporary superintendent about future behavior problems without PBIS training and the Safe Schools Initiative. I'm not a rocket scientist, but it was no surprise that schools had issues with behavior, students, and capacity four years later. This was in many buildings, but not in all buildings, since there were pockets of us still using these systems and approaches with students. By the end of the next superintendent's term, he brought in MTSS-B and appointed a person to bring Positive Behavioral Interventions and Supports back. It finally rolled back around, but this concept should never have left. Now, the new principals and other leaders will get more of the training they need and be able to implement these processes with staff.

A powerful vision for a school includes teaching students about common areas--teaching what they don't know. It all fits together. Teaching guidelines for success and expectations around all the different areas of a school is important, and should cover all aspects, including common areas and buses. Collaborating, teaching, and developing a common language to support students at all levels. There is no quick fix and working with students takes more time to be effective. It is not the easier solution, but it is the best to equip staff and students to succeed.

When we began PBIS at the high poverty building, our success guidelines were based on the program *Character Counts*. The tenants were: Trustworthiness, Respect, Responsibility, Fairness, Caring and Citizenship. We quickly learned that this was too many guidelines for success. Despite the concepts being useful for our learning, we had to limit our guidelines. We then moved to the three B's: Be Respectful, Be Responsible and Be Safe. These guidelines worked well and helped us move forward.

Then we narrowed it down. After a few years, we used one main building guideline, Be Respectful. We found that everything we needed to teach our students had something to do with respect or the lack of respect. This was one clearly focused area we could teach around, and it made a difference. We taught social skills and Character Counts concepts as support for our main building guideline.

As we formed the Focus School, we decided as a staff to use the three B's: Be Respectful, Be Responsible and Be Safe. It fit our needs and we established posters and expectations for what it looked like in the different areas of the building. We established teaching points and taught the correct procedures and routines for students to be successful.

As a staff/team, you need to decide what are the best guidelines for your building. Then you can expand out to the many areas in and around the school, and teach the procedures and routines needed to be successful throughout the building and grounds. The guidelines should be a normal part of the building's culture and we need to teach and show how to follow them.

Many times, students just want to be heard. I love what Randy Sprick says about making a targeted request, preferably not calling out a student. He says, make a specific request and back off, just get away. Keep teaching and eventually the student will comply on their own terms. This only works if you back off. It works and is a solid strategy. I have taught this to many.

It is hard for some people to make a request and back off, so they end up escalating the situation. I guarantee there is going to be more talk and work of de-escalation since many staff have difficulty with this. They turn it into "I can't let them get away with this!" They take things personally. You can't take things personally! Remember what I say, "Dislike the behavior, not the student." I have already completed many staff trainings on de-escalation. We have seen an increase nationally with law enforcement in de-escalation training. Nebraska's State Legislature is considering funding for schools to train their staff in de-escalation. It is much needed!

I recently consulted in a school building with acute needs. During my stay, I had to be in a fifth-grade room with unruly students who didn't let the teacher start the day. Some students were being disruptive, and instead of calling them out, I used a technique from *Love and Logic*. I interrupted them and said, "Students who follow directions and listen may stay in the classroom!" One student jumped up and gave a verbal response about always being picked on. I responded calmly, "I was talking to the entire class, not you in particular." Many of these students think you are singling them out. I didn't want to get after the entire class. Here, most of the students were misbehaving, and calmly making this statement made it clear to all the expectations. It wasn't said in a threatening manner. I was simply restating the expectations. The tack in how you address things matters!

I had a student with emotional needs in my office who required special education. His behavior was labeled ED, which stands for emotional disturbance, and includes emotional and behavioral disorders. I like the term better than in the past, since the descriptor is about the behavior itself, not the child. It is all semantics and education is big on new acronyms and labels! What I was getting to is this: I had this student sitting in my office waiting for his grandmother to pick him up. We were just talking at this point, and he said out of the blue, "This is the office of Hope!" I asked what he meant, and he said, "We sit down and have a conversation and solve our problems." This was a third grader, and I would say he was pretty intuitive. I couldn't have said it better. I loved how he saw the interactions in this office! We problem-solve with students and help them change their behavior positively. I want them to succeed, and I think they know it. This was validation. Never underestimate the interactions and connections that you are making. Many students just want to be heard and know that you are listening.

My guidance teacher at Wilson Focus was doing a lesson, having the students write letters to me on why Wilson Focus School was excellent. One girl said, "It's because of Mr. Anderson–he's nice." She told me this later in a note and it was nice to hear since culture starts with leadership. This was further reinforced when I was greeting the arriving buses. I had a student assisting me that morning. The student was a high energy student who sometimes benefited from being given extra tasks or duties. I asked about their last principal, and they said, "I don't even want to say her name, she didn't talk to us." High expectations matter, but so does the relationship. The relationship makes things work better.

Developing your ability to work with students is an ongoing effort. This is especially important for students who have recurring issues.

This is one of those Professional Learning Community (PLC) concepts for staff to think about: "What do we do when they are not learning?" Since behavior is a part of instruction and it is another subject area, "What can we do better?"

One role in which I have served for several years has been assisting one of the large medical facilities in the area. They have a Residential Treatment Center (RTC) helping students challenged with behavioral issues. I have been the principal/superintendent for them since 2006. I used my vacation days to evaluate the teachers at the facility during my off time as a principal elsewhere. These appraisals had to be done to meet the state requirement of having a certified school administrator observe and appraise.

There have been two teachers, and they oversee elementary, middle and high school students. The students are the tough cases from all districts, and their prior building has transferred them out. The students stay at the RTC, get treatment, therapy, attend school and can be there as long as it takes to correct the behavior. It is a lockdown facility. The students complete their schoolwork independently while in the classroom, using the Accelere program on a computer system. It allows the students to hear tutorials and complete work, and even maintain credits for high school. They usually have at least two assistants in the room who also work with students. The teachers do extremely well working with the students, and it all comes down to relationships. The students know the expectations, procedures, and routines.

Upon one visit to the RTC, I had just visited the older students and had left the younger student room. I was in the hall completing my notes as they escorted the class to a 10-minute snack break in another area. Out of the corner of my eye, I noticed a high school student I will call

Adam sitting on a bench by the double doors that would have to be opened by security. He was making noises and talking. It was obvious he was on a break from the room or somewhere. As one of the teacher assistants passed him, he was making noises and said, "I don't care! "F**k this!" He was using the "F" word frequently. The teaching assistant tried to calm him, but it didn't help. A security guard tried to give him instructions, but he didn't listen and remained in the hall.

Adam was curious about me, and I have had many students with emotional difficulties, so to help de-escalate him, I asked, "What is your name?" He told me he was Adam. I said I was there observing his teachers. He didn't really care about that, but it was small talk and let him know why I was there. I asked him where he went to school, outside of this place. He said in Bellevue. I told him I was a principal and probably knew his principal. It did not impress him since he wasn't happy with the school he thought had put him there.

I said I grew up in Bellevue and started talking about the high schools. As we talked, he lightened up. He then started listening, since we had a connection. He started telling me why he got in trouble and how he ended up there. They had moved from another place to Bellevue, and he was a new student at his building. As we talked and discussed things in a calm voice, he settled down and we talked about different parts of town. I stayed listening, leaning against the wall outside the classroom, and he was still across the hall in his corner. I told him some good things about the schools and as he explained what he did, I could get him thinking about his behavior. He wanted to get out, and I said, "Do you think this behavior is going to get you out and show you are ready to leave?"

You could tell his wheels were turning as we talked. I even said that his behavior probably made the situation worse at one point and told him he needed to get this taken care of and get out of here and get it back together. Soon, the class returned, and I followed them back into the classroom, observing and taking notes. The assistant complimented me on how I handled Adam in the hall. When I came out to leave, there was a security guard talking to him and another assistant. I jumped into the conversation and went over and told him to keep working at it and do what he needed to do to be released. I told him it's not worth it to make matters worse. He finally realized that his actions didn't match his words. He was going to have to change if he wanted to leave. I gave him a fist bump, and we both said goodbye. I need to illustrate a point. Earlier, I wasn't reacting to his shouting of obscenities and just started talking *with* him, not *at* him. I also ignored what he was trying to do to get attention. Mutual respect goes a long way, and he also calmed down. We often see directives as directives. I was hoping the adults watching learned from my lead. You can't really force compliance, in leadership and with people. These people are doing well with challenging children in many difficult situations, but on this day, he just wanted to be heard.

Once, as principal of the last building I was in, I had a student come up to me on the playground and say, "You are my favorite principal!" I, of course, thanked them and asked why they would say that? They said, "because you talk to us." This is important to children. I asked about their last principal, and they said she just told us what to do, gave orders and didn't really talk to us much. Ouch! Obviously, whoever this was did not affect them positively. It is so important to make connections. The students need someone they can trust to listen and problem-solve with. Therefore, check-in and check-out systems work well. Students with potential difficulties can benefit from a morning routine to stay on track. As they check in, there is time for reinforcement, problem-solving, and reconnecting to keep them focused.

My first high poverty building had issues with gangs in the neighborhood. There was also a local gang that was affiliated with the projects in which most of our students lived. As discussed in an earlier chapter, we worked with the Omaha Police Department, South Omaha Probation, and the gang unit. Our focus was on gang intervention groups led by Beto Gonzalez and promoting career awareness and positive activities for students. We wanted to become their other family, a school family. It was important to our culture that students also knew they could not wear gang colors or bandanas in school. They could not have a pant leg up, or any other obvious sign of affiliation or disrespect. These non-negotiables became a part of our positive culture, and the students showed respect by adhering to them. We had to ask them to remove or correct their dress, but we handled it respectfully and with tact. We faced a challenge from external sources that would step in as their other family or connection if we didn't create a strong support system. This was outside of their *real* family, and we needed to fill the gap or someone else would.

Keeping students safe is a priority now, more so than in the past, with school shootings, pandemics and other disasters. As I was ending my career as a principal, there were all kinds of national and state initiatives directed at keeping our students safe. One of those came from the I Love U Guys Foundation. The foundation supported schools, districts, departments, and agencies with operational guidance. They have wonderful materials. There are protocols for lockouts, lockdowns, evacuating and sheltering. Most of the districts in Nebraska are using this standard response protocol. This makes it easier for city agencies, first responders and law enforcement to assist schools in emergencies. Our safety department gave us information to use as standard procedure during lockdowns in Nebraska districts.

The complexity of running a school has become more of a challenge and the more procedures and routines that are in place, the better the school can respond. As the world changes constantly, safety measures for students are also growing, and even school buildings are promoting safety. Office areas are located to clearly view who is entering. There are cameras, buzzers to enter, and most school buildings operate with secure doors. As society changes, schools will have to strengthen around what new threats are present, and what the needs are to keep our children protected. This is an ongoing goal and will continue to develop and change with the times. Schools must continue to be a safe place for our children to develop and grow, socially and academically.

"It is not fair to ask of others what you are unwilling to do yourself."

— *Eleanor Roosevelt*

Chapter 8:
Getting Things Done

Many companies have created whole campaigns around this focus of getting things done. As a principal, "Let's get to it" is an excellent motto to have and can function as a positive mantra. I am not saying to use it to be a dictator or use poor leadership skills barking orders at everyone. I mean, doing what is necessary as you need to. Job descriptions aren't everything. Do what is necessary to assist your team.

Over the years, I have done everything from painting lines on the playground to cutting down trees with my chainsaw. I've drilled holes, hung pictures, ordered parts, and fixed a variety of things. I've washed lunch tables, planted bushes, painted walls, and cared for landscaping. My wife and I are both handy and can repair things, which has come in handy in both our leadership roles. Once, when the water was off for part of the day, I had to carry five-gallon buckets of water to make the toilets flush in the school!

Another time, I had a teacher, Ms. Fischer, come to me and say, "We have a mouse in the ceiling, attending fourth grade!" She said during class, the students see him scurrying through fluorescent light fixtures as he makes his way across the ceiling tiles. I had to look and sure enough, every so often you would see this mouse body shape moving inside the light to another area unseen above your head. After school, we watched for him until he came out. We had a plan! I stood on a table, opened the ceiling tile, and was ready to tilt the tile when he came along. Mr. Anderson (no relation) and a 6th grade teacher grabbed a small trash can and held it up to catch the mouse. It was a good plan...or so we thought. The mouse did not come back--he was on to us! I put a few traps in the ceiling, thinking we would get him overnight. In the AM, I opened the ceiling tile and checked so I could remove him before students arrived. Guess what? He was gone, and we didn't see him again. Maybe he found his way back outside. Maybe he had had enough of fourth grade! This was just another day in the life of a principal.

There was even a time one of our down spouts off the side of the gym fell off. It was about a 50-foot spout. We put in a work order and even though we have excellent service crews, something kept coming up. Our district also only had one large lift, and it ended up being in the shop for repairs. To make a long story short, this went on for months, with no repair being made. We started having rainstorms and the water would fall out of the remaining spout on to the playing field and directly on some of our classroom garden boxes. This started eating holes in the ground and causing all kinds of damage.

Finally, when they came to repair it, the lift was down again. I had gone through the channels and tried to get this completed. I didn't have money in the budget for contracted services. Guess what? This is when you roll up your sleeves and do what needs to be done. I ended up loading up my 28-foot ladder on my SUV roof and stopping by the hardware store to get parts and sealant. Then I fixed the gutter, added a bracket, sealed it, and the following week, repainted the sealant areas to match the rest of the building. I did this on a weekend. Our secretary cancelled the work order later, and when they arrived to finish it at last, she calmly informed them that our principal had fixed it. "That's not my job" is *not* a phrase that gets things done.

There are certain things you can do to keep your grounds and building looking nice, and that should be a priority. This is part of your culture and climate. This willingness to do all kinds of things to make your school better rubs off on your staff and the district staff. It also influences the neighborhood. Leading by example and taking on what is necessary helps your credibility. The creed of being a servant leader is true. Leading by example and modeling this type of leadership is powerful. Doug Reeves even talks about doing "the scut work" as a leader. This is work that may not fall within your duties. There are enough people out there who will say it's not in their job description, but don't be one of them. Servant leaders do what needs to be done.

I always kept in good with all the tradespeople and craftworkers of the district, and they would do good solid work for me. It gets around who they like doing jobs for. I consistently made time to communicate with them, clarify my intentions, and show appreciation and admiration for their work. This is another area of relationships that really matters if you want to make things happen.

There was another time we wanted to create an outdoor classroom area. I purchased benches for our bus loading area. I ordered two metal benches for our school in our colors, but the concrete crew was too busy to install them. So, I took matters into my own hands, bought concrete anchors, and installed the benches myself on a day when there were no teachers or students. They were so nice and worked so well that I ended up buying two more and installing them to have four benches for our outdoor bus waiting area. They also could hold a classroom for reading or learning outside. Some things need to be done in a timely manner. This is especially true if it influences instruction or the classroom.

The first building I was in as principal did not have air conditioning, and I was there from 1998 to 2008. This is not exactly the era you would expect to still have schools without air conditioning, but this was the case. The office and the cafeteria were air-conditioned. There were some window units around. I brought in an electrician and installed ceiling fans in classrooms and industrial fans in the gym.

I continually built dollars into the budget to use contracted services in increments to improve our building. There were no bond dollars or renovation plans. I started adding window units to every classroom with any spare dollars outside what I needed for curriculum supplies. I learned quickly the district-approved units to buy, and put in work orders for the district electricians and carpenters to install the units.

This was also the era of zero-based budgeting, so I could move some funds toward contracted services. The maintenance supervisor said to stop ordering units because I was installing them too quickly. I was almost finished air conditioning all classrooms when the district put me on hold. A local benefactor who frequently made large donations to the district and our school heard me talking about this and said what do you need in dollars to complete the building with air conditioners. I think it was about $6,000. She said it was no problem, that they could do that. The district contacted me and completed the process. They also added a larger electrical panel, beefed up the wiring, and installed window units into the rest of the building, which was a great help. This was still a temporary fix until future bond issues, but before this, we were one of three buildings that still did not have air conditioning. We also were the only three who could cancel school due to the heat if needed. After I left to start another school in 2008, the district wrapped up a bond issue and my old building finally got central air in 2016, with much needed renovations. It had taken eight more years after I had added the last of the window units as a band-aid.

The bond covered many additions and needed improvements across the district--most of which are completed now. As I write, they are working on Phase II of the bond issue, to complete work and continue to add needed buildings, space and improvements. Supporting schools through property taxes is important to me as a homeowner. It helps improve education, facilities, and prepare students for society. Bond issues are often a way for school districts to get funds for much needed building improvements and resources.

This resourcefulness pays off in all areas. If you are trying to get curriculum that is needed, materials or instructional needs, fight for your cause. Develop a case, a rationale, share the logic, and specific reasoning. What are you doing to support and develop your students in your school and community? They are the priority. They also deserve the best resources, facility and surroundings you can offer. Equity should be across all areas and buildings throughout a city, but the reality is we know they often are not. I know that any school I lead will compete with any school, aesthetically and academically. That is driven by my inner achiever. We are always striving to be the best. If you don't believe this about your school and are not willing to do what it takes, you should probably find a new job. Blunt, but true. Our children need educators willing to go the extra mile and push them toward success.

The students need advocates. When buses missed students, I would go pick them up. I wanted them in school and sometimes that was the only way to do it. Once I picked up two students in the first week of school, since the contracted bus company refused to go back and get them. I informed the transportation director about the issue, and the company called to apologize, stating that they usually go back. I was not upset in the email, but was letting them know, if I must pick up children to get them to school I will. It is a priority for them to be in school and I need them--all of them--here.

At another point, I needed to add equipment to the playground and approached Susie Buffett, daughter of world-renowned investor and Omaha native, Warren Buffett. She is a powerful supporter of public education and early childhood development, and founder of the Sherwood Foundation. I asked if she would come to the school to meet about adding to the playground at this high poverty inner city school. With a different topic in mind, she arrived at the school to talk. She then laid out the plans for an early childhood center on our campus. She suggested, "What if we give you the playground and establish an Educare that would benefit the community?"

This was an enormous project that could inject hope and early childhood care into a much-needed area. If you are not familiar with an Educare, they are state-of-the-art facilities for early childhood with excellent high-quality teachers and staff. They are promoted as "A catalyst for change sending a bold message about investing in the first five years." Look up Educare and you will find they are being funded all over the United States. The goal is equal opportunity for all and a leveling of the academic playing field. This was a much-needed facility that would prepare our Pre-K students for the now all-day Kindergarten program we housed. Wow! What do you say to improvements like that? This was a major move that had the potential to change the community. They would have parent classes, infant support and training for new mothers. We were excited for the opportunity, and plans started to get underway.

I remember carrying around a proposed plan of the layout for the Educare in my professional portfolio that I could show at a moment's notice. I did this for two years as our district fell into some local politics and the project was put on hold. In fact, I remember the day before construction, I received a call that said we were putting the project on hold for now, until some district and city issues get straightened out.

I was highly disappointed since I had spent the last year assisting in moving a row of houses that were across the street from the school, and talking to homeowners about how this step would get us closer to having top notch early childhood education in the community. The houses were purchased by the district and removed, and everything was set until this hold was placed on our construction. When I say assisted in moving houses, I mean I had to convince the homeowners that it was a good idea to sell to the district and let us demolish their homes for this future early childhood care facility. We also had a plan to move portables and to add four classrooms to the existing school building. This project prompted some much-needed improvements. Unfortunately, this construction was started two years after the intended date, but there is good news: it is fully functioning and there have been other Educare facilities added to the Omaha area and around the nation. I was invited back for the groundbreaking, since, by this time, I was starting a new school elsewhere. I was glad to be included in this piece, after having assisted with the work to get this project started.

In the meantime, there was what I would call a turf dispute among the districts which came out of the "One City, One School District" dispute. This is what caused the original construction to be on hold for two years. As a response, the Nebraska Legislature created the Learning Community, made up of 11 districts within the Douglas and Sarpy County areas. They also included in the legislation the proposal for what they were calling focus schools that could be created within each district. This is the trajectory my career would eventually take as

I would soon become the original leader of the first collaborative multi-district focus school in Nebraska.

It reminded me of my dad's favorite turn of phrase: "A fella could..." and he would get a twinkle in his eye as he'd continue with his latest innovative idea. He was creative, inventive, and always solving problems. He never let grass grow beneath his feet and I think I inherited that trait as well. I have always been action-oriented and into making things happen (I think it's an Anderson trait).

"We cannot always build the future for our youth, but we can build our youth for the future."

— *Franklin D. Roosevelt*

Chapter 9:
Doing What is Best for Children

At my first principalship, we needed to make many changes to set our students up for success. In this high poverty environment, we needed supports and ways to provide opportunities for children.

One of the things we found we needed was more time with our kindergarten students. They were coming in behind, lacking social skills, and having a great deal of ground to make up. I had an early childhood portable, an early childhood special education room, and four half-day kindergarten rooms. This was a time that early research was showing the benefits of having high poverty students in longer day sessions.

I wanted to remove our early childhood room, which did not serve us at the time, and add a couple of all-day kindergarten rooms. I am all for early childhood, but at the time, I needed more space for kindergarten, and time to try two all-day kindergarten rooms. I also kept two half-day rooms that year. The students in the all-day rooms ended up doing better socially and academically. It took a while to convince the district to try these all-day rooms. To make this work, we also had to turn an old locker room into a kindergarten room, with all the requirements and codes being met. We ended up doing this with the other locker room as well, and within a couple years, we had five all-day successful kindergarten programs going strong. I had solid, excellent teachers who would run our own benchmark test and gauge where the students were upon starting. They documented how well students knew their ABC's, numbers, colors and name. Now, there are screening tools and ways of benchmarking how your students are entering school that are utilized. Our immediate goal was to give our students more quality social growth and instructional time.

Another thing we found is that with a large population of high poverty students, there were many who were struggling with reading. We were using the standard Basal Reading Approach and teaching skills, but the students would say they had difficulty reading in the "big book." The research was also showing students needed more time for learning skills and reading.

The teachers solved this since many had been to conferences and were interested in Guided Reading. They explained to me what Guided Reading was, and we piloted it. Soon, we started a book room of leveled readers, and we continued to add to it over the 10 years I was there. Now, this was also not a district practice. It wasn't until later that the district approved of and started adding Guided Reading and book rooms to schools as a strategy for improvement. There was a cluster of us using strategies like this that were working with acute needs students. Our teachers were getting excellent results, combining Basal work with Guided Reading. Soon we were benchmarking each quarter and showing some excellent growth. The four quarters of data enabled us to see individual student growth. These data points helped to direct our teaching throughout the year. It was an indicator of progress!

We focused on promoting mental health services as a major component of our Positive Behavioral Interventions and Supports at Indian Hill. I recall a meeting with a philanthropist who inquired about the biggest need in schools. I answered it was mental health services and support.

This was around 2005 and was an ever-growing problem. The evidence was the growing number of students we were assisting and problem-solving with daily--many with extreme needs. This continues to be a big need in many school districts and school buildings. Mental health has no boundaries. Since we were a high poverty building, it seemed that our needs were even more extreme.

In an effort to help, we partnered with Terri and Brent Khan through Alegent Health. Terri was with Alegent and her husband, Brent, was with Special Projects at Clarkson College. This partnership with Alegent and the Omaha Public Schools developed a school-based integrated mental health program. There were three schools in the Omaha Public Schools involved in the three-year grant: Indian Hill Elementary (where I served as principal), Kellom Elementary, and Wakonda Elementary. The initial goal of the project was to implement a school-based integrated mental health program focusing on elementary schools who educate children in high poverty and potentially traumatic environments in Omaha.

This model program included: addressing the needs of school children who cannot access needed mental health services due to resources, implementing the HeartMath program which addresses stress in teachers, testing anxiety in staff and students, and using of tools to promote internal changes in behavior and to provide support through teacher and parent coaching (source: October 2007 Overview and Description of Project). The grant provided a Licensed Mental Health Professional (LMHP) on site, four days a week, eight hours a day. I selected Lori Montano as our LMHP and she could assist with intervention plans, getting students evaluated and getting them referred to needed services. We also worked with families on getting them to appointments, which was a challenge.

We had Brent Khan present Test Edge Training for teachers, and conduct Teacher Resiliency Training and Stress classes. The training was offered at a couple of different sessions, and ran from 4:00-6:00 PM right after school, and we provided pizza during the training. The strategies we employed were designed to assist teachers in working in this high needs, high stress environment.

Brent also did the executive stress coaching, providing tools and techniques to assist me in my leadership role. He provided us with the training to use HeartMath techniques (like Freeze Framer) with students to help them start controlling their behavior using breathing as a powerful tool.

At one point, the grant allowed Brent to assist in our building two hours a week outside the other training. Terri Kahn was excellent in setting up our LMHP services and creating processes and procedures while applying strategic practices. The results and data our LMHP collected showed the positive impact of having these supports available onsite for our students and families. As they were preparing documents they asked for a quote for the results paper. The following is what I wrote: "The integrated mental health approach has enabled us to address the needs of our staff, students and families. This has been through HeartMath and the expertise of an LMHP, tied with our positive behavior supports, to increase the capacity to keep students in the classroom and learning. Many of our high need students have improved on attendance and achievement." This was definitely true with the amount of needs our students had--many were extreme, and the support applied was assisting them.

The behavioral services program was still in place when I left the school in 2008. The funding source changed, and many high schools added district social workers in-house to support families. Medical clinics within schools, such as Charles Drew, are now offering more support, including mental health care.

There is still a large need. I assisted a building as principal in 2019 which had on-site services, and was at a meeting where we added 12 more students to the list who needed to be evaluated. They most likely will need some kind of support and an action plan. This was on top of what they already had as a caseload. Mental health support is a growing need in schools—one that seems to be continually increasing.

The evidence continues to show itself. Look at the many mass school shootings and incidents most likely related to mental stability. It is important to assist our students in need. I believe in providing more mental health support for elementary schools to prevent future problems. They need regular counselors, social workers and specialists suited to assist with mental health issues.

Outside of mental health were general health issues. Students in poverty often have less or no insurance, and rarely have access to adequate health care. They struggle with health needs despite having Medicaid. As a high poverty school, we worked to help provide access to health services, general, dental and vision. The vision and dental truck could visit and assist on site. The establishment of school-based clinics in needed areas led to improvement in our district. This improved access for families--especially those with transportation issues.

Having the resources needed is another way of doing what is best for children. At my first building, we were Title 1, so had extra funds to support staff and instruction. This was until some of the federal guidelines changed. The district also used what was called an equity formula within our budgeting system. This formula was used to weigh students against factors like poverty and other high risk and potential needs. Our building, with 675 students at 90% free and reduced lunch, was equivalent to a building with 2,100 students because of our acute needs. The formula made sure you had adequate funding to provide extra supports.

In contrast, my colleague up the road had the largest elementary school in Nebraska, with 1,200 students. He catered to the needs of his population, and as a result, it weighed his building at about 1,500. Our building and students needed many more supports. This formula is no longer being used and they allocate buildings FTE (full-time equivalency) and resources based solely upon the total population number, not needs. This makes it fair for building sizes across the district, but not fair in terms of need and support for the demographics of the students. They do still get allocated Title 1 funds based upon the federal formula, which continues to change. I always have worked to find grants, partnerships or other means of support to assist the students under my watch.

At the focus school, we looked at what would allow our students to grow, socially, and academically, within an innovative environment focused on strengths. The students became owners in the culture of the school. They were active contributors, which increased their success, no matter what their background was. We talked about our uniqueness and how important that was to the concept of this school. The students were empowered through this philosophy and, in turn, grew by leaps and bounds. We provided opportunities and let all students into programs that could improve their development. We didn't strictly adhere to test scores for selection into programs, and all our students increased growth--especially in STEAM areas (science, technology, engineering, arts and math). We restructured all the old tracking, and weeded out many exclusionary systems which only allowed middle-class, high scoring students to excel.

If you are this far in the book, you have probably picked up on the fact that I am all about providing opportunities for students. I am talking truly for *all* students. This can be done by breaking down those barriers schools have ingrained throughout systems, and those old tracking mechanisms which silo students into groups. As educators, we often become the gate keepers who keep students from gaining opportunities and developing to their potential. Test scores alone do not inform us of the potential of students and cannot be used solely in selection criteria. If you want to see all students excel, give them opportunities. I have had students terrible at math and science learn programming/coding skills and increase their ability and achievement, turning these areas into strengths—all because they could learn in a different manner. It is important to offer opportunities for all students. Increase opportunities and increase achievement!

I have always felt blessed with the intuition to move toward effective practices before they are mainstreamed or become the norm. This has helped us stay ahead of the curve. I guess this is due to following trends, consistently reading research, and watching our in-the-trench data. The feedback we get from staff helps to show what is working. I am also willing to take risks while following the data and observing results. I have moved with what works and have built a substantial toolbox of successful strategies, especially in turning around a building.

It is easy for central office to get entrenched into politics and the workings that can impede progress. If you bring it back to doing what is best for children, this simple statement can be a guide in an otherwise foggy sea of confusion. I have used this strategy with staff and at committee meetings. Keep the focus on the children and on doing what is best for them.

"Leadership is the art of giving people a platform
for spreading ideas that work."

— Seth Godin

Chapter 10:
Motivating Staff in Effective Ways

Motivating staff is something you must do as a leader, and--as a principal--it is no different. Dialing in the right factors to motivate staff is a combination of many things previously discussed, including relationships. If you encourage your staff to use their strengths and talents, and put them in positions to utilize those every day--staying in their zone--they will soar.

Positivity and the ability to stay optimistic are qualities that principals must possess to effectively motivate. Even if you have a bad day, have problems outside of school, etc., the baggage you bring in will affect everyone. Like it or not, the leader sets the tone. If staff members have the attitude of "I wonder what kind of mood they're in today," that is not good. Consistency matters. You must *walk the talk* as a role model of the positive culture you wish to build.

Staff members need to know they are part of a team and that the leader cares about them--each one of them. They need to know you are protecting them and have the best interest of the organization at heart. There are days when I might've been run down or tired, but I knew that, when the rubber meets the road, I'd better be ready to find that positive energy.

One asset that helped me is we had student-led morning news in each of the buildings I served as principal. This was a school-based news station which began as a live-feed video and eventually moved to being streamed to classrooms through Wi-Fi. I was big on having this in place to communicate and push out messages, as well as give students an outlet to promote events and show leadership. The students loved being on air throughout the building. I would also go on every day. Going on live gave me a chance to promote positivity and set the tone for the day. It was consistent daily messages from the principal. Leaders must communicate purposefully and consistently.

Before the morning news, I was always out greeting buses and students as they arrived, which is another way of setting the tone. Staff was encouraged to do this as well, in the hallways and at their classroom doors, and it was infectious. The extra supervision is excellent and touching base with students starts the day off right. This not only sets the stage with students, but it does affect the staff too! It is all an intertwined part of your culture. Years ago, a big business concept was Management by Walking Around (MBWA)! There is still truth in this method for getting to know your staff and developing positive relationships. Being out and about is important to an organization. You get to rub elbows and really see what is happening.

I still believe in banking many positives, so when you need to address issues, there are bonds formed that make it easier to confront and deal with the negatives. Positivity is contagious; so is negativity. It only takes one person to start a cancer that can spread throughout your environment. How do you fight it? You make that environment one of the most positive places and you work to ensure it is a place where positivity is the norm. It is part of your culture. This usually drives someone away that does not hold the same philosophy or optimism. The old saying of "You get what you give" really does apply.

In Jon Gordon's book, *The No Complaining Rule* (2019), he talks about having this attitude of gratitude and says everyone needs to get into the habit of saying "I *get* to..." instead of "I *have* to..." I've done this with staff and used this book as well. Negativity can take its toll on an organization. If you get staff into thinking about it, this common language develops and even becomes infectious and humorous. My staff would say, "Oh yeah, I *get* to..." As Ms. Carole (our focus administrative assistant) kept saying, "It's another chance for a golden opportunity!" I love this and have adopted it. Everything is a new opportunity. It's how you look at the circumstances. It does all end up being a part of your attitude, and having a positive one is much better for everyone.

As a leader, consistently talking to staff, joking and lightening the mood can make a big difference. Why is it so many educators (not everyone, but many) are so serious? Gone are the days when educators must be stiff and controlled--never to break a smile. There is so much research on the importance of relationships that it is hard to refute. Find the levity!

I have always liked the Gallup Organization's Q12 that gives you a list of the 12 things which must be present for people to be effective at work. They call it "The 12 Questions That Matter." Look it up, they have great materials and have thoroughly researched many aspects of leadership and using your strengths. People need elements in a workplace that make them happy--make them feel they are part of a team and are valued. It is what I call collaborative ownership. If a staff member has strengths, use them. Put them in their strength zone and they will excel. This will increase productivity and happiness.

It takes time to talk to staff, check-in on them, and hear about what matters to them. These conversations make a difference and can be a catalyst for team improvement. You do have to be sincere and really listen and understand, using empathy with emotional intelligence. Don't underestimate the power of empathy and understanding people. This also helps build trust.

Positivity is highly contagious if the leader exudes it with a "We can do this" attitude. Like it or not, staff will always look to the leader--if trust has been developed--and watch for reactions and direction. Letting staff know you believe in them as professionals and giving them opportunities to try new things without it counting against them is a huge step forward in building a strong team. This has been a strong constant in my leadership over the years. Learn together, work together and collaborate. If you have a leader that is controlling and stifling, you can tell the minute they walk into the room. The climate changes, conversations change, and productivity as well as positivity goes down. This kind of energy is not needed.

It is important for the leader to have no fear, "We can do it no matter what" attitude. There are always alternative ways to solve a problem and often positives can be found within anything that comes up. You cannot be afraid to act, and decisions must be made as needed. This is not always easy. There are many educators I have come across who do not possess this attitude, and are held back by fears like, "The district won't let me do that," "What if it fails?" and other excuses for not taking the reins. You must have an attitude of "How can we improve?" "What if we try?" "Are we getting the right results?" You must make decisions and stick to your mission and vision. I'll be frank, sometimes district protocols hinder progress. You are the CEO of your building. For me, I have always had that inner achiever, wanting to improve, do more, and increase my effectiveness. As a result, sometimes what our staff is doing is ahead of general practice.

As a leader, I have studied Shawn Achor materials and resources. His research on what makes people happy is interesting and enlightening. I think his materials would surprise you and help you see what is at your core. I also use Jon Gordon materials on the power of positivity. I have used his book *The Energy Bus* with staff and students, and it is a good way to wrap some common language around positivity. The story presents good principles as well!

Storytelling and sharing your journey are wonderful ways to get staff involved and connected. Showing you are open to sharing your life experiences and your ups and downs only makes you more human and personable. As Brene Brown has taught us, being vulnerable only makes you stronger as a leader. Everyone has struggles and there is nothing wrong with sharing those at the appropriate time. I often do this to illustrate a point or to develop further learning or understanding. It also helps to laugh at yourself. You cannot underestimate the power of storytelling with your staff.

Each year, I like to start the year off with staff in-services with a purpose. I do one morning on setting the tone for the year. This is an overview, looking at our vision, goals, school improvement plan, and data. It includes some team building activities and helps in understanding everyone's strengths.

Ingra started me using a template with our school branding for slides for presentations. This is used to create a PowerPoint which usually starts with a welcome back, introductions of new staff, and what's new. Then it moves into the importance of everyone in the school building, and a rationale about how we all make a difference. I call this building the strength of our team. It is important for all staff to realize the importance of their role in the organization, and that no one role is more important than another. This develops into the importance of teaching, and I often show them visuals of other super challenging and less appealing jobs and remind them how much impact they have as educators.

I review the philosophy of the building, our instructional template (what has developed into the best practices framework for our building), and goals for the year. Some goals are around instruction, behavior, and especially learning target goals based on our data. Teams and communities then use our school plan to improve based on data. Our grade-level teams will make connections and clarify targets.

I review what solid instruction looks like, using effect ratios established by Marzano and other authorities. We also use some of Mike Schmoker's information based on what is effective, and create strategies based upon that research. We go into being self-reflective, talk about coaching visits, what's important, and how we can improve as educators. By the time I am done with this session, we have set the tone for the year.

The next session I lead helps staff prepare for the upcoming year by building relationships and using PBIS to motivate them. My overall goal is to increase the teachers' and staff's capacity to work with students. I train in de-escalation and strategies for working with challenging students and behaviors. Our training teaches relationship building, restorative practices, and positive behavior supports for student success. I focus on giving them tools and building that proactive philosophy of problem-solving and re-teaching. We discuss the importance of procedures and routines while setting up our building guidelines and supports.

I concentrate on the impact of positivity in teaching and the various positions that support it. We look at where we have been and where we are going (mission/vision), celebrate successes from the previous year, what is new to the building physically, and make introductions of new staff members. By analyzing our academic and behavioral data, we determined the course of action. We discussed changes we need to make. We set goals for the year and most of all--as stated earlier--I set the tone. The principal--the building's leader--*must* do this. Leadership teams can contribute, but the bulk needs to come from the leader.

It's okay to have guests, speakers, and staff members present at some meetings, but the first meetings are important to set the tone and pace for the year. You, as the leader, help set the course. I spent a great deal of time preparing those two opening meetings. I often include humor, activities, brief video clips, discussion and a chance to collaborate on working toward our vision. I feel so strongly about this that I did multiple sessions for two different years at our district's principal summit on "Pumping Up the Positives." One year, at the summit, I had sessions on creating the healthiest climate, and another year was on how best to craft these opening meetings--setting your team up for success. We give time at team meetings for staff to contribute and develop strategies within the school and infuse strong ownership as a group. I love the quote by Ronald W. Dollens: "Leadership is about the psychology of helping cause people to do exceptional things." Then, throughout the year as a team, we continue to do a needs assessment, revise strategies, and rework our approach as needed.

Motivating staff is about relationships. Knowing the staff and being able to use emotional intelligence to understand where they currently are is important. The idea of the *Friday Focus* weekly one-sheet I borrowed from Todd Whitaker has been a proven staff motivator for about 19 of my 21 years as a principal. He talks about many versions of this, like *Friday Highlights*, etc. This tool can be an excellent leverage piece to promote a positive culture. Ours started as the *Indian Hill Weekly Bulletin* and developed into the *Friday Focus*.

Then I was in a new principals cohort with Ann Mausbach, who taught us to do a weekly bulletin as well, summarizing all the great things happening. She talks about this in her book, *Align the Design* (Mooney, Mausbach, 2008). Early in my principalship, I started doing weekly "Look Fors." These would be positive things happening in the building. I had a steno pad labeled "Look Fors" with the year on it and took that around all week as I visited classrooms. My version changed over time from a Weekly Bulletin to a *Friday Focus*, where I could summarize my week and highlight important things. These early "Look Fors" were also a version of coaching, promoting strategies and the positives I would see and wanted continued.

I always ended *Friday Focus* with a Love and Logic quote, and my name at the bottom. The Love and Logic quote promoted and reinforced the strategies we had learned from Jim Fay and kept this tool constantly in front of them. The other quote was just uplifting or selected to help the staff self-reflect and stay motivated. It was never over two pages, so it was an easy read. I did it on golden rod paper and it would be in the staff mailboxes by Friday morning. I was the only one that used golden rod paper, so when the staff saw this, they knew it was important. This is an excellent strategy as a principal. They had access to all kinds of other colored papers--not just goldenrod. It worked for me. It is a technique that might work for you. I gave them a paper version and a digital copy sent through their email. By providing different formats, it offered many chances to be read. I also included when our next meeting was, so you had to check it to see if we had a staff meeting the following week.

The *Friday Focus* I produced summarized the week. I had a section on coaching and "Look Fors". These were the positive instructional practices I was seeing and wanted to promote. Don't take this lightly. What you write about, they will do. This is a great way to move instruction and build culture. When I was promoting anchor charts, for example, as the weeks progressed, I saw more anchor charts. When I pointed out first-grade students were having success with Lucy Calkin's writing system, second-grade teachers took notice. It surprised them how students were progressing, and strategies changed when they observed first graders were outperforming second graders.

Much of the *Friday Focus* is about being a cheerleader and keeping the positivity flowing. This helps to counteract the state of negativity that often creeps in and is prevalent in buildings. It is a never-ending battle and as the leader, you set the tone. The language was intentional and in my voice. The following was an e-mail I received from a special area teacher that was only in the building on certain days. "I just want to tell you how much I enjoy and appreciate your *Friday Focus*. Particularly, just being in the building for a day and a half a week, it helps me stay in touch and know what is going on. Plus, I like the way you share things that you do out of the building, your readings and trainings, how the school activities are incorporated with your goals and philosophies. Your weekly bulletin is helpful in remaining in touch, too. So, for what it's worth, I do really appreciate you taking the time to do all this!"

The email was a great example of how it keeps people in the loop and connected, which is essential in communication. It helps them understand everything that is going on behind the scenes. It can also help your staff regroup at a time they need it. I had a teacher write, "Thank you again for the *Friday Focus*...it does help to refocus. The fact that you are consistent about it encourages us to be consistent in our perspective and noticing the positive around us and keeping the vision. Thank you."

As I was leaving my role as a principal, I received this response from a teacher: "Mr. Anderson, Thank you for the excellent *Friday Focus*. I will miss those when you leave. You had excellent reminders in there. Today was challenging for me. I made some good decisions and then I allowed my frustration to impact me too. Thank you for the reminder to help students with their own talk outs, as well as the final quote about control being like love and respect. Also, your last comment about sledding made me laugh. Sometimes I feel like I am learning more than the students. Hopefully, we are all learning together! Thanks for the positivity and excellent reminders."

The previous responses give you a glimpse of how this weekly *Friday Focus* can affect staff. It can be the catalyst in keeping the staff motivated. It may be the words they need to hear on a really tough day. Create your own version of this effective tool!

A pleasant feature of *Friday Focus* is it becomes a record of a school year. I put a copy into a binder each week and by the end of the year; it was a compilation of everything that happened that calendar year. There are many binders with the covers and sides labeled with our school logo and school calendar year. I learned this organizational system from Ingra, who created the most organized binder system I have ever seen. It can also be handy if you need to look back, reference activities and find something, or see the instructional practices that were taking place. If you are big into archiving, you will love this to keep and record the history. It is also an easy way to check progress.

I share positive messages on social media by taking photos on my phone during coaching visits. It is a quick and easy way to promote your building. Social media helps you to push those positives and get messages out to a large audience fast. Twitter has become a good promotional tool for buildings. Now I am using Instagram as a promotional tool as well. I am sure there will be many more new social media platforms soon. Keeping up with these tools can help you promote your organization.

Another strategy I used with staff was giving what we called "Teacher Tags", and these were nomination tickets given while at the larger building. They were coupons or tickets that said: "Teachers Achieving Greatness Nomination! I would like to tag [name of teacher] because [reason]," and there was plenty of space to write in what they were being recognized for. I would often read a few of these at staff meetings to give public recognition and allow them to select a prize. These were often staff-friendly prizes: a restaurant card, or something they could use in their room. We also created a certificate. It said, Congratulations! You've been tagged! Indian Hill Proudly Presents This Teachers Achieving Greatness AWARD to [name of teacher] for [reason]. I had a wonderful leadership team that helped to make this a successful process.

Giving plenty of opportunities for your staff to have a voice is important. We have different options to do this, such as PLC groups, team meetings, staff meetings, in-services, or surveys. A culture where staff members are free to share is important! A principal who only meets with each staff member once a year, and doesn't allow them to give honest input, is a weak leader. Urge employees to provide honest feedback and show how it's making a difference. Empower your staff.

One year, I gave a sheet that explained that--in planning for the next year--our leadership team would like to get some input. We split it into sections with "Things I've appreciated this year." The T-chart had two columns: one titled "Problems I've noticed" and the other "Suggested Solutions," with each column numbered one through three. This helped to refine our answers and give us some feedback to work with. This type of document can be created and changed based upon your needs. Keep it as positive as you can. If they are sharing a problem, there must be a suggestion or solution.

Over the years, I used different methods, including online surveys. The important piece is doing some compilation of data, sharing results and bringing it back to staff to brainstorm and problem-solve. Discuss results and give your staff opportunities for involvement and ownership. Feedback is important and just like our student and building data, it needs to be used or people may realize you are just blowing smoke. The feedback must be discussed, applied, and put into action.

It is also important to laugh at yourself, have a great sense of humor, and have fun doing your work. Learn to laugh. This is a hard business. Everyone can be so serious. As a principal, you just never know what could happen. I came back from a principals' meeting once, bent down in my office to pick something up, and heard a rip in the seat of my pants. I wasn't sure how bad this was and everyone who knows the pace of a school building knows you can't always stop. This day, of course, we were out of our meeting earlier than normal, so I was on my way out to supervise lunch and recess like I normally would. I had a suit coat on, but it didn't completely cover where the rip was.

It was winter, so I just put on my long black wool playground coat and went to duty fully covering whatever mishap occurred. When I came in from recess, I left my coat on in the cafeteria until we got our last group out. Once the teachers picked the lunch students up, I returned to my office. I worked on some things in my office during the afternoon. I did not do "Look Fors" on this day! Then I put my big coat back on to supervise recess and helped get the students to enrichment classes. Then I continued working in my office, threw on my big coat, and assisted with student dismissal and buses.

When I got home, I told Ingra what had happened, and she had a good laugh. Doing yoga has made me more flexible, but I realized my suit doesn't allow for those movements. That is when I heard the damage. While changing clothes, I found a 10-inch rip in my dress pants at the rear seam and laughed about it with Ingra. I was so glad I kept throwing my long wool coat on and it was a good thing I avoided coaching or classroom visits that afternoon. As a principal, you don't need that kind of exposure! Relying on my big coat was a good move. Good thing it was winter. Sometimes your instincts are right on! Learn to laugh at yourself!

This was something I later shared at a staff meeting and, of course, the staff thought it was more hilarious than my wife did. Being vulnerable to your staff is important. Being big enough to admit being wrong and even discussing mistakes makes you human, which you are, right? I love the work that Brene Brown has done. She has written books based upon the importance of being vulnerable and allowing staff to be vulnerable. The book *Dare to Lead* (Brown, 2018) is an excellent book about effective leadership. She has many wonderful resources with research to help you be a better parent, teacher, leader, person, etc.

If you are a superintendent leading district meetings, think of the information you need to get out and how positive you are being. How about building everyone up? My excitement at district meetings as a principal for 21 years was often overshadowed by the overwhelming amount of information from different departments and initiatives. It is a challenge to sift through what *must* be done and what you can protect your staff from. Focusing on the priorities of what really matters is important. The principal handles everything within a school. It is one of the toughest jobs there is. Thus, many don't remain as principals and switch to other positions. How about rallying principals and building them up for all the tasks required as they return to their buildings, rather than overloading them with paperwork?

As I left the role of the principal and became a consultant, I invested in becoming a certified Behavior Consultant through People Keys. Ingra also took the courses with me, and we are both certified, and we can team up as needed to work with organizations or leaders. It has also helped us to understand each other at home and in our marriage. You can take these assessments with a work perspective or a home perspective, depending on your purpose. People are different within a work setting and home setting. The core remains the same, but characteristics can change.

One course was on understanding the DISC assessment instrument, and one was on advanced behavioral analysis. DISC is an acronym that stands for the four main personality profiles described in the DISC model: (D) Dominance, (I) Influence, (S) Steadiness, and (C) Conscientiousness. You learn how to apply materials to become a better leader, coach, and team developer. They have tools to assess teams, values, and leadership strengths. The ratings give excellent insight into the tendencies of the unique character traits. As a leader, these can be useful tools.

The DISC is a tool, similar to Gallup's StrengthsFinder, that helps people understand themselves better and work well with others. Getting people to understand one another and to self-reflect is an important skill to developing powerful leaders and teams. The more you understand the type of leader you are, the better you can relate to others and understand how to motivate them in a more effective manner.

It's like that famous Francis Bacon quote: "Knowledge is power!" That is so true. If you are like me, you always want to know more about your own characteristics and hone your skills. Emotional Intelligence and understanding people will always be at the core of being a successful leader. Daniel Goleman's research in this area is another resource that can help you understand all the things that make us human. I love the books *Primal Leadership* (Goleman, 2018) and *Emotional Intelligence: Why It Can Matter More Than IQ* (Goleman, 2006). As a leader, you are always continuing to learn, grow, and fully develop. Learning never stops! To motivate people, understand them.

"Leaders create and inspire new leaders by instilling faith in their leadership ability and helping them develop and hone leadership skills they don't know they possess."

— *John Maxwell*

Chapter 11:
Mentoring New Leaders

Developing leaders and bringing out the best in staff is part of the mentoring process. The more experience you have, the more you should share. Let me clarify this though, there are many people who have received numerous degrees, yet still do not have common sense or the ability to be an effective leader. A certificate or title is not a guarantee you are set up to be a successful leader.

Early on, I looked for leadership experiences. As a teacher, I looked for experiences to develop as a leader within the school, as well as outside of the school, in the community. Eventually, I was nominated for our district Leadership Institute by Matilda Browne, assistant principal of a building where I was teaching. She saw some potential in me. Robert Jorgensen, my principal at this time, then joined in and approved my practicum in leadership.

Both Ingra and I looked for leadership opportunities and became officers with the Jaycees in the community in which we grew up. We stayed with the Jaycees until aging out at 40 and could coordinate many projects to assist the city of Bellevue. For years, Ingra and I worked on drawing and painting a large street mural for the city, right before the Arrows to Aerospace parade. We also had fun volunteering and calling bingo for Hillcrest for nearly nine years. Excellent volunteering and community service can add to your development.

Eventually, we aged out of the organization and our community support was more tied to our career roles.

Through my father-in-law, Dr. Larry D. Winkler's connection to the Air Force and UNO, Ingra and I painted a 150-foot mural at Offutt Air Force Base. This was in the building's hallway that housed the offsite university offices in Building D (the old Martin Bomber Plant). The artwork showcased the University of Nebraska at Omaha. We created it as if you were right on campus with a stone wall along the bottom and the hills and landscape of the university. This included buildings and landmarks, trees and perspective. It gave a feeling of being outside. We each received an Outstanding Service Award from the University and were recognized at a private celebration as well as the unveiling ceremony of the mural. Community service experiences help develop character, and discovering the joy of giving back is also important to developing good leadership.

These experiences also shape who you become. I am an achiever, so I have always studied on my own. Ingra is an achiever as well. I have a passion for leadership, so continue to read leadership books and look for better ways of doing things. As an aspiring administrator, I had my sights set on the principalship and being an effective leader. I looked for people doing the job well and had many mentors along the way. One of those was Ray Perrigo, a long-term principal who shared insight early on. I remember my first year as principal, going over to his building where we worked on our budget, and I learned much from him. We created zero-based budgets, so you had to think of what your goals were while planning for the future, and the needs of your particular building. Matt Ray was one of Perrigo's teachers, who was also learning and was interested in pursuing administration and supervision. Matt has served in several leadership roles and, as I write this, has just been named Superintendent for the Omaha Public

Schools. Ray Perrigo ended up being a principal for 30 years--an accomplishment rarely held today. We still are good friends and have breakfast meetings periodically to catch up.

Another mentor of mine was Thomas Warren, former Police Chief of Omaha, CEO of the Urban League, and current Chief of Staff for the city of Omaha. Encouragement has always been his forte. He has supported me and has been an excellent role model. He is another mentor who helps bring out the best in others. I have seen him mentor so many people and future leaders. He had some excellent mentors, and he is passing it along. I will continue to do the same. I have had many other mentors, but these are two who are still in my life and continue to multiply their talents--great role models!

I find great satisfaction in continuing to pass this legacy along, helping others to grow. I've helped new administrators develop their leadership skills at the University of Nebraska at Omaha as a resource mentor. I was called on to share my knowledge especially around the issue of urban education and building successful leadership and community. I did this for many years and was always open to discussing the success of the schools I was in or the new concept of the focus school.

There is a vast collection of resources on effective leadership. Principals need to study effective leadership skills both within and outside of education. Make sure you are well rounded in developing yourself. I have subscribed to *Leader to Leader*, which gives the most up-to-date writing and research on leadership. The journal, which Peter Drucker started, is now being run by Frances Hesselbein. It comes out four times a year and has a lot of great articles and research on everything from teamwork to effective leadership skills. I also used a monthly booklet called *Bits & Pieces on Leadership*, which was published by Lawrence Ragan Communications, Inc. It contains short stories for leaders and quotes around leadership that I would use frequently.

Joining your professional organizations can also provide you with research and effective strategies. I like the Association for Supervision and Curriculum Development (ASCD) and have continued to be a member. They provide an excellent monthly magazine and many wonderful books. They provide an outlet for education and instructional practices. There are many resources out there that can assist in your development as a leader. It is important to stay in touch.

The more you develop yourself, the more you will develop others. As leaders, we do not complete our learning. While at Indian Hill Elementary, I helped and encouraged 17 members of my staff to get into leadership positions. We had a cycle of developing leaders and the skills people had. Seven became principals, two moved up to even higher-level positions, and the rest are in some form of administration. They developed into what I would call a "Dream Team" before moving on and, as I would lose people, we would add another that was also strong, keeping the cycle going. I encouraged staff with the potential to get involved in the Teachers' Corp. It is a program that helped educators earn a master's degree in educational administration and supervision.

This cycle of producing leaders strengthened our school. Some of the excellent people were Tim Hamilton, Ryan Kaiser, Dwayne Chism, James Cunningham, Charla Johnson, Teresa Heimes (now Hamilton), Melissa Schroeder, Tynishia Northcutt, and Nicole Longlee. Many more got degrees after me, but these are people that developed into successful leaders as we had this process in place. We encouraged people to grow.

As a leader, try to be a leader that inspires others to be better and to fully develop their strengths. At the focus schools, I continued the cycle and excellent people that developed into leaders were Deb Gernandt, Jean La Grone, Angie Wright, Garret Higginbotham, Scott Hilger, Joe Eckerman, Glenn Mitchell, and Christine Moats. As a leader, you can affect many others and help them along their journey. It is reciprocal. I wish more leaders were more comfortable helping others be successful. Try to make this one of your goals. It only makes you and your organization stronger. I still maintain this goal of developing and mentoring leaders. Most of these people I am still in touch with and continue to provide dialogue and encouragement. We continue to learn and grow together. Once a mentor, always a mentor!

I also learned and gained insights and ideas from colleagues, other leaders, and principals. Learn what you can and continue this developing process. All during my administrative leadership, I looked for opportunities to be on boards, advisories and committees. I talked about many of these in a previous chapter. These experiences are all a part of your growth as a leader. Contributing to your community or organization makes you a better leader.

At the focus school, seven individuals got leadership positions. Four became principals, two went to other districts, and the remaining received diverse leadership roles. Then, during my last years as a principal, I had more staff work on advanced degrees and looking for leadership roles. I even was able to mentor our niece's husband, Joe Eckerman. I worked with him for a year when he switched from a high needs building to teach 5th grade in my building. He then became an administrator in another district and, as I write this, he has been a successful principal in Grand Island, NE for several years. We talk about the role often and share experiences.

Developing people takes work, but it pays off for your staff and for your district. Be secure as a leader in helping others to grow, achieve, and excel. Not very many can or want to do this well. My wife, Ingra, is a good example of someone who others did not always support. She has worked as a director in marketing, public relations, resource development, and sales for over 30 years, and was the first executive director of a school foundation in another district.

Ingra was the second in Nebraska to become a Certified Education Foundation Leader (CEFL). She is sharp, highly talented, and is an excellent writer with a broadcast journalism degree. Skilled in social media, web design, branding, marketing, graphic design, broadcasting, and public speaking, she is super organized and develops efficiencies in all the jobs she takes on. I have seen her work hard in various positions, running circles around most people. Yet, I have also seen her undervalued and not always appreciated in some of these roles. My perception is her wide variety of skills intimidates them and they discount the value of her abilities.

This is exactly what I was talking about. These leaders have not realized what they had, how her strengths and talents are actually helping them, and they were not secure enough to have strong, talented people as part of their team. The best leaders wrap other gifted, confident people around them and create a collaborative, effective team. They develop, encourage and support staff growth to help them be the best they can be in their roles.

Ingra finds she is much happier running her own business, and enjoys a semi-retired lifestyle, selling jewelry and other gadgets at IngraAnderson.Magnabilities.com. She loves using her broadcasting degree, having hosted close to 700 live shows on Facebook.

The point is not, look how many people I helped. It is more to look at all you can do as a leader. You hold the power and opportunity to assist in the growth and development of others. The power to influence someone's career path lies in your hands, and it's a responsibility you must take seriously. You can give people experiences to help them grow, encourage the use of their strengths, and help them develop their talents. In the long run, they benefit your organization and any organization as they move up or take on other roles. I make it a habit to give leadership books and materials to the people I work with, such as John Maxwell's *The 21 Irrefutable Laws of Leadership* (1998). I have given this book out so many times, and often will write words of encouragement on the inside cover. It would be great if others would start making a supportive gesture with a book as well.

I still love the feel of a *real* book and like having them on a shelf for quick access. I do read some digitally though. I mark up my personal books with highlights and notes for presentations and discussions. They are a great reference. I know Ingra would love for me to cut down on my book collection!

Take advantage of the wealth of knowledge available through technology and social media to keep learning. Never stop learning! After retiring, I started a podcast called *Urban Principal: Leadership Lessons* and have posted this weekly. It is a great way to share information and discuss issues. My goal is to continue to mentor and assist other principals and leaders in being more effective.

I aim to help districts and leaders become better prepared by increasing leadership capacity. When asked why he continued to practice at 90, the famous cellist Pablo Casals replied with words that resonate with me. He said, "Because I think I am making progress!" I feel the same way. I am always learning through studying leadership. I get better and better, so I am still practicing!

Joining boards and committees can help you develop your own skills and talents. I have been in so many groups and on many district committees which have helped shape and form concepts within the organization. Helping to shape our district leadership, and mentoring new principals was enjoyable for me.

I was a part of our District Coaching Team for six years. We helped train over 400 administrators every year, coaching teachers and moving to best practices. My partner was Dr. Christina Warner. We had fun presenting and did well together. She is now a principal in my past district. We challenged each other and helped others grow at the same time. Experiences designed to help you stretch and grow, do just that. Try to move out of your comfort zone and step up to get involved.

I joined the Principal Pipeline Design Team, and we spent a year developing a program to produce powerful leaders for our district. We worked with a consulting firm to identify the qualities and characteristics that need to be developed to succeed. Rubrics of skills were designed to show leader competencies as a way of developing the principal talent pool. We brainstormed, researched, and looked at what makes principals effective.

I was also on the Launch Design Team. Our district's Launch Program was used as a steppingstone for people who want to enter district leadership. District leaders give lectures and have discussions with them throughout the year to help them learn. Launch participants also do some shadowing of effective leaders. Our district also paired up experienced principals with new principals as mentors for a year. This process enabled us to work with other principals, sharing our experiences--what worked and what didn't. It was an in-the-field mentorship.

You can develop your reputation as a leader and a person who can add value to many groups. Don't just settle. My goal after retiring was to not really retire, but to use my experiences and skills to help other leaders--especially principals in the field. This includes problem-solving with districts and buildings. My consulting services cover positive behavior supports, trauma-informed teaching, restorative practices, and leadership skills. There are lessons I have learned along the way, and it is good to pass those on.

After retiring, I became a student supervisor for Iowa State University. I have coached student teachers and helped them become effective professionals in Omaha. I've also worked with the University of Nebraska at Lincoln, coaching in the Para-to-Teacher Cohort program to produce more teachers. We will continue to need many more effective teachers. I have added this to my variety of consulting areas.

There are many people who helped me develop, and it is just natural to help others move forward—a way of giving back. I still have a passion for leadership, education and children and that does not end. It has been my life's work, and it will continue to be so. It may develop or change, but I have a feeling I will continue to contribute in some capacity.

"Education is not filling a bucket but lighting a fire."

— William Butler Yates

Chapter 12:
Launching Instruction / Assessment / Coaching

Instruction and being an instructional leader are now at the forefront of being a principal. The current principal must know and be up on best practices, and how to get the most effective instructional strategies out of their staff. To me, instruction, assessment and coaching go hand in hand as a multifaceted catalyst needed to get results. Each district provides its leader with a core base of curriculum. My experience as a principal showed me that supplementing the provided materials was the best way to improve student instruction. It isn't necessarily more, but the right things. I am a firm believer in a professional learning community and the positive outcome of collaborating with staff. To improve student instruction, it is essential to examine how teachers carry out instruction and the learning materials they use.

I reviewed my past practices and noticed I made changes based on student progress data. I added materials or changed the curriculum and delivery methods accordingly. The teachers and staff I have had have been my best guide to what is working and what is not. If you listen to them, you will find out strategies and ways to improve while getting your staff excited about the curriculum. If the teachers are excited about what they are teaching and have ownership, it will translate to their students. The assessments we give have always been a guide to what is working.

Follow the data. It tells the story of what is working and what is not. I am lucky enough to have belonged to a large district that has had a strong research department. They provided an ample amount of data information about our school. This included demographic data, like attendance, mobility, free and reduced lunch status, and diversity. They also gave standardized test scores and other baseline data.

They need assessments to gauge where teachers are and where classrooms are within the realm of the standardized state tests. We must use consistently formative and summative tests to guide the learning process and make it possible to make needed adjustments. Teachers use formative assessments to identify and help learners while they're learning. Summative assessments are standardized tests which summarize the learning that has happened. These standardized assessments are often driven by state and federal requirements. If you are an educator, please know I've felt your pain since I'm aware you get inundated with assessments.

If the data is showing you are not getting results in a certain area, you need to look at that area closely, and see what can be done. I don't mean to make this so simplistic, but sometimes it is not as hard as we make it. Investigate the area where you're not getting results closely and figure out which actions you can take to improve the outcomes. We should not assume that the way we have been doing something is the right way. I have always had my staff look at the data with me and develop conclusions. Why is this happening? What is [name of teacher] doing to meet that standard within their classroom--especially when the data says something is working? This may still seem simplistic, but getting to those hard questions and opening discussions about instruction and data is not a simple task. What are the strategies we need to move our students? What strategies are working? Richard and Rebecca DuFour's work highlights the importance of deep collaborative discussions in professional learning communities. Constructive dialogue makes a difference.

There must be a culture of success and a climate of growth. This growth mindset is popular right now. We should combine it with staff trust. My staff made their own assessments during team meetings to track student progress. This included tests for kindergarten students and evaluating student writing. Staff members created rubrics for many areas to monitor success. Student portfolios can be a useful tool for demonstrating growth.

Standardized tests are used to evaluate the success of schools and districts within the state. It is not always apples to apples, since demographics vary. The media leads us to believe they do not use assessments for ranking schools or districts, yet these are the stories run by local newspapers in most areas: district-district comparisons, including rankings. Again, they're not comparing apples to apples.

For years, educators had to be extremely resourceful in reviewing the data. We used data walls during the *Adequate Yearly Progress* (AYP) years and within *No Child Left Behind*. Some of our best tools involved using individual classroom student data to gauge exactly where each student was in math, reading, and writing. Then we knew how much we needed to move them to increase achievement. Once the teachers had a handle on their classroom, they realized that, as a building, we could move the dial. Then the rules changed again, and the AYP results were a combination of grade levels. This made it more important to look at how each classroom could affect the whole. The federal rules and state requirements are always going to be changing, and our goal is still going to be to increase achievement and success.

During my last few years at the focus school, the staff developed a matrix to keep track of data by student. This was teacher-developed and kept online. The online version became our replacement for a data wall and gave an accurate picture of our building and student status.

As a building, it is important to look at trend data and the impact that is being made. How is the data progressing historically? If it is not working and achievement is not taking place, it is time to review data and make changes where needed. It's time to change course. Through my experience on the district coaching team, I believe in the power of coaching to improve instruction. I have had the opportunity, over the course of six years, to train and coach over 400 administrators. Gone are the days of seeing any teachers shut their doors and deliver ineffective instruction. It is no longer a time of tossing a coin and hoping you have an excellent staff.

If you are coaching, you are visiting classrooms weekly and promoting best practice strategies. What I always did with my staff was illuminate the high yield research-based strategies that can move achievement and learning. Basically, be focused on those strategies that give you the most bang for the buck. Effective instructional strategies are powerful tools for constructive dialogue during coaching, tailored to your building needs. You develop a culture of constructive dialogue.

Before formal coaching, I did "Look Fors." I visited classrooms each week and wrote about the positive things I saw. I wanted to highlight those positive strategies throughout the building. This also promoted the all-important productive conversations with staff members around instruction.

I believe in the power of building wide learning targets as well as individual learning targets for each lesson. It is extremely important for students to know what they are learning. As I did coaching visits, I quickly learned that when I asked students what they were working on, many were unsure and couldn't provide an answer. When they had no learning target, they were as confused as I was, and I could get many responses about what the goal of the lesson was. Once they had a student-friendly learning target, reviewed it and posted it, they could easily tell me exactly what their learning goal was, and what they were learning during the lesson.

Our school studied *Classroom Assessment for Student Learning* (Stiggins, 2006) and *Seven Strategies of Assessment for Learning* (Chappuis, 2009). Then we found out how important learning targets are. When we started having students write learning targets at the top of their assignments, the answers they gave me changed. We were much more focused on our actual learning. I would visit a classroom and ask a student what they were learning. They would tell me about writing a persuasive paper or adding and subtracting numbers. This clarity improved the teaching and improved the students' view of what they were learning. Clarity makes all the difference in the world. If you match standards with strategies and teach with targets in mind, you end up having success.

I love Mike Schmoker's material and books he has written, like *Results Now* (2006), *Focus: Elevating the Essentials* (2018) and *Leading with Focus: Elevating the Essentials for School and District Improvement* (2016). In fact, his *Results Now* (2006) book helped to form the backbone for the focus school curriculum. His direct study on much of what schools really do, and how they can get back to spending more time on reading and writing and solid basic instruction, is powerful. His simplistic yet targeted approach to teaching what really matters makes a difference. He shares a truth rarely stated about schools and his books are well worth a thorough read! My copies are dog-eared, highlighted, and have many note flags and post-its sticking out. I used these frequently with staff.

Our basic curriculum foundation started with clear learning targets. These were for every lesson and posted throughout the building for assessment targets. Clear "I can" statements as part of our building headings--created by students as student-friendly learning targets--backed these. Our approach involved modeled, shared, guided, and independent learning. The gradual release of instruction framework became our model. We broke lessons down into smaller parts. There were regular checks for understanding, and extra teaching if necessary to adjust the learning. These are simple yet effective principles.

As a school, we spent most of our time on checks for understanding and giving strong descriptive feedback to students. Does this sound familiar? It should. It is pretty basic, boots-on-the-ground stuff. We spent more time on learning and making sure students understood by reteaching and using additional strategies as needed. These concepts, reinforced through coaching visits and "Look Fors", made the difference. We spent more classroom time on reading and writing. We developed students' higher-level thinking skills, pushing Bloom's Taxonomy, which moved us from the low levels of knowledge, comprehension and application to analysis, synthesis and evaluation. To address the needs of Special Education (SPED) and special needs students, the teachers created Individualized Education Plans (IEPs) and specialized action plans.

There is great stuff out there. Robert Marzano's research-based strategies in *Classroom Instruction that Works* (Marzano, 2001) were useful tools for me. I like the strategies in *Teach Like a Champion* (Lemov, 2010), *Visible Learning: A Synthesis of Over 800 Meta-Analyses Relating to Achievement* (Hattie, 2008) and the research work on the effects of strategies. There is a large body of work out there and it continues to grow. Use the research and the data. I have listed some more useful resources at the end of this book in References.

Look for high yield strategies encouraging students to think critically and providing opportunities to develop questioning skills. This is crucial. Success requires finding effective strategies and promoting discussion, implementation, and reflection among your staff. They are experts and by getting your best teachers to work with everyone, observe and follow the data, you can't go wrong.

There is power in simplicity and protecting staff from excessive initiatives so they can spend time on quality instruction. Getting the most out of your time with students is extremely important. Even a few minutes a day can add up to a tremendous loss of instructional time over a week, month, and year. We always practiced 30-second transitions within classrooms and other ways to get the most out of your time. If you have strong procedures and routines, you are gaining back precious instructional time.

What is the big deal with lesson plans? If you're a principal and want to get me going, tell me you are collecting lesson plans weekly or-- dare I say--daily! I am all in for well thought out lessons and the use of the gradual release framework for modeled, shared, guided and independent. I know some principals force their staff to turn these in weekly, and many have immaculate plans, checklists, or even provide templates. These may have a place but should not be a gotcha for an otherwise strong teacher.

If you are using a checklist as a reflective discussion tool positively, it might work. Let me say this: I have had excellent teachers who could plan and start an excellent lesson plan developed on a napkin and include all the needed components. I have also known teachers who can make the best-looking lesson plan, with a binder, examples, etc. and still not be able to pull it off in the classroom. A well-written lesson plan does not guarantee an engaging lesson or excellent teaching. Just collecting lesson plans every week won't ensure good teaching, but teachers must learn to make effective plans. This is only showing compliance. If you want to drive staff morale down drastically, collect lesson plans.

In my first year as principal, I made a checklist and collected lesson plans every week because I was told to by higher-ups. I received a stack of these by the end of the week and guess what? I had the utter joy of reviewing these sometime over the weekend and filling out my sheets. I would have them back to them on Monday morning. Did it help? No—it's one of the worst strategies I've ever tried. My recommendation is to get into the classrooms, observe, collaborate, and coach. This is where the rubber meets the road. You will see if there is real teaching taking place, student engagement, and a solid lesson framework.

When dealing with new, struggling, or intervened teachers, it's important to focus on creating and reviewing lesson plans. They are still mastering the skills they need to succeed. They need to be thinking through the thought process of planning and problem-solving. If you want to kill morale and micro-manage, collect lesson plans and see what happens. I have had many interviews where one of the big questions from the teacher being interviewed is, "Do you collect lesson plans?" It is also often a red flag of the environment they are coming from. If we are truly professionals, we should discuss, share and collaborate on our practice, anyway.

Coaching teachers out of the profession is another type of coaching, and we discuss it more in handling difficult conversations. The coaching process still requires tactful handling and focuses on bringing out the best in everyone. However, when coaching teachers out of the profession, it may also require a plan of action. This may include lesson plans, strategies, goals and the meeting of deadlines.

Help your staff learn from outstanding teachers by observing them and hearing about their successful methods. I gave my teachers the opportunity to do peer visits and have the benefit of learning from each other. They scheduled their own visits to observe effective strategies and lessons. All they had to do was tell me about it and they received a jeans day that they could use any time. This was for the observer and the teacher that had the visit. They both benefited from this collaboration. Jeans days--or another incentive they like--can be a powerful tool.

The important piece is getting staff to see what is working throughout the building and if they can replicate the successful results or process. This helps build in the self-reflection needed for staff to improve instruction. Many staff members shared their ideas during staff meetings and in-services, which empowered them. The atmosphere and culture must be collaborative and open to truly assist students in learning. Open dialogue and self-reflection can make a big difference in improving instruction in a building.

At the high poverty building, our students needed extra support and tutoring to succeed. We used Title 1 funds (Federal funds available to schools meeting the required poverty status) to create a tutoring schedule. We did this for 31 weeks, from September to May, and it comprised tutors at every grade level--kindergarten through sixth grade. It comprised 23 staff members meeting with targeted students before school (from 8:00-8:30 AM at the time) and after school (from 4:00-4:30 or 5:00 PM). It totaled 899 hours and provided many opportunities for reteaching and developing understanding. These teachers were dedicated individuals who wanted what was best for the students. It was just a matter of finding resources, grants, or ways to support their dedication.

Through tutoring, our students improved their scores in math, reading, and writing, as tested by the required Adequate Yearly Progress (AYP). We used the quarterly benchmarks in guided reading and came up with many of our own formative assessments to gauge growth. Teachers are professionals and can often develop many outstanding rubrics and check point assessments. Each teacher can view where students stand in terms of scores and identify how to boost their achievement. Give them a voice, collaborate, use your data, and watch out! As their enthusiasm increases, student achievement will climb. It is true in the right environment that people excel. The culture you develop makes a difference.

"In learning you will teach, and in teaching you will learn."

— *Phil Collins*

Chapter 13:
Establishing Professional Development

Professional Development (PD) is one of those areas many districts will control. They set forth the objectives that follow the districtwide school improvement plan and the district strategic plan. Curriculum departments and professional development coordinators are common in many districts, particularly urban areas. This may drive some of the professional development principals are required to give. The district usually has specific curriculum days planned according to teacher union contracts.

As a principal, I tried to protect my staff from things that took us off our primary goal of improving instruction. I geared the professional development I offered around our school improvement plan. We developed it through staff collaboration and input. It was specific to our school. The School Improvement Plan and data also drive some of the professional development. I will discuss this more in the chapter on School Improvement. Your school data could show you need more support in reading, math, science, or other areas in which you are checking accountability. Behavior runs parallel to achievement and there must be a pyramid of supports for both.

The professional development I provided helped develop staff capacity to work with students. The goal was to improve their delivery of instruction while building strong relational skills. Supporting teachers to connect with students will improve engagement and achievement. When teachers are excited and energized, their enthusiasm will translate to students. Employee ownership of their professional development and skills can help meet the established vision.

It is hard to say what individual buildings need without looking at your data and demographics. Doing an overall needs assessment of your school can guide your professional development. I always stuck to the high yield activities--reinforcing practices that are showing excellent results. These were often strategies and concepts we were already doing or had built into our school improvement plan. One of my continuing goals was always improving staff capacity to work with students and develop positive relationships.

We can do this training through having the staff take part in delivering professional development. It is important to have your leadership teamwork with staff in defining training needs and developing skills in specific areas. If your professional development doesn't align with your work or instruction goals, it may not be useful. Staff members can see right through this and know when it is not really relevant to learning.

Staff development direction can be determined by using a survey to identify and more clearly define the needs you have. There are many instruments you can use for this. You could do a Strengths, Weaknesses, Opportunities and Threats (SWOT) analysis and one I like is the NOISE analysis. NOISE looks at Needs, Opportunities, Improvements, Strengths, and Exceptions. It could be a simple needs, solutions, and actions chart, prioritizing areas. Look them up. There are many options in this area, and they usually point you in the right direction for professional development.

The best professional development treats teachers like the professionals they are. They need to guide some of their own professional development. We can do this through outside courses, colleges and district non-mandatory options. Often, teachers create their own individual PD around the areas that interest them. This can increase their expertise in a subject area and increase their strength to assist staff. If there is money for professional development, we can bring in experts to reinforce concepts, or further training in areas of specific needs.

A more expensive option is sending staff to professional development out of town--usually for several days. This can be highly positive. Many times, the teachers come back refreshed, full of ideas, and excited about the content learned. Leaders ought to take advantage of this learning and prompt their staff to share instructional strategies. Enthusiasm can be contagious in your culture!

This is also true for principals. I remember working on feeling comfortable going to professional development events like the Association for Supervision and Curriculum Development (ASCD) national conference. I had to be secure in leaving the building for a few days. The good thing was I was getting to hear the best of the best, surrounded by colleagues, with dialogue and discussion around my craft. When I came back, I felt energized and excited to reinforce, present, train, and use strategies with the staff.

In order to become a true instructional leader in your building, it is important to keep up with learning and research. I always focused on giving teachers more open-ended strategies to meet the state standards but allowed them the creativity to make it happen. Everyone in your building is involved in supporting the core skills in classrooms. All subject areas need to support skill development and progress. This is especially true with math, reading and writing.

I have found that teachers are highly interactive. They learn better through practical experience, discussion and sharing. There is nothing wrong with making it fun. I tried to make my professional development enjoyable, interactive and fun. A little humor can increase learning. It is just like engaging students. As a leader, work to get high engagement. If you are excited, they are more likely to get excited as well. The staff needs to connect to the vision of the school and share ownership.

There are different ways to rotate your staff through professional development--including the PD they help provide. Allow team leaders and all staff to present on areas of their strength. It is often best to hear from peers. I still push the importance of the principal in presenting--especially at the start of the year--and frequently to keep the vision and focus of the school alive. That said, I worked at keeping our PD targeted and tried to avoid lengthy unneeded sessions.

Even some of the district PD provided, I would pare down and make sure it meshed with our building focus and needs. I always had a core instructional framework around which we would create PD. Protect your staff and guide training around your building's needed support.

PD is for everyone, not just teachers. We even developed PD for our bus drivers at one point and had them attend--promising a free breakfast--after delivering our students. The PD was how to use positive behavior supports productively as a bus driver, and what tools to use that connected to the school. This helped them in working with our students and prevented future problems. It also allowed us to give them training and support in working with students that they didn't always get in their other trainings. They received some district training, but this went further and more related to our students that they saw daily.

I have also run special PD for paraprofessionals and other different school teams. Again, professional development is not just for teachers. Anyone who has contact with your students and is part of your staff, should be involved in your professional development. All districts promote teacher training, but if you want to really get everyone together, train all staff members.

I have enjoyed building professional development around our school needs. It is important to pull in many resources to develop the capacity of your staff. As a leader, you need to gather resources and provide training, reinforcement, and support to your team.

We need to be cautious. Too many initiatives and PD can overload your staff with information and reduce effectiveness. Put your learning into context and use it to improve your current instructional and relational capacity. A professional development plan can help your staff grow and become better at teaching and working with students; plus, getting the staff together and moving toward a common goal or vision can be exciting. Anytime you can inject enthusiasm into the professionals you're developing, you're building a strong school community aimed at successfully accomplishing common goals.

I would like to end this chapter with some examples of when we started the focus school concept. We had extra funds available which allowed us to send a team to the Apple campus in Cupertino, CA. We were getting ready to start a 1:1 (technology-to-student) innovative school and were looking for ideas. Apple gave us many creative possibilities, and we walked away learning that it is better not to limit our students.

Let them learn and discover, create and develop. We learned many ways to use technology as a tool within instructional learning. The trip was highly successful in getting us motivated and on track for collaboration.

As the focus school prepared to open, I saw that one of my favorite leadership authors, John Maxwell, was coming to town, and we could sign up for teams to attend. I had heard him before and thought this was a great opportunity to bring my new teachers to his seminar and hear some of his knowledge of positive leadership practices.

If you are familiar with John Maxwell, you may know he has a Christian base and works with many church leadership teams. He also works with the business world and is one of the top authors on leadership. Maxwell often tailors his seminars to a specific group. Well guess what, I did not see all the information, and I arrived with my new hand-selected teaching staff at this big speaking event. He started with some good stories and illustrations, and then he got into biblical illustrations. They had geared this event toward church leaders!

The information was good, but at one point, he even did an altar call. I didn't have knowledge of the staff's spiritual beliefs since we had just met, and I felt uncomfortable during several parts of his speech. I thought to myself. Great, I'm the first principal of this new innovative school, and now I just brought my staff—unaware--to be witnessed to!

I talked to them afterward, and we all had a good laugh. I'd guess most were Christian, but you don't usually discuss such at school. I think it actually helped unite us. They would have a running joke around this for years as we became closer. It still ended up being good professional development, a bonding experience, and certainly an event I will never forget!

"It is easier to build strong children than to repair broken men."

— Frederick Douglas

Chapter 14:
Embracing Diversity

Our classrooms and schools have become increasingly more diverse and there are many cultures represented. The National Education Association (NEA) has said: "Cultural competence is a key factor in enabling educators to be effective with students from cultures other than their own. Cultural competence is having an awareness of one's own cultural identity and views about difference, and the ability to learn and build on the varying cultural and community norms of students and their families. It is the ability to understand the within-group differences that make each student unique, while celebrating the between-group variations that make our country a tapestry. This understanding informs and expands teaching practices in the culturally competent educator's classroom."

Staff in urban districts must comprehend the diverse mix of students and their cultures. Cultural proficiency is crucial for teachers in all districts and states to provide the best education for students. All buildings and communities have different demographics.

Matt Blomstedt, a Nebraska Commissioner of Education, wrote a letter to all the superintendents of the state during the 2020 rallies for George Floyd--a 46-year-old black man who died during an arrest by Minneapolis police. Blomstedt's letter read, "We must create space to genuinely and intentionally embed racially diverse perspectives into our conversations and actions." He says, "The conversation about racial inequities must occur everywhere to prepare our students in every corner of the state to better face the challenges of our nation." Many such statements were made throughout the nation during this historical timeframe. The fact remains that our schools need to be culturally responsive, and hopefully we will continue to move forward in this manner. Throughout history, there have been many mistreatments of various cultures, and these are things that need to change. As leaders and educators, we can create courageous schools who are not afraid to talk about race and culture. If we want our children to change this world, these are important discussions to have and teach about. There has been systemic racism built into many systems of our American society. As an example, they mapped cities out to keep certain people and cultures in specific parts of cities. Areas early on were "redlined" and became void of opportunities for growth, housing and improvement. These practices need to stop. Banks and lending institutions need to support all families and housing growth.

We developed our focus school with a goal of promoting diversity and equal opportunities for all students. Cities have groups that encourage growth for all by aiding diverse families with business models and financing. We still have a long way to go, and most of the learning starts with our children, families, and our students in school.

If you are a principal or leader, you can help make this change happen. If you choose to be a courageous school, you can set up initiatives, as we did, to promote "No Place for Hate," encourage acceptance, and elevate understanding. Your school can become a place for change as your students develop an understanding of history and productive problem-solving. We created the focus school from scratch with the goal of promoting diversity across 11 districts through an open model. It was still a public school but had a magnet school year-round theme that celebrated the unique qualities of all students and cultures.

At the start of the school, we had many intentional discussions about cultural diversity. Here is where the staff needed courage. After discussing and reflecting about it, they discovered their lenses influenced their views of different people and cultures. It is advisable to broaden your understanding of cultural diversity through self-reflection and learning from others, despite limitations. It's common for biases and preconceived notions to be exposed when discussing issues with staff. There is healing in dialogue.

We emphasized recognizing and accepting differences among students during school assemblies. We were intentional in our discussions. Our students were aware of the community we were building and why. We were planting seeds for the future. The students from other districts were not used to the diverse mix of students in our urban district.

Focus on acceptance became a positive, as I have seen many young people of all cultures standing together in solidarity, wanting improved cultural relations. We were fortunate enough at the focus school to have grant dollars bring in various experts to help work with staff and set us up for our mission. Bonnie Davis, author of *How to Teach Students Who Don't Look Like You: Culturally Relevant Teaching Strategies* (2012) and Curtis Linton, co-author of *Courageous Conversations About Race* (2006), worked with us. They assisted us in generating some excellent discussions about race and helped us to self-reflect on diversity. The book, by Linton and Glen Singleton, has some excellent tools for having productive conversations about race.

This ties into the chapter on professional development, which must be specific to your building and needs. There needs to be more professional development around being culturally responsive as educators, and leaders can provide it. All buildings need to be addressing cultural proficiency if we want to break down barriers and create more collaboration in society. As schools, this is the starting point for creating a better society and world. It is important to understand each other, and everything starts with the leader.

As a principal, I have always worked to help my staff understand the demographics and cultures of the students within our community. If you are not doing this, you are missing out on a great opportunity for your staff and students to make better and stronger connections. These relationships, connections and understanding develop into a positive school culture. There are many wonderful resources I have used over the years, and leaders can find a seemingly endless stream of materials to assist in staff discussions.

I had a perfect example of racism when we were starting this innovative focus school concept within another district. A teacher I recruited to promote diversity and create opportunities had a curious encounter with a parent. This parent from another district, whose child was going to be attending our school, asked the teacher a telling question. The parent actually asked if he had a teaching degree. Talk about an unintended insult. We had work to do!

This African American teacher not only had a teaching degree, but a master's degree in social work and another in administration and supervision. He was on his way to being a principal. Surprised, the teacher briefly explained his degrees and education. He then came to me afterward, and I explained this was why we were doing what we were doing. He handled it really well and said, notice they did not ask any of our Caucasian teachers what their credentials were! I responded with you are an excellent teacher and the best thing you can do is prove their doubts wrong. Change the narrative! By the end of the year, that same parent was saying this was the best teacher her child had ever had. He had proven them wrong and destroyed any misconception they had around skin color and abilities. I am happy to say he is a principal now and still a friend. It may be incremental, but it was a step in the right direction. We had some other interesting situations, but that is why we were working to bridge this cultural divide.

Parents from across the city came to our school, resulting in the strongest parent group I've seen. They came together with a common, unifying purpose. They also developed more of an understanding and respect for each other. This is an ongoing process for districts and schools, and there is still so much work that needs to be done in cultural understanding.

Educators need to address issues of race actively as they occur, and not allow them to be disregarded. It is important that we teach history--all history--while promoting understanding. We are the role models as adults, and the things we let go, the students notice. The things we address, the students notice. How we address things and the tact we use, the students notice. It is important for staff to practice better listening skills, which can aid in better problem-solving and understanding. Our students are watching, and it is our opportunity to be positive role models who can influence generations.

"The best way to predict the future is to create it."

— Peter Drucker

Chapter 15:
Branding and Marketing

The principal or leader is an ongoing marketer of their school or program. I am a firm believer that the principal, CEO or leader in charge needs to know the most about the organization. They need to deliver facts, demographics, and a concise summary of the organization effectively. To everyone they meet, they are effectively selling their school and organization.

The image and branding of an organization are extremely important. Ingra, my gifted spouse, taught me about branding and marketing. She knows about templates, mascot designs and the significance of font and color choices. Being meticulous and detail-oriented is her nature. For example, when we were making choices on logos and mascots, she explored options which could reproduce well in both print and embroidery.

The messages you are sending can sometimes be subtle, but they are always present. A clear brand gets that name recognition. You don't have large companies changing logos just for the heck of it. They need sometimes a redesign to promote change, but it must still maintain the integrity of the message. Ingra has created highly professional designs for me in many different formats. She is a perfectionist and pays attention to every pixel.

Make sure your designs are professional. Not everyone with design and illustration programs can create top-quality designs. I have a

Bachelor of Fine Arts as one of my degrees, but still don't have the graphic design knowledge Ingra has. Quality work matters! Ingra created many designs for me that maintained the branding of the school. Her work involved designing templates for school visuals such as presentations, newsletters, logos, etc. She created graphics in TIFF, JPEG and PNG useable formats that I could use for all kinds of needs. She created a focus STEAM logo, a VEX Robotics school logo, and many other professionally designed resources.

The image of your organization is important. I also worked with the district in creating a district standard trifold brochure about the focus school. I still used my logo and graphics in the piece the district artist created for the focus school. The trifold contained information about the school and, when fully opened, the back side became a large poster for display. The design of this piece was very nice.

The district had a communications department that worked with all schools to promote news and public awareness. Ingra also started me creating a press release with information I could pass along to the district Public Information office. During my last few years there, they finally had a person who encouraged branding and marketing. Each building had to select a branding ambassador. This is a growing area where more support is being provided.

At Indian Hill, we became an academy program, which focused on keeping numbers lower in classrooms of high-poverty schools. I changed the name of the school for several years to Indian Hill Academy. I felt like it gave us a unique name and sounded more like a specialty school. We actually became a school with a credible, solid program and gained the reputation of a building that could work with all kinds of children. Ingra helped me modernize the logo for the school. Eventually, the district wasn't fully able to support the academy program concept. Then we had to go back to Indian Hill Elementary, which changed our branding, stationary and minor graphics, but the bear logo stayed the same.

I have designed quick fact sheets for every building in which I have served, and they are a great way to give a quick list of demographics and important information. Now, many are creating infographic sheets. The technology of today makes it easy to promote your school or organization. I am a firm believer in websites, and they must be current and updated regularly. I posted calendar dates, pictures of past special events, and advertised upcoming special events. There was a lot of relevant information on our website. I made sure I could add or change items on our website, even while having district web teams. We posted it when our school, students or staff received recognition. The ability to access the internet opens many doors.

Signage can make a big difference. You can order all sizes of large vinyl banners at a reasonable price. I would make banners of student progress, or for the VEX robotics team, or other important features I wanted to highlight. I could hang them in the gym, office, hallways, cafeteria, or any large open areas. I also had the large lion's head banners made for each light pole in the parking lot. They displayed our mascot image and had "Welcome" in large letters, which also helped our image. Directional banners identified rooms and locations throughout the building. I framed our awards and would add these to the main office area or in our trophy case. A large display case at the second focus school location held trophies and memorabilia of the school, including plaques and news articles. It not only showed success but displayed history and school pride.

Social media is a growing way to support your school and must be a part of your branding and marketing. We set up a Twitter window, so if I tweeted from my account, I could have it show automatically on the website for more timely information. I used Twitter to promote and share positives about the school. It was great for classroom visits on instruction and celebrations. It helped get information out fast. There are many other platforms available. The point is: use social media vehicles where it makes sense to promote your organization!

Facebook is one of the few that started it all. LinkedIn became a business tool, and now everyone has a resume on LinkedIn. Social media is a growing industry and students are often the first to make a change to the latest platforms. Information gets out fast, and it is important to be riding those waves. I now use many types of social media to support my business.

I would also suggest if you hear something negative is bouncing around, take care of it right away. Nowadays, you do not want a negative perception surfacing through social media if you can help it. A teacher talked about a student's personal problem in a restaurant, and an employee who heard it called the school, concerned. Her question was, "Is the school doing anything about this or trying to help the girl?" Without giving her details, I could call this person back and assure her we are aware of the situation, and we have things currently in place to help this girl. This had to do with the possibility of sexual abuse--not a public issue. Luckily, we had things in place, and it ended up not being an abuse case. I had to talk to the teacher about confidentiality, and being careful where and what she shares about her students with others. It was a learning experience.

It is important not to air anything you want to stay confidential. This person could just as easily have posted what she heard on social media but, thank God, she didn't. Like I said, this is the information age and if you must do damage control, it needs to happen fast.

Building a reputation takes time but--it is sad to say--destroying a reputation does not take long at all! It is so important to keep banking those positives. All staff members should build a positive narrative around your school. They should all have a positive elevator speech for your organization (like the example in an earlier chapter). Having staff excited about the school, and able to articulate what makes it excellent, is a wonderful promotional tool. This will happen if you have built a positive culture. The flip side of this is having people talk about the school off hours. You really can't control this and, if you haven't built the right culture, those remarks may not always be positive!

Newsletters are another way to get information out about the school and, for me, it was a major promotional tool. I had the *Bear Facts Newsletter* at one school, *Underwood Hills Focus Newsletter* at one school and the *Wilson Focus Newsletter* at another. There was a *Principal's Corner* section at the school with a bear mascot, and a *Principal's Pride* section at the schools with the lion mascot. At the last two schools, I pushed out the newsletter twice a month and had plenty of information to add. I did the newsletter myself to maintain a positive slant and promote school pride. I included dates of upcoming events, as well as small stories about all the happenings around our school. Staff and organizations could contribute to it as needed. Ingra created an amazing template with super graphics. I included our mission, vision, quick call school numbers and transportation numbers. To show our success, we included our STEAM logo and national accreditation by AdvancEd, as well as our AQuesTT excellent school award and Apple Distinguished School status. We distributed it to all central office departments, all our families, and made it available digitally on our website.

During school assemblies, I displayed banners on the side of the gym which highlighted our school's successes. Then, if we had news media or any other photos taken of an event, we would have these positive messages shown in the background. It is important to keep these details top of mind--you are promoting your organization. We used a podium on wheels with our mascot graphic on the front for audiences and photo opportunities. These things are sometimes subtle, but they give an impression of your school. As you are taking school photos, look at the backgrounds, etc. and decide if those are really what you want in your photos? Again, aesthetics matter. What is best to represent your school?

Install a decent sound system as well. Why is it schools often have crummy sound systems? I installed a wireless microphone receiver setup with a speaker system in the center of the gym ceiling. The focus school changed locations and got a new speaker system. To improve the sound quality in my second building, I upgraded the wireless system and added high-quality wireless microphones. Also, I bought some good portable systems that are suitable for both indoor and outdoor events. It's fantastic to have sound that is both clear and adjustable. This also promotes a professional image. Communication is key, so we might as well be as clear as possible coming through a sound system. It is also a good practice to always have a spare microphone or extra set of batteries in your coat pocket or nearby, since these usually go out at the worse times!

"Ultimately, human intentionality is the most powerful evolutionary force on this planet."

— *George Leonard*

Chapter 16:
Organizing with Intention

Great building principals and other leaders can organize well. They all have what I call an intentionality that is present. As a principal, it is important to figure out effective ways of planning which keep the organization running smoothly. The staff may or may not be aware of these things, but they would notice their absence. The inner workings of a smooth-running organization are not always clear.

Early on, I started creating a weekly calendar and put it out to the staff. The calendar shows the day, date, cycle day (needed for scheduling), and events for that week. The schedule included team meetings, events, due dates and grading periods, and everything else happening in our busy building. I soon realized, once I started, that this was as much for me as it was for the staff. It helped me prepare for the week, look ahead, and always be ready for what was coming. It made my planning easier. I would complete it on Friday before the next week, so it was always looking ahead a bit. We also had a master calendar that we would plug everything into, looking further into the year. Eventually, we digitized all of it and sent it out to the staff. They then could print a copy and have it by their planner for easily accessible reminders.

This weekly bulletin soon developed into the *Friday Focus*, which was also a means of giving a recap and upcoming events. I also started putting all the events listed by date into my bi-monthly newsletter for families and staff. This was a running list of dates and events. As I added new dates, some old ones dropped off the list. I created a template for my staff agendas, and we could easily change it as the topics change, but they always posted the vision on top, and the format remained. Speaking of templates, once created, they are a great way to save time. Have digital folders and templates for frequent items, and you will save time by just rewriting copy as needed.

Lists are a wonderful tool. Don't underestimate the power of a list, and if you have an inner achiever like me, you'll love to cross off those things as they're completed. If you are a list maker, you know what I am talking about. If not, give it a try! It gives you a feeling of accomplishment, especially if you must prioritize and plan for deadlines. As a principal, it is common to have many district deadlines, as well as building deadlines. Therefore, it is important to develop systems to make your time more efficient and keep your sanity. I have a start-of-the-year list and an end-of-the-year list. The longer you are a principal, you learn certain things happen at specific times of the year, so you can have a rough plan at the outset.

I was also the king of small sticky notes or what most of us know as post-its. These are a wonderful invention and allowed me to write small reminders, numbers, etc. and stick it somewhere I would see it. There are digital solutions for this as well, but I like tactile visuals. I found great joy in being able to throw one away as a symbol of completion. I think we all love being able to cross something off that may hang over us. Sometimes, I had way too many of these small colored notes all over my office. I think this just shows all the tasks that a principal completes or keeps up with--especially with daily interruptions.

There are always going to be instances that arise needing your immediate attention or pulling you off task, but then you can get back on course. Meeting with students, parents, and staff may be necessary and can take precedence over other tasks. You can arrange meetings with parents, unless it's a surprise visit (which I would try to accommodate). This conveys that our visitors are important to us. Often these types of visits involve something that needs to be addressed right away. Talking to them right away is a good way to head off a problem before it gets bigger. You can establish a visiting time if it works for you. That didn't for me. However, having a time or days for visiting classrooms and coaching worked well.

I set my office up for productivity. I had the same setup at two buildings, since it worked for me. I had a large U-shaped desk setup with a laptop and desktop to the side and a printer accessible to my right. The phone was easily reachable to my right, and I had a steno pad, which I made every year that had a label on the front: "Phone Records" and the year. As I talked to people on the phone, I would jot down a date and quick reference of what it was about or what action I needed to take after the call. I used steno pads to stay organized for different situations like meetings and documentation. Later, I started using my smart phone and laptop.

I could easily keep track of time during meetings without seeming rude by having a clock on the wall in front of my desk. It helps to keep you on track and moving. If I had used the mounted clock on the other wall—where I'd need to turn my head--it would be easy for others to tell "he's checking the clock!" It always worked for me. I also placed it well so I could still meet with a small group around my conference table, and I would select the seat on my usual side where I could still see the clock. Using your time well matters!

At the start of the year, I created various binders to keep me organized. I had a binder for assessments with the name of the school, a title, like Assessments/Data, the year, and a school graphic/logo with a theme or phrase. I had this digitally, but often wanted a quick hard copy reference. I had a template with graphics and would just change the date and print the covers out for a new year.

I had another binder with the name of the school and the title: Professional Development Plan. It contained schedules, class lists, etc. I kept this right in front and directly under my desktop monitor as my keyboard was a pullout style. Then I had another binder with the school's name, titled Contacts/Directories that was kept on the floor next to the computer tower. I could easily grab this binder or use the digital directory on my laptop. Why does the location matter? It's all about creating routines and procedures to streamline a process and eliminate wasted time--just like classroom transitions. It is developing efficiencies. Those add up. Any extra time needed over weeks and years adds up to inefficiency. I am surprised to be sounding like my wife--I think Ingra might've influenced me here! I have had my classrooms use 30-second transitions to gain instructional time. It can be the same within your office.

Develop a system with filing, digital folders, etc. which allows you to organize and find what you need without searching forever. Things you access daily, you can organize in folders or quick links on your computer. This varies with individuals and often your system may not make sense to anyone else, but if it works for you, use it. I made a binder called Curriculum. It contained information associated with instruction, state standards, and anything specific to our school. I had a binder for my *Friday Focus*, which I could look back at every week and see what I said to staff over a year. I filled these *Friday Focus* binders with best practices and what I was promoting as an instructional leader. It is a great way to archive your year and be able to grab one from a previous year to look something up. These contain a lot of useful information, and someday, I could compile these into a book! Most of them comprise the best of what I was reading and what I was finding out from research. It was the best on how to work with students and increase achievement--wonderful stuff compiled for staff weekly. By the end of my career as a principal, I had quite the binder collection. I kept most things digitally as well, but again, sometimes you need to quickly grab a hard copy.

Another useful tool for a principal is having an alphabetical roster of all your students handy, and a roster by class--including a list of locker numbers and bus numbers. It is easy to grab or look someone up quickly without having to go into the computer system. I also keep a specialist/class schedule on my desk as a reference. I often had a laminated version or would have the copy in a sleeve for reference.

I also had our lunch schedule with times, classrooms, etc. laminated on small 3 x 5 cards. These could be a quick reference in your shirt pocket at lunchtime and have been useful. Each card listed classes, teachers and times. I also had the class order posted to help line students up from recess. I could give these to cafeteria or lunch supervisors to assist them in learning the schedule. These are little things that add up to a very organized, smoothly run organization.

The administrative assistant/secretary can make or break the school. I have always worked at developing a strong relationship with this person. They may have some excellent ways of organizing information or assisting the running of the school already. Inheriting a leadership role requires reviewing processes and building relationships to identify areas for improvement. It is important to value their input and skills.

It also involves them learning how you, the principal/leader, work and the kinds of information you want. It takes a while to get into sync. Eventually, you fall into an effective rhythm and back and forth of positive productivity. If you don't, you should. A collaborative leader is important for developing a successful team. At my first school, Indian Hill, I had Mary Vinzant as my administrative assistant, and we worked well together. At the Focus School, I had an excellent administrative assistant in Carole Yanovich. We were in sync really well and she became part of our leadership team. Her tasks are too many to mention and were highly valuable to the efficient running of the building. The administrative assistant position is an integral part of the smooth running of a building, and we cannot ignore its importance.

At the larger school, we used a supply sheet to be turned in on Thursday, with people receiving their supplies by Monday. It was a long checklist of resources, where the staff could highlight or mark them off as requested. At the other buildings, our administrative assistants received verbal requests, and filled them as soon as they could. Ms. Carole kept the important supplies locked up but would give people what they needed. This helped her keep inventory and reorder supplies as needed, as well as help me in watching the budget and gauging our needs. Create a system that works for you and your school or organization. Trends help you see where money is going and how to adjust the budget annually as needed. It is important to provide needed resources for teachers and staff. Our district budgets had the previous year listed with the current year, where you could see spending patterns and do some long-range planning.

The staff can help plan and organize different parts of the building, such as arrival, dismissal and bus transportation. The staff collaborated and shared great ideas during meetings. They implemented these ideas proactively as solutions to existing problems. Having an ongoing needs assessment by staff can help them be a part of the solution when planning, or when issues arise. Shared leadership works!

I had a sheet with school information, like demographics, achievements, programs, and community groups. I often memorized these for my elevator speech. Businesses use fact sheets or infographics to display information visually. I later had a nice glossy brochure and it opened into a poster which included this. These resources help you get information out to visitors and people or organizations with whom you speak.

The lines I painted on the playground were helpful for organizing recess and lining up. You cannot overlook the importance of firming up your procedures and routines. There may be some work upfront, but the headaches saved are totally worth the extra effort. Think ahead, assess, adjust and plan.

Toward the end of the year, as I would be getting ready to look at staffing, I'd send out a half sheet to staff that has the sole purpose of finding out what their career plans are. Many principals try to get a feel for their staff and where they stand in personnel, and forms like this can assist in doing so. Principals can adapt this staff input form to their specific building. The information can set up the staffing needs for the following year. It gives a way to plan for the next school year and possibly a heads-up on what staff is thinking. Things could still change over the summer break and could still have a domino effect on staff, but at least this helps get in the right mode of thinking.

I also used the gold paper I used for the *Friday Focus*. It said:

To: Staff Members

From: Bret Anderson

Date: _____

Re: Staffing

As I consider staffing for the [year] school year, it is important that I have input from each of you. Please fill out this form to the best of your ability and return it to me before you leave on Friday, [date]. Thank You.

_____ *I plan on remaining at the school next year in my current teaching assignment.*

_____ *I plan on remaining at the focus school but would like to move to _____ grade.*

_____ *I will request a transfer from the school next year but will remain in the district.*

_____ *I plan on resigning from the district.*

_____ *I am planning to retire at the end of this year.*

_____ *Other (explain)_____*

The nice thing about this sheet is it often can be a precursor to conversations with staff. If you find out another grade level becomes available, you can see if someone is flexible to moving. This is not a new idea--many leaders have their own version of this—but it is worth sharing in case helpful to assist in the next year's staffing.

I enjoyed the funny responses I would get from some of my staff who were just messing with me. You could tell these responses since they would be like, "I am planning on running away and joining the circus!"

These teachers were the best because of their sense of humor and relationship skills.

The running joke with Ms. Carole was, "I need to fill out a gold sheet." As an administrative assistant, she did a ton, was very good at her job and would often say, "Where is this in my job description?" I would quip back "You didn't read the fine print" and say, "The extra addendum with all the extra pages." I would add, "It's just like my job description!" We would then have a good laugh. This became her common response when we were going through incredibly busy or tough situations. She would ask for a gold sheet. She has a great sense of humor, and we both would often lighten it up when needed. This is part of being a good team!

Another tool I found useful was a message note. I used a small sheet that was about 4" x 5" in salmon-colored paper, and I would cut it on a paper cutter. The small message notes said:

MESSAGE FROM BRET ANDERSON

TO: _____

DATE: _____*TIME:* _____

_____ *PLEASE SEE ME*

_____ *FOR YOUR INFORMATION*

_____ *JUST A REMINDER*

_____ *I NEED*

_____

THANKS [Signature]

I would also add a graphic of our mascot on the sheet and run off a bunch of copies to keep a stack of these on my desk for use with staff. It made it easy to drop a note in their mailbox or attach it to something else. I still like it and have used it at all the schools. This is something I picked up from Joan McCrea, my mentor when I first became a principal. It was a useful tool, and, like the *Friday Focus*, I reproduced it on goldenrod paper. I used email and text as well, but sometimes a note is better. It can be quick and easy and to the point. It is hard to beat a handwritten note sometimes.

We have always provided our students with tools to help them learn to be organized. I have used student planners at all the buildings in which I have been a principal. These are wonderful tools to teach daily and weekly planning skills. When I was at the building which had primary students, I had a simpler version (age appropriate) starting at second grade. Then I had a different version for third through sixth. There are all kinds of fancy versions out there. You can also tailor these agendas for your building with mascots, messages and inserts.

I finally found a company that was very reasonable and had a long-lasting cover--which many will use as a selling point. They give the ability to add your school's name and mascot logo within a window. Then I also got in the habit of ordering these early to get a discount. They can also be a vehicle for messages between home and school. Many have sections of helpful information or positive character reminders. If you have a print shop or district printing and publication department, you could create your own.

At one point, I purchased heavy vinyl home-to-school folders into which we could insert a logo page and they were pre-labeled Home to School and were in school colors. The folders had good durability, and we could reuse them for another year. Anything that helps to organize papers, flyers and information going home can be useful.

Another tool we provided the children with is water bottles. You can get a simple water bottle at a good price and add a logo. At the focus school, we gave them to all students with an agenda at the start of every year. The students get in a routine of getting these filled and have water available as needed. Hydration is good for the body and brain, and we want students to function as best they can, so water is another tool which helps them be their best. I will take any edge like this that helps health and achievement!

An activity we did to assist the usability of our playground in the winter was to get the students involved with clearing snow on the playground. Our playground had a hard surface area and a rubber surface around the playground equipment. In the winter, the head engineer could use a tractor blade on the hard surface, but not the rubber area. We purchased a bunch of plastic blade shovels (a metal blade or scoop can damage the rubber surface) and had the students help clear it during recess time.

It was just like a Tom Sawyer moment: I would often start, or the security guard would start, and soon the students would be asking, "Can we shovel?"

The next thing we knew, they were helping. We ended up allowing them to take turns, and they loved to do it. It got to where they would expect to help shovel at recess. I'm not sure if they are that willing at home, but they sure enjoyed doing it at school! Actually, some did not have a shovel at home, so they had to learn to use one correctly. I saw this in developing our school community garden beds. We had to show many how to use a regular shovel or garden tools. These are worthwhile teachable moments!

At one building, I helped organize the supply room by taking pictures of what was in each cabinet and added a label with the contents-- almost like you do in a primary room. We then laminated these to put up on the cabinet doors with Velcro. It made it easy to locate items and restock shelves. It was another strategy to make finding supplies easier.

When I think of good organizers, our computer specialist at Indian Hill—Nancy Johnson—comes to mind. She helped organize our book room, distribution of supplies, and initiated the Light Span school-to-home reading program, which was of great benefit to our students.

There are ways to make your building more effective by organizing it intentionally. Look at what other buildings and principals are doing, share ideas, and look for ways to improve processes and procedures.

"It is our attitude at the beginning of a difficult task which, more than anything else, will affect its successful outcome."

— *William James*

"If you're going through hell, keep going."

— *Winston Churchill*

Chapter 17:
Facilitating Difficult Conversations

I thought this chapter deserved two quotes since having difficult conversations is an area where procrastination can dominate. As Winston Churchill implied, when going through something challenging, it is best to go forward and get it done! Developing relationships and motivating staff are two crucial elements to effective leadership. Another not so pleasant element is having those tough conversations.

One factor that is helpful in working with people is being able to listen and listen well. Effective listening skills help you understand any situation and move forward. The tone and tact you use are extremely important, and coming from a base of care doesn't hurt either. I have had many tough conversations with staff, parents and families.

There are things you can do to diffuse situations with angry parents. Many come in extremely angry and wanting to fight. In these cases, they often come into the office with an aggressive stance and remain standing. I have found that moving them out of the center of attention (out of the hall or into your office) can help diffuse the situation. If you take away the audience, communication can improve. Also, taking a breath and sitting down helps. Showing you will listen and really want to hear what their concerns are goes a long way to solving any issues. If you sit down and start speaking with a calm, non-escalated tone, you can diffuse the heat when someone comes in ready for a battle. Listen and repeat back the concerns you are hearing--demonstrating your understanding.

Giving positives based upon what they say, like "I can see you have high expectations for your [son/daughter], and I respect that." Give them some positives based upon what you are hearing. These need to be complimentary. "I can see that you are a highly involved parent, and we need more of these! We appreciate this at our school!" Use statements that affirm they want the best for their children, and, as a school, you do too. Make your compliments sincere.

I have always found it useful to maintain a sense of humor, and my goal has been to help people leave in a better mood than when they came in. I love what Oscar Wilde said, "If you want to tell people the truth, make them laugh. Otherwise, they'll kill you." This may be extreme, but there is a bit of truth in what he said. Bring people out of their anger, if possible, and move them in a positive direction.

I usually do well defusing irate parents, but every year it seems like there's at least one who is out to get you. I had a single parent who had a child of whom she was very protective, and we had been working with her since a few students had picked on him. We had many pieces in place to assist this student, but it wasn't enough in her eyes. Other students received consequences when appropriate and we had a sound system of positive behavior supports in place. This did not matter to her. I met with her at the school many times and she was not happy. I finally had a liaison from our central office attend a meeting with us. I actually thought she would be more tactful, but she still ended up screaming and complaining about me and the school. Then she bypassed me and arranged a meeting with one of our assistant superintendents at the central office.

I came to the meeting with a stack of materials and all the things the school had been doing to ensure her son was getting the best experience. Again, I thought--under the assistant superintendent's presence--she would be more professional. She was not. She started screaming and laid into me for a long time. In fact, this meeting lasted 90 minutes and I could barely get a word in. The assistant superintendent let her berate me for the whole time. I lost respect for him on this day.

He could have stopped her after she started repeating herself and continuing the rant. I kept trying to interject respectfully, to no avail. I later realized she was trying to get an inappropriate reaction and was ready to use it against me. It is so important to keep your cool. Acting professionally and respectfully can prevent accusations of unprofessional conduct against educators. I call this the professional trap. They will also use anything said against you, so watch your words. The next day, human resources called me and allowed me to present my case. I could show all the things we did to support her son, and things seemed to calm down after this meeting.

I learned to stop complaints from going to the central office by contacting student community services to inform them about the situation beforehand. They would get back to me and remind the parents to meet with me, the principal. Then I would work with the parents to come to an agreeable solution. The superintendent at that time—Dr. Jon Mackiel--once said to me (when one parent had gotten all the way to the top), "Work your magic!" He was aware I was at one of the hardest buildings in the district. His faith and support in me were excellent and much appreciated!

Some of my toughest conversations were with staff members at the first school where I was principal. The staff is much trickier. You want to motivate your staff and bring out the best, but there are certain circumstances that need to be addressed. Some issues need to be handled right away and others take time. Inappropriate behaviors can become part of the culture. This is something nobody wants to have happen. Build a positive culture that addresses problems when necessary.

I had a staff member who was very intelligent, had a PHD, and was helpful in many of the literacy interventions. He had some personal problems, and, as an outlet, he had increased his drinking. It started outside of school and soon came to work. It was a way of coping, but not a good way. We had suspected something was going on and we were observing his behavior. Some staff had come to me and wondered if something was wrong with him.

All you can do with staff is thank them, let them know you are aware of and addressing it, and that you appreciate their concern. I had been in contact with Human Resources (HR). They wanted me to continue to monitor him and, if it seemed like he was under the influence, to send him to be tested. I kept my eyes on him until one day he was at his desk with his head down like he was asleep. I called HR and met with him. I told him I am not sure what is going on, but we would like him to go with our nurse to get drug tested. I also told him this was a district directive and failure to do so would cause actions by HR.

He complied but wasn't sure why I needed to do this. Before he left with the nurse, he asked if he could go grab something from his office.

I said yes and had my assistant principal watch him. He didn't go out the back door or anything like that, but he tried to hide the evidence. She said she had seen him put something in the large, covered trash can by the restroom near his desk. I knew after I got him on the way with the nurse, we could check this out. The nurse drove and accompanied him to the testing facility used by the district.

When clear, we checked the trash can and found a large size bottle of wine. This was then moved to my office as evidence. When he returned, they had the results in an envelope. I opened them as I was talking to HR on the phone, since they wanted to know what the reading was. Their response was, "Are you reading that right? He is three times over the legal limit for alcohol. How is he functioning? I explained that he wasn't functioning very well. The nurse then drove him home.

On the way out, he was apologizing to me and was so sorry to have let me down. I was just saying he needs to go home and take care of himself and get his personal issues back in order. I then called his wife (I was unaware they were no longer together), explained the situation, and that someone would have to come get the car. She came the next day to get the car, and he was done. HR cut him loose. This was a tough conversation with someone who was at one point a strong, respected part of my team.

People come from all kinds of backgrounds and have many different life experiences which can influence their work. Difficult conversations will sometimes need to happen. I don't know how many staff members over the years came to me with issues taking place in their lives which they wanted advice to help them solve. Effective leaders become counselors. It may not say that on your degree, but you are a counselor and a life coach. People will come to you--especially if you have developed trust and respect. They will seek your counsel.

I had another staff member--an outstanding teacher--who called me once on a weekend and said, "I need help to move my house." He informed me his stuff needed to be moved within a certain time frame, as the house was inaccessible. I didn't ask him questions, just showed up and helped him clean out the house in the designated amount of time. He needed help. I don't know the circumstances. He didn't share that, but no problem. To this day, we are good friends. He is still a top-notch teacher and one of the most loyal staff members I've ever had. You never know what staff members are going through. He needed help, and I was there.

I had a para-professional once who was acting erratic, similar to the first example. She was definitely under the influence. She was acting weird--not what was normal for her. I had a staff member come to me with concern and I thanked them without giving details of anything (we were already observing). I had to call her mother to pick her up and take her to the Employee Assistance Program (EAP) provided by our district for counseling. I had also been in contact with HR, and per protocol, they said when we saw the behavior again, to have her go with the nurse to be tested.

Then it happened again. A staff member said something was up with her. On this day, I even had a student who worked with her ask me what was wrong with her. I called HR, and I did a similar process to what we had done previously. I told her it was a directive from HR that she goes with our nurse to get tested. As I was making preparations, I had her wait in the assistant principal's office. She was kind of oblivious to what was going on.

While in her office, she started eating stuff she had with her. I saw this when I was walking past the office door. I stepped into her office and told her she could not eat at that moment, and I removed the food. This could change any reading. When you are testing someone, this is a priority. It is important to monitor them and send them as soon as you can. The nurse and assistant took her to be tested after I told them this must happen now. Then when she returned, we called her mother to come get her. HR then called me and said she tested positive for drugs and would not be returning. She was a fantastic para with a lot of potential but made some bad choices and went astray.

Some things you handle will be more subtle. I once walked into the engineer's office and four of them were sitting and visiting. It wasn't lunchtime, but no one was working. I didn't need to address it. They knew I saw them. They were uncomfortable, and this behavior improved. Knowing what to address and what not to is part of leadership. Walking into the room addressed the situation.

Over the years, I had to address other staff who had issues and needed to pull it together. Some did, some didn't. I always approached them with how we could help them get better. This was always true with staff members who were put on intervention. The goal was to give them the chance to improve and succeed. We provided resources, support, and a plan of action.

After a while, I became pretty good at these conversations since they can affect a whole classroom and, in turn, generations of students. The district processes in place can be long and tedious. There is due process in place and usually, as in our case, they set it up through the union to protect rights. Our district process for teachers was to notify them they were being moved to informal intervention. This would comprise an improvement plan for a certain number of weeks. If they have improved after the time is up, we could pull them off intervention. If they were still struggling, they could continue with the informal process longer or we could move them to formal intervention. This was after encouragement, coaching, and mentoring.

The next step was a formal intervention that included weekly meetings, a review of lesson plans (which I believe are necessary in this case), and additional personnel support. We developed the plan with the district HR department and often a teacher union rep (who could also be involved anywhere along the line). I have completed many of these plans, especially at my first building, where I inherited many staff members.

The goal is to do what you can to assist and support, but if they are not putting forth the effort, including self-reflecting, it will not happen. They must take an active stance and show progress. The hope is if someone is told to pick it up or be put on intervention, they would produce the best lessons ever. This is their moment to pick up instruction and work to impress everyone. Everyone is different, but what is a priority for the school needs to be a priority for the staff.

Unfortunately, the majority of everyone I have ever put on informal intervention moved into formal intervention, and they could not change. We did remove some from intervention after seeing improvement, but they still required help and professional development. If they have character flaws or are not good at relationships with students or adults, they will probably have the same problems and fail. It's difficult to change things that can't be hidden, because they eventually resurface. Many of these traits are just a part of their personalities. Excellent communication skills are needed in the world of education.

As I mentioned earlier, in Coaching and Instruction, there are times that--instead of coaching to improve--you are coaching someone out. Coaching out is helping uncover a realization that the teacher may not be in the right career placement. I call it self-reflection coaching or reality coaching. This is where you may end up coaching them out of the profession.

I had a staff member show up frequently late and wondered if this would be a case of reality coaching. She was tardy many days, and it became a burden for staff who wondered if she would be there that day, and they would often have to cover her class for a bit. I ended up using our district Employee Consultation Form, which laid out the problem and an action plan for improvement outlining what needs to happen.

This was a district form and way of documenting what was taking place. I kept doing these and documenting the dates on the form, consistently addressing her. She would say, "You are giving me one of these again," and I would explain it is not fair to the students if she is not there. I wanted to help her get better and explained she needed to be there on time every day. The form helped guide the conversation. We had an idea something else was probably going on outside of school, but she kept saying it was her alarm.

She was getting better, but this was after setting high expectations and being consistent in confronting the problem. Many times, she would get angry and cry. I knew something else was going on, but I stood my ground and kept giving her the forms and having meetings with her. I explained it was for her own good, and for the students who depend on her. Her behavior was getting close to HR intervention. She needed someone to make her accountable.

She improved her behavior, but I wasn't sure if she could maintain it. The next year, she was like a different person. Her attendance improved, and she started being punctual and really turning things around. She gave me a card to express gratitude for my belief and support, and she ended up becoming one of my better teachers. She changed her ways completely, showing up early, attending family nights, and even optional PTO meetings. Nowadays, she actively takes part, jokes around, and has truly transformed herself. This type of consistent coaching worked. She became a loyal staff member and said she will never forget what I did for her, which really was holding her accountable in a caring way.

I had another teacher I had to coach out of teaching. He was struggling, had been late for some meetings, and was appearing more unprepared for lessons. It eventually came out he was having a drinking problem, and it came to school and affected his performance. I knew we were in trouble when I got a call as my wife and I were getting ready for bed one night. The woman who called said she was his friend, that they were at his apartment where he was saying weird things, and that he seemed really out of it. I was ready to go see what I could do. His parents then called me and said they were on their way, so I stopped getting dressed to go. They assured me they had it under control. I am sure he really didn't want me seeing him in the state he was in.

By the end of the school year, I had created a document titled Classroom Performance, which was a brief letter and action plan. It read, "It has become necessary for me to apprise you of some concerns I have regarding your teaching performance during the [dates] school year, and to suggest ways in which you can be successful in the following [dates] school year." Then I outlined areas from our teaching rubric that I needed to see improved. For this, I asked for lesson plans, since we needed to see how he was preparing for classes.

The action plan included a list of detailed requirements that need to be evident by Open House in September of that year. The letter concluded with the following statement: "These are our expectations. Failure to get the discussed items in place will cause you to be placed on informal intervention. As stated in your appraisal, your overall performance rating was [rating scale placement]. We expect you to improve your performance, based on your past two years with us and previous experience with another district. Check your appraisal for more information. The actual work should be focused on increasing effectiveness in your instruction and engagement."

This teacher was excellent with students and had a natural talent for relationships that many didn't have. We also told him we were there to support him, but he must be attentive, motivated, and committed to his job. His personal life cannot influence his ability to provide solid instruction and teaching. We have created our school with high expectations for both staff and students. We had hoped his summer break would allow him to recharge and renew his dedication. The timing of his personal problems did not permit any kind of intervention this late in the year. I copied this document to our human resource director who worked with teachers. This was not informal intervention at this point. I could turn the detailed action plan with a review date into an informal intervention process if needed.

I wish I could say everything was better, but over the summer break, he went into a rehab facility for alcohol. I was informed by his parents the rehab facility had released him right before our opening days of school--not ideal. I was keeping my fingers crossed, but these can be tough battles for people. He had a doctor's release. We started by addressing a few last-minute things that were supposed to be done before he had left for the summer. He completed documents and the new year began.

We started following the plan, but he was struggling. Then our assistant principal viewed the lesson, and it was rough. She was prepared to discuss and suggest improvements to prevent it from falling apart. He went out to lunch. I went to a principal's meeting and then received a text from the assistant principal that he was not back to pick up his students from lunch. I said to have our administrative assistant call his mother, since his mother and father were emergency contacts. He ended up being out driving around. He was upset by the observation he knew wasn't good. This observation ended up being a trigger and not in a good way. Then, an hour and a half later, he still was not at school and his students were being watched by someone else. His mother called him during his drive, asked him what he was doing, and said to get back to school.

When he came back to school, I had a closed-door office meeting with him. I talked about his class scores (his were the lowest, about being fair to the students, and that he can't continue like this. I told him about his strengths and about my concerns. He was not keeping up, it was almost open house, and he still hadn't completed some deadlines from the previous year. He said he didn't have time at night to focus on strategies and lessons since he was in group therapy and recovery. We had to figure out how we could move forward.

We discussed his addiction and what he was going through. Then I asked him a hard question, "How much do you like teaching?" He said, "I do like teaching. I may need a break, but I do like teaching." I reminded him of the open house deadline, that it was coming the next week, and that he could not keep up on the plan we currently had in place. This was our pre-plan aimed at setting the groundwork for any next steps. That meant the next week we would be starting on informal intervention. I said this process will be an official informal intervention and more rigorous.

This informal intervention meant we would have a plan that runs for 8-10 weeks, with the union and HR involved. This will also be a more detailed plan of action. If he could not do our building-created action plan, I did not see how he could make it through a real district intervention plan (reality coaching). Then, we would put him on a more intensive formal intervention if needed after this plan. Failure in the intervention could cause his release and inability to ever continue teaching—basically a revocation of his state teaching license. This was a fact based on our current progress.

This is where we had a serious discussion. I went back to the fact that, if he truly enjoys teaching, he needs to really think hard about his current situation. He asked if I thought he should resign, and I explained the decision was up to him. I said, I could not make this kind of decision for him, but based upon current circumstances, I had strong doubts about him being able to manage the stress and pressure. If he really wanted to teach, my suggestion was to take time off and get his personal life back in order. We talked about him living with his parents back home as he pursued the needed help.

I gave him examples of others I have known about with this battle. I told him to use his sponsors and family to think hard about it and do some soul searching. I had already sent him to the Employee Assistance Program (EAP) for extra help. We planned for a substitute teacher for the next day, which was a Friday. At the end of the meeting, I told him to make sure he talks to family or a sponsor, and not to turn to substances. I was worried this might be a trigger again. His mother called me in the evening at home, since we had been working together, and I told her what I had explained to him. His parents were supportive and understanding, trying to get him help and keep him on the right path. He was from a smaller town, so his parents would have to drive to our city to assist him.

The next day, I tried to call him to see how things were going. This was in the morning. No answer. This was not a good sign. I called his mother, and she said they were in town looking for him and could not contact him. They also could not get a hold of him the previous night after we had talked. To make a long story short, they finally got him by phone and could tell he had been drinking. They told him to leave his car. Earlier in the evening, he checked into a half-way house, but they kicked him out. His sponsor was trying to find him, and we discovered he had checked himself into the Nebraska Medical Center.

As he became clean and after talking to his parents, he resigned, and I received a resignation letter by fax. He decided it was best to resign, get straightened out, and re-evaluate his career. Then we worked on getting a sub while we sought a permanent replacement teacher. This was not great timing, but it seems like it never is. I sent a letter to the families explaining he was leaving us for personal reasons, and we would have a substitute or replacement at the open house. It is important for people to see the process which took place. Not all people are cut out to be teachers and sometimes, for the benefit of the children, leaders must move in and make some tough decisions.

I have learned you have to develop a thick skin as a leader. You cannot always please everyone and they may not always agree with your decisions. However, it is important to respond tactfully, with a good demeanor, combined with understanding, to cushion the impact. It can make a substantial difference. I love the quote by Maya Angelou: "People will forget what you said, people will forget what you did, but people will never forget how you made them feel." This is often true, and emotions can run deeply. Therefore, I work at bringing out the best and believe in the positives of others.

One of the best things I did as a leader was to continue to hone my people skills. I learned about emotional intelligence, problem-solving, building relationships, and developing people skills. I continue to study people, because I want to know what makes people tick, where they are coming from, and how to best work with different people. I want skills and tools to help assist with more positive interactions and team building.

Dare to Lead (Brown 2018) talks about having the courage to be vulnerable, while still managing everything that comes your way as a leader. All leaders have insecurities. It's what you do with these thoughts that make a difference. Honest sharing with staff can bring you closer and help develop trust. I find it comforting that probably all leaders throughout history have dealt with self-doubt. Most effective leaders, who want to continue to improve and be the best at what they do, are self-reflective leaders.

I like to use Gallup's *StrengthsFinder* (2007) tool to build teamwork and encourage staff strengths. Being aware of individual strengths and backgrounds can assist in tough conversations. It can really help in mediating situations with staff.

At conference time, I stressed to teachers the importance of being good listeners as well as clearly presenting information. I always said to use the sandwich technique. Start the conference with positives and strengths, then address areas for improvement and create a plan, then end on a positive note. Everyone loves a sandwich!

Some parents come to the meeting anxious about their child, and with personal problems which can affect the meeting. As parents, they are often on the defense, and you do not need to fuel this fire. It is better to put them at ease, and this sandwich technique allows you to give positives. It is a partnership of collaboration that can make the difference. How can we work together to help [name of student] improve in school? Together, build a productive, positive plan.

Ingra and I became certified behavior consultants to learn more about how people lead and behave. Learning about human behavior makes it easier to understand and connect with others. The more common ground people see, the more they communicate and connect. We cannot change the lenses people are using to see the world, the experiences that have made them what they are, or how they have developed. It is possible to listen and develop an understanding and see multiple perspectives while connecting on a human level. This really matters.

As leaders, one of the best things we can do is self-reflect on our current status, skills, and what we need to do to improve. If you are not happy with how you handled something or if you lost control, you can change it! True leaders continue to learn, grow, and develop through experiences along the journey. You have the power to develop into a strong mediator, problem-solver, and someone who can handle anything that comes your way.

"Creating a collaborative culture is the single most important factor in school improvement for those seeking to enhance the effectiveness of teaching and learning."

— Richard and Rebecca DuFour

Chapter 18:
Starting School Improvement

Improving schools is required by the state, school district, and Federal mandates. All districts spend a great deal of time on school improvement. What does school improvement mean? To most in education, it means meeting those state requirements and having a strategic action plan to improve the school. Yearly goals and strategies are focused on areas that need to improve based on standardized tests and state benchmarks. Many districts will set guidelines and a bar for improvement.

School districts use AdvancED for national accreditation, which is linked to their improvement plan. The plan really is like a yearly business plan, with goals and strategies to meet these goals as well as address deficiencies. Such plans focus on increased achievement, increased sales, goals, and customer base. Schools are very similar. They are like large businesses, with the principal being the CEO. Schools create an individual school improvement plan that falls under a larger district strategic plan. States often rank schools and districts based on criteria developed at the state level as well as federal guidelines.

At the first school where I served as principal, we made tremendous gains because we focused on bringing behavior in line so achievement could happen. Using PBIS allowed teachers to make gains in academic achievement by improving behavior. During the 2001-2002 school year, our fourth-grade state writing assessment (state reported requirement) went from 40.32 percent to 74 percent meets or exceeds standards. This was a 33.7 percent increase in a building that was about 89-90 percent free and reduced lunch. These are excellent gains I think anyone would appreciate.

Our school at the time had focused on writing and writing prompts. Teams had collaborative scoring and sharing sessions. They used six trait writing sources and the lower grades (Kindergarten through third) were using Lucy Caulkin's writing series. The teachers wanted to pilot Caulkin at the lower grades, and we did this with outstanding success, even though this was not a district initiative.

We also did quarterly running records supplementing the Basal reading series with Guided Reading. It was a way for us to show growth in a high poverty building and was a part of our school improvement plan. In 2004-2005, we had 58 percent of first graders reading at or above grade level, and by 2005-2006, we had 91 percent of first graders at or above grade level. That's another 33 percent increase! Our plan and the teachers were doing an incredible job, and our progress was showing. In 2004-2005, we had 66 percent of second graders reading at or above grade level and by 2005-2006, we had 88 percent of second graders reading at or above grade level. That was a 22 percent increase! The impact of moving our lower grades influenced the entire building and prepared our students to succeed as they moved up the ladder.

We accomplished this success through a strong collaborative effort. To assist students in learning, we employed diverse strategies, like grouping by performance and grade level, flexible grouping, and teaching reading skills in different ways. We also used after-school tutoring and reading assessments. We still used the required Basal reading series as well.

The staff teaming and the "whatever it takes" attitude are more of what led to our success. During my 10 years at this building (nine as principal), we worked to move math, reading, and writing scores, and we did just that. This was a total team effort by all. This was during the Adequate Yearly Progress (AYP) era and No Child Left Behind (NCLB). The behavior was getting better at the same time, and there was a parallel of success with a positive progression of behavior and achievement. When negative behavior went down, achievement and academics went up!

Another piece that changed was the culture. It became more positive, and success oriented. We increased our community involvement by having family events to make connections. This was definitely a contributing factor to our overall success. By tracking attendance at events, we collected data to measure our impact. We intentionally looked at what was bringing our families to the school, and how to increase family involvement. The development of staff capacity is crucial for behavior and achievement strategies. We worked on professional development and quality training specific to our building needs. This included de-escalation and intervention techniques, relationship skills, and restorative practices.

A dedicated leadership team with representatives from the staff helped develop ownership, which made this process more of a true building plan. I discuss many of these variables in other chapters, but they all work together to make effective school improvement. It is not just one thing, it's many facets coming together to influence the whole culture.

Another factor in school improvement is the availability of needed resources. Because we were originally a high poverty building, we had Title 1 funds which assisted many of our staffing, instructional, and resource needs. When the federal government changed funding from elementary to secondary students, it affected programs for kids at a critical age. It spread out the money more, but we really needed it early on to develop a strong learning base for children. The primary years can make such a difference in growth.

Our district had an equity formula that considered many factors affecting student success. This formula tipped the scale in favor of funds for higher poverty buildings with higher needs. At one point, my building--at its height--had a population of 675 students. Under the formula, it was equal to a building of 2,100 based on the number of needs we had (as discussed in Chapter 9: Doing What is Best for Children). It allocated resources to the areas that had the highest need.

A building in a high poverty area will have more needs than a building in a middle class or upper middle-class area. The students are going to come with many of those *Developmental Assets* met (Search Institute, 1997) met. We need more resources in a building with high poverty and different demographics, where students will have an asset deficit. You cannot treat all school buildings and areas the same.

Many districts use a formula that considers student and staff numbers to distribute resources. This does not work in a high need, high poverty building. A building of 400 in one part of town may need more resources than a building of 400 in another part of town. Additional staffing and resources may be necessary to be successful with the demographics. The equity formula used for a while was one that allowed funds to follow the needs of the students. These and many other factors have an influence on school improvement and the school's ability to successfully move forward.

Our goal at the focus school was to help students grow and achieve more by giving them better opportunities. Over the 11 years I served as principal, we moved our students socially and academically. Our trend data was excellent, and, in our standardized math test, our scores went up four years in a row. Then the state test changed from the Nebraska State Accountability Test (NESA) to the Nebraska Student-Centered Assessment System (NSCAS). I will share more focus school data in the next chapter.

The focus school received extra funding and support through grants. I continued to write these grants all the years I served at the focus school. We needed the two-year Sherwood grants to fund this innovative learning program. Sherwood funded many programs to provide more opportunities for students in our district.

Another resource was the Omaha Schools Foundation, and the support we received toward our programming was excellent. Our results showed the power of using resources in a thoughtful, planned manner to assist students. Schools can seek other ways to provide resources for students. Solutions like these were often the avenues I pursued. Just like our students, schools can be very resilient and resourceful themselves!

For 13 years, I was on the district's School Improvement Planning Team. We worked to make state requirements simpler and to create rubrics. These rubrics were used to identify a school's current status and determine the areas that needed improvement. Being a part of this team also helped me understand what was coming down from the state and the current requirements to be followed. The requirements routinely changed, and the district plans also changed with the current trends.

In my 21 years as a principal, I have completed my share of school improvement plans. We have worked on both large plans and smaller, more focused plans, with strategies to enhance the school. One binder was so thick, it could have held a door open! If you talk to educators, many of these types of plans are documents of compliance—district and state accountability. An action plan or strategic plan is good if it fits the school. It is important for your team to identify the strategies you will use based upon the data observed, while addressing the needs of your specific building. I always posted goals and had what our current targets were for the areas of academics and behavior we were looking to improve. Always refer to the destination and track the progress toward your goals.

If you work with staff on studying the data, showing progress and what it will take to move achievement, you will make even more gains. Leaders should keep growth meetings positive instead of being a dictator about score improvements. Be motivating while celebrating the minor victories along the way. It is important to follow the data. You must identify the progress together as a building, as grade-level teams, and as a school team.

Everyone must have agreement and ownership of the success of the school. The goal is to turn a school improvement plan into a usable action plan that is ever-changing, based on the building needs and data. All school improvement is in a constantly changing cycle. It should be a developing plan. The actions and strategies around the plan matter. It must be a tentative guide to moving your progress forward. It also should echo the needs of your community and demographics.

"Whenever ideas are shared, the result is always
greater than the sum of the parts."

— *Rich Willis*

Chapter 19:
Forming the Focus School as a National Model

It was 2008. I was still at this large urban school with the Educare construction on hold. Our district had collaborated with two other districts about a focus concept. The legislature at our state capital was circulating all this talk about a proposed Learning Community. There was legislation that developed around this school concept. The legislation was going to allow school districts to have focus schools. I had been watching the news around education, but really never gave this a second thought.

My district had sent out a plea for ideas for a so-called focus school. I remember talking to Ingra and saying a brilliant concept would be to base the theme around leadership. I have always loved leadership, and it is my hobby to read about it and study it. My wife suggested I send in the ideas I had, which I ended up doing--not thinking it would go anywhere. I also shared my concept with an assistant superintendent at the time who was gathering focus school ideas.

The multi-district committee creating the concept for a focus school surveyed parents to learn what they wanted in a school. I thought little about it and then about a year later, a citywide posting went up for a focus school principal to lead and drive the development of this school. It would be a new school model focused on leadership, technology, and communication, and would be a partnership with three different school districts.

Through her non-profit connections, Ingra had become a community representative in the school district's Special Education Advisory Council (SEAC). They specialized in assisting children with special needs. One day, she came home and told me, "They are incorporating your leadership idea into the theme." I wasn't sure if it was solely my idea or if others had also mentioned it. Her point was maybe I should consider throwing my name in the hat, since I had many ideas for this new concept school, and a passion for leadership. I am also a risk-taker and was open to improving the design of schools.

I remember printing out the actual posting for the focus school principal, bringing it home, and showing it to Ingra. Her response was "Leadership was your idea and—with all the things you've shared with me around it--aren't you going to apply?" She encouraged me and reminded me of all the ideas I had been tossing around and said simply, "This is a sign. You should apply!"

This collaboration for the first focus school in Nebraska involved our superintendent and two other local superintendents as three districts were in the mix of this intriguing concept. Their idea was to make focus schools a collaboration between districts. This is an improvement over the original idea of the learning community, which was to give students an option in all 11 districts, where each district would have their own focus school.

All 11 districts would still be welcome at the collaborative focus school. At this time, the Learning Community concept was in the process of development at our state capital. Our three superintendents wanted to beat the legislature to the punch, and create a working concept of collaboration. We wanted to change the legislation to make focus schools collaborative in design. This would be a model for future schools and districts.

There was a team made up of administrators from the three different districts, and they got direct input and feedback from families. They accomplished this through a survey. The survey asked parents what key concepts they would like to see in a school. Two of the big themes were technology and communication. Leadership also joined the mix.

I was reluctant to apply since it was a time when the Educare was back on point for construction at my current school campus and would start soon. It would provide early childhood education to the neighborhood and community. I had now been with the district for 20 years and had been the principal here for nine years, and one additional year as assistant principal. I had relationships built, and strong community support. The staff was behind me and held the same philosophy. We were productive and had turned the school around. We were a strong cohesive staff.

The vision we held was taking hold. We were collaborative, and it was running smoothly--like a machine. Sure, we had normal problems here and there. Organizations are always a work in progress, but the major stress of the building was not there. The reality was, I still had an itch for new challenges, and, after serious thought, I applied. My inner achiever had kicked in again! The concept intrigued me, so I thought, "Why not go for it?" I applied and waited.

Someone called me and invited me to the first round of interviews. Soon after, I found out I had an interview in the evening with a representative from each of the three districts. It went well, but it was hard to see where you stood--a typical challenge during an interview process. After the initial waiting period, I received a call that I was in the final interview selection process. It would be at one of the other district's community centers during the evening. I prepped for the interview as much as you can and thought about my philosophy of creating an innovative model for a school, promoting diversity. When the day finally arrived, I was relieved just to get it over and done with.

Any potential life changes can take their toll on you, and this was no different. The interview itself was interesting. It was with the three different districts' HR directors, and there was also a room full of community representatives. I sat facing the panel of three directors, and the other community stakeholders were on the side of me at tables. It was like having a classroom watch while you answer questions from the panel. The HR directors took turns asking questions, while the community reps took notes and wrote feedback about me. The information and insights were important, and the search committee would review them later.

It was an intensive process. Being satisfied with my current position as principal and our progress, the interview was more comfortable. I was fine either way. This was not a do or die for me at this point in my career. This is an excellent position to be in throughout an interview process. I knew I could continue to make a positive impact where I was, but I was also excited about the possibility of starting this unique school from the ground up. It would be a once in a lifetime opportunity if they selected me as the leader.

The process was normal, and of course, I had to wait. What is it with these waiting periods? Then finally, I received a call from my district superintendent that I would be the first principal of this new focus concept school. Somehow my name got out before it was official, and the newspaper printed some speculation about me. Then, at a district meeting, an upper official announced that the paper could be wrong, and the person was not official yet. It kind of made it anti-climactic and put me in an odd position. I do not understand why they did not handle this situation better. The three districts were all vying for a principal from their district to be selected as the "chosen one". Luckily, I apparently fit the bill and they chose me!

I was excited to be offered the position. Public Information Director Luanne Nelson—who was very supportive of principals--informed me I was one of 36 applicants in the metro area. It was an honor to be selected. I would have to work to prove myself again. Once they officially announced me as the new focus school principal, things took off. I had board members saying, "Make us look good" and "Make sure you represent us well!" No pressure, of course, but I quickly learned I was right in the middle of citywide school politics!

Before finding the principal, there were committees made up of people from each district. They were formed for different areas such as curriculum, transportation, and technology. They were ready for the selected principal to collaborate with them in making school decisions.

I learned a lot navigating the various committees and collaborating to continue moving forward. I had three school superintendents and three school boards. There were various groups involved. This included the Learning Community Council, the Superintendents Advisory Council, and the Nebraska State Board of Education, among others.

A year later, the legislature formally created the Learning Community. They set the Learning Community up representing 11 districts of Douglas and Sarpy Counties. The goal was to provide dollars and a tax levy to support the needs of high poverty students. The legislation talked about creating focus schools in every district. Each district could run these schools and attract students from all 11 districts-- almost like an open magnet school.

The option enrollment that was in place had been dropped and now there was the Learning Community Application. This enrollment application was due every March. It would allow students to apply for any school within the e11 districts. The goal was to allow for demographic changes to provide more equality and better opportunities--balancing the socio-economic diversity of an area. It was an ambitious goal!

If you were a school that had a high number of free-and-reduced-lunch students, you would try to add more students who were not. The opposite was true if the school needed more of a free-and-reduced-lunch population. The idea was to get to this ideal 35 to 40 percent free and reduced population. This would offset schools that were highly slanted, balance the community and create equity. It would also open up more opportunities for all students.

At one of my earliest meetings, I met with Senator Raikes and several superintendents. We were all at another district's central office discussing this new focus concept. They started saying things like "If we don't get enrollment" and "If this doesn't happen," and kept going on as if it may not work.

I remember finally raising my hand and saying, "I fully plan on making this concept work and getting enrollment. I did not leave a school where I was happy to fail in this venture. We will get the enrollment." The looks I received were mixed--some filled with doubt about whether this concept would work. I realized what I had walked into. The stakes were not as high for them. They could always say we tried a collaborative concept, and it didn't work. In contrast, I did not consider this something from which one could simply walk away.

I remember starting this school and for years it always felt as if I were out on a limb, and it could break at any time. There was never a year that people in the legislature didn't work to shut down or change the Learning Community. This is still going on at the time of this writing.

Let's discuss the focus school and effective leadership, rather than the politics of the Learning Community and tax levies. These are often the things that work against us, making it hard to concentrate on the students and what we need to succeed. Our focus must be on the students and fighting for what is needed to advance success for all. A big part of this was proving the focus school is a valid, effective concept. There had to be positive results!

We created Underwood Hills Focus School as an example for the Professional Learning Community legislation in Nebraska, with the help of three school districts. The three districts were the Elkhorn Public School District, the Omaha Public School District and Westside Community Schools. Underwood Hills Focus School opened for the 2008-2009 school year and was open to all 11 districts within the Learning Community, with students chosen through a lottery system.

In some ways, the school was like a magnet school with no boundaries. We started the school by making an agreement between the three districts to share staff, budget, and resources. We wrote extra value standards to emphasize the theme of leadership, technology, and communication. The diverse population, with extended day learning activities (enrichment), added to the unique school. This, with the extended calendar, are a few features that set the focus school apart from traditional schools. After three years, and despite the law allowing partnerships with other districts, the school moved to Wilson and is now run solely by Omaha Public Schools. It continued with the same qualities that made it unique and successful. Willie and Yolanda Barney and other parents presented to Nebraska's Unicameral to change the original focus legislation. They stepped forward when the districts were looking to close the school after three successful years. The problem was the legislation was not changing, despite student academic and social success in the collaborative experiment.

Mr. Barney and others attended board meetings and presented on the achievements of the school. When he started the "Keep the Focus" movement that took two coach buses of parents and students to the legislature to testify about the success of the school, I thought, "How many schools have this kind of support?" It was an accurate indicator of the success of the concept. This push changed the legislation and made it possible to continue the focus school concept.

The school promotes a wide mix of students and is still open to all 11 districts, supporting socio-economic diversity. The school was officially the first focus school of the Learning Community in Nebraska. At this writing, it is still the only one. One other district I am aware of tried to get a focus concept approved, and they denied it. The focus school became a successful model of one.

None of these innovations would have happened without the support and commitment of The Sherwood Foundation. Also, the powerful family and community support contributed to its success. I had spent time--when the school first began--sending letters to senators and legislators, hoping to change the legislation to make focus schools a collaboration. Many families and staff members also wrote letters and worked hard to change the legislation in our favor.

I eventually got the state education chair and his wife to stop at the school while on their way to an event in Omaha. It gave me the opportunity to show the things we had been doing and talk about the success of this unique program. All these efforts no doubt made a difference when families held meetings and went to hearings at our capital in Lincoln, NE.

The staff was originally comprised of people from all three districts, with parents coming together from the surrounding areas. The thriving school community cultivated community partnerships. This was a unique collaboration. The focus school was like a large family. It was truly the Learning Community concept of everyone assisting with learning.

Throughout the next eight years, we continued to add sections and classrooms. We started as a third through fifth grade building. We added more capacity until we had three classes of grades third through sixth with 240 students. About 63 percent of them had free-and-reduced lunch. As I was preparing to leave the focus school in 2018-2019, after 11 years, the population had moved to 62 percent free-and-reduced lunch.

It always bothered me that the Learning Community had set a target of 35-40 percent free-and-reduced lunch. It went up every year for most districts throughout the state, and the mix we were serving had significantly higher needs. I knew we could still get measurable results--even with higher percentages of free-and-reduced lunch--and we did. Our district had an average of 78 percent free-and-reduced lunch, having the majority of students coming from our district pushed us up some. I knew the concepts and strategies we were using would work with a higher poverty population. Most of the things we did that made the focus school strong will work for others and are effective practices that could be applied to any school or population.

Our initial goal was to start with two sections each of third through fifth grade. Each classroom would have 20 students and we had 120 students to start the concept. This was not very many, but it would allow us time to hone the ideas. The school was open to all 11 districts of the Learning Community, and we had 800 the first year for our 120 spots. Remember, the original committee was worried about getting enrollment! The families were hungry for something different, and we showed promise.

In 2008-2009, we were 39.5 percent free-and-reduced lunch, and in 2009-2010, we were 38 percent free-and-reduced lunch. We added two sections of sixth grade and included 40 new third graders into the program. The following school year, we maintained students from various districts and started in 2010 with 41 percent free-and-reduced lunch—which later became 44 percent (due to adding new students). In the fall of 2011, we were at 48 percent free-and-reduced lunch and had students from four districts. By 2013, we added another fourth grade, making it three sections of third and fourth and two of fifth and sixth. This put our enrollment at 200 students, with the population coming from seven different districts. We were then at 54 percent free-and-reduced lunch--still mirroring what was happening in the Learning Community. Our attendance rate was 96.8 percent and mobility was low, at 3.3 percent.

For the 2014-2015 school year, we added another fifth grade, making three sections. We had 220 students with seven districts represented. This was a diverse socio-economic mix of 54 percent free-and-reduced lunch, 8.5 percent mobility, and an attendance rate of 95.7 percent. Fourteen buses brought our population from all over the Learning Community. Even with students from many districts, families and parents still strongly supported the school and its programs.

In the 2015-2016 school year, the school added the final sixth grade, making three of each section, third through sixth. The population was at the goal of 240. In 2016-2017, we were maintaining the 240 population and started climbing more in free-and-reduced lunch, and still maintained a diverse mix. In 2017-2018, we were at 65 percent free-and-reduced lunch. In 2018-2019, it dropped slightly to 62 percent. Our original goal was to mirror what the Learning Community goal was but, as it happened, we moved beyond it. We kept the concept and were intentionally providing a diverse mix of students from around the 11 metro area districts.

Our mobility rate was 6.5 percent compared to the district rate of 13.4 percent. Our attendance rate was 95.1 percent, and we attribute solid positive attendance rates to our innovative program and enrichment offerings. The students wanted to attend and enjoyed the programming and curriculum offered. Attendance in the district was 94 percent. In 2017, the district introduced a program called *Strive for 95*, designed to promote individual student attendance.

When we dig deeper and look at some of the subgroups, we find our Special Education population at 9.2 percent in 2017-2018 had dropped to 7.9 percent in 2018-2019. It varied by year but was always lower compared to the district average of 17.4 percent. Our English Language Learner (ELL) population was growing at 17.9 percent, with 5.2 percent of that being brand new to the English language (non-exited ELL). This was interesting compared to the district average of 9.4 percent with 26.8 percent of that being non-exited ELL. Our Refugee population was at 1.3 percent in 2017-2018 compared to the district's 4.2 percent. We strived to maintain a diverse mix, with a range of abilities and talents, from different socio-economic backgrounds and cultures.

An interesting note was that the population continued to change, and even the free-and-reduced lunch percentage was creeping up closer to the district average of about 78 percent. The 240-enrollment goal continued through 2017-2018, and in 2018-2019 (the year I retired), the demographics were: 240 students, 34.7 percent White, 32.2 percent Hispanic and 23 percent African American. We maintained an extensive waiting list and, when I left in 2019, we already had a full school for the 2019-2020 school year. They rated the school ninth among 62 elementary schools in our district. This showed a significantly higher success level than other schools in a similar 65 percent free-and-reduced lunch range. The school was beating the odds and showing gains beyond expectations!

There are many things that made this school unique and set us apart from a traditional elementary school. The school was like a magnet school but had some extras. Our school had a 190-day calendar, but the way we structured our day allowed us to gain the equivalent of 41 extra days. This was an increase in instructional time compared to the regular district. Thirteen buses with students arrived at 7:20 AM for breakfast. The Grab and Go breakfast began at 7:30 AM and school started at 8:00 AM. Most elementary schools started in the 9:00 am range with breakfast at 8:30 AM. We gained some time by starting earlier.

Ms. Carole, my administrative assistant, did an amazing job working with tours and balancing our enrollment. Our student ambassadors kept the tours rolling while explaining about our school. They were proud, and it showed. The unique challenge was promoting the school and keeping enrollment up from the 11 districts. We did this through making our program attractive and successful. Another challenge was that not all districts saw the value of promoting socio-economic diversity and recognizing the goals of the Learning Community.

We decided, to compete with surrounding districts, we selected the route of being AdvancED accredited. We received national accreditation from AdvancEd in 2009 and met *high functioning* in all seven areas of school improvement during the first visit. This was not a minor feat! To the credit of the staff and our leadership team, we had effectively created a model of success.

In 2014-2015, the accreditation team visited us and gave us an extremely high rating. The focus school continued to be a place of innovation and collaboration with staff, successfully integrating technology into the fabric of the school. We included project-based learning using capstone activities for all grades, to engage students in real-world experiences.

From 2012 to 2015, we worked toward becoming recognized as an Apple Distinguished Program, and in 2015; we were acknowledged as an Apple Distinguished School. The school maintained the Apple excellence for seven years, demonstrating innovation in education. Wilson Focus was again recognized as an Apple Distinguished School from 2017 through 2019. This is something we wanted to maintain as I was transitioning out (2019), and we wanted it to continue to move forward into the future. It was another type of accreditation. To maintain this status, we had to meet requirements. To succeed, we had to make an Apple book, lead effectively, grow professionally, innovate with technology, and show success.

Our school offered an enrichment program that enhanced the curriculum with a Science, Technology, Engineering, Arts and Math (STEAM) focus. The school had a goal of being a model of innovation, showing success while demonstrating positive trend data in all subgroups. The student engagement was high, and we built in supports to help our students be successful.

There were many key stakeholders as our school developed into a professional learning community. All staff collaborated and looked for the best ways to move students forward. Shared leadership was a common theme, and I empowered staff to make a difference. As a school, we pushed to stay a model--moving beyond the district with technology. My philosophy encouraged experimentation and collaboration among staff.

The staff excelled and so did the students. The data results and engagement were our guides. Many staff members were in leadership roles, especially within technology. We used Gallup's StrengthFinder to identify our strengths and talents in an effort to work in a productive strength zone. Many of the teachers had advanced degrees. Several won the Alice Buffet Outstanding Teacher Award--named after the 35-year teaching veteran and aunt of World-Famous Investor Warren Buffet--recognizing exceptional educators. We encouraged teachers to present at staff and team meetings and share best practices and other strategies that were working. We selected all staff for their ability to be innovative and engaging with their students. Everyone's ideas mattered. Staff members wrote the goals, mission, and vision as the drivers of the school's unique program.

As the principal, I set the tone and promoted a positive culture of success. Our meetings were productive, and the students were at our core. We all worked to achieve our learning targets and still had fun. The students enjoyed coming to school, and we worked at building strong relationships.

The principal and assistant principal coached teachers in classrooms to make instruction better. We had received professional training from Kathy Kennedy and Jim Knight, who are instructional coaching experts, which helped us hone our methods. We provided digital feedback data to teachers with a dashboard, assisting further in the collaboration and needs assessment process. I always did "Look Fors" and classroom visits. Dr. Kehrberg, an assistant superintendent, also helped us advance in classroom coaching.

I was also serving as a district coach under our curriculum department, and we continued to implement additional things I learned in this type of coaching at the focus school. We applied Jim Knight's coaching and training methods and observed progress in our instructional coaching and academic achievements.

I loved getting into classrooms, talking to students and staff, and finding out about the learning in progress. The students seemed to love me being present in learning. It was very collaborative, and we adjusted as needed around student success. We started the school from scratch to become a model of innovation and creativity, which it had become.

The school was always reviewing data, noting progress, and adjusting to engage student interests. It incorporated technology into *real world* learning. We were a STEAM school, and, for enrichment, we developed classes and concepts around this broad career base. Coaching, collaboration, and mentoring were a large part of this school.

I was excited to serve as a mentor as we developed our own leaders within staff. I continued to mentor around the district as well, and still believe leaders should create leaders. Several staff members have since been promoted to leadership positions.

Four staff members completed a Master's in Math program and three others were seeking administrative positions. Our school became a positive training ground with a record of success. People wanted to be a part of this successful school. This is ideal for a leader. If you are getting requests from people to join your team, you are doing something right.

The students were stakeholders as well. One of the main areas of our theme was leadership, and developing student leaders was a priority. Our students received many opportunities to gain experience in building leadership skills. They took part in our Focus Council (Student Council). They could become a Focus Ambassador (these students gave any visitors and prospective families a tour). The students managed their own library check-outs and returns through a scanning system. The lunch serving line and cleaning were both assisted by the students. Students could be a part of the Flag Corps, which raises and lowers the flag daily, as well as presents the flag in full dress at assemblies. A paraprofessional had started the program, and all we had to do was supply the resources for her to take off with it.

All students took part in the live morning news, ran cameras with a MacBook Pro, and delivered the program through Wirecast Professional Streaming Studio. They created music beds in Garage Band and used Keynote slides to highlight special activities and promote our positive character. We also did service-learning projects. We had former students of our program who had continued in the Focus Pathway at Burke High School come to help us work on our landscaping. Bryan High School had students in an agriculture program who worked with our students in planting raised garden beds. South High School students came to tutor third graders, and also assisted with our fifth grade Kindness Retreat as counselor helpers.

There was a Civil Air Patrol, run by the same para as the Flag Corps. We even had students form a Bully Squad (on their own) to reinforce our anti-bully stance. They did reminders that connected to our "No Place for Hate" initiative through our partnership with the Anti-Defamation League. Our goal was to give students opportunities and a voice.

Our school was involved with our community stakeholders, and we had many connections with the surrounding businesses. Our Halloween Harvest Parade went around to nearby businesses, and they were incredibly supportive. We worked with Arrow Stage Lines (a charter bus company) who provided a discounted coach bus for a fourth-grade history trip to our state capital (the kids loved this trip). Coca Cola, another nearby business, provided treats before the winter break.

A local radio station (98.5 FM) also recognized the school in its *98 Days of Love Campaign* for making a difference in the community. I enjoyed spending some time on the morning show, talking about what sets us apart from other schools.

One of our most active partners was our own Parent Pride (focus school parents). Members represented families from all over the city and multiple districts. They were very supportive, planned many activities with us, and donated throughout the year. We partnered with many agencies outside of the school to build a powerful community.

Another partner was the First National Bank of Omaha. Our students underwent interviews and training to work as tellers for an in-school bank counter our carpenters had built. Students could deposit money into actual accounts linked to the bank. Financial literacy was a subject they learned in this process. They could take their savings out after completing sixth grade or continue their account at one of the bank's branches, which many did.

We included all these groups in a list on our website dubbed Wilson Partners. Many of our partners also collaborated with us on enrichment classes and activities.

In the early years, as the school was forming, I spent a great deal of time speaking to clubs and groups around town about the focus program. I helped them understand the concept of an innovative school. I was creating an awareness about this unique model and building interest and support.

I was involved with many boards and groups while leading this school. The Empowerment Network Board and the Cradle-to-Career Advisory worked together to uplift North Omaha schools. African American Achievement Collaboration, Omaha School Administrators Association (OSAA) Board, and the Omaha STEM Ecosystem Group (creating a STEM network for all districts).

I was also on the District Coaching Team for six years (assisting in ongoing training of over 400 administrators in effective coaching). I joined district committees and assisted with a pipeline for leadership. As principal, I continued to mentor other administrators while also promoting the success of Wilson Focus School. Many of these presentations were for colleges and university programs and, for years, I was a resource mentor for the University of Nebraska at Omaha. This was important early on, as we were developing, and helped get the word out about our school. It also kept me in the educational arena. As a principal, you are the chief promoter of your building.

Our goal as a school was to set up sustainability. The district was continuing the Wilson Focus School as an innovative model of excellence as I retired. I established a funding formula which successors could replicate and adjust. A portion of the budget was coming from a consistent Sherwood Grant for which they could write every two years, with a stipulation of showing ongoing successful results.

There was a contract variance built into the teacher union contract that covered the extra hours our staff worked at the focus school. Now, other schools are replicating some of the success pieces. This made Wilson Focus School the place to work within the Omaha Public Schools system. Human Resources incorporated our current unique staff makeup into the allocations for our school. I also built in a succession plan for future leadership. I set the school up to continue to be an innovative school of technology and exemplary learning. The development of the leadership and continuation of the model is now in the district's hands.

Wilson Focus School concentrated on keeping learning innovative— creatively going beyond the traditional classroom. The teachers designed their rooms to be student-friendly with couches, bean bags, exercise balls, and other choice seating. There were no rows of desks, and all students were set up to facilitate teamwork. One room used almost all exercise balls, one room used a cafe style setup, and many incorporated bean bags and other alternative seating, with the students often transitioning to different places. The teachers had flexibility in creating their ideal learning environment.

We were 1:1 in technology, with each student using a MacBook Pro or an Air Book. I worked hard at keeping the technology in good working order, and in the hands of students. I became an expert at ordering new hard drives for computers, and salvaging parts off old units to keep computers working. The techs I had were supportive and assisted in the upkeep. We also planned regularly and ordered replacements every year to accommodate damaged or broken hardware.

All the rooms had LCD projectors, document cameras, and Smart Boards with a Mac Mini attached, which allowed the teacher to keep their laptop from being tied up. There were also wireless keyboards and track pads to allow teachers to move throughout the room. LCDs projected our morning news, which was streaming from the studio to the classrooms. We networked printers at each grade level, and they were set up to assist grade level team planning.

Students ran the morning news, and rotated through all the tasks involved, allowing time to be anchors as well as other positions needed to run different aspects of the cast. The large painted green screen wall enabled the students to create a variety of effects. We used computer programs as needed. We moved to an updated version of Wirecast Pro and incorporated two cameras through a MacBook Pro at one time. We then moved back to a single camera after the district changed some network systems. We updated programs and software as needed. Each day, we went live with the broadcasts, and recorded them to later post on the website.

The morning newscast was an excellent tool for me to get out daily reminders and keep the positivity and vision of the school going. It promoted consistency and common language. I was on nearly every day for 11 years. The students were on daily as well and rotated throughout the whole student body. They loved learning the news process with our library media specialist.

At Wilson Focus, we had student-focused learning, and we encouraged students to learn at whatever level they were at any given time. The school started using a Learning Management System (LMS) during my last few years and was improving the effectiveness of this tool. We used a program called Schoology for this purpose. Among the many platforms we reviewed, this one was the best fit for our needs.

We integrated technology into our learning, giving students experience in many areas. The students used StrengthsQuest from Gallup to find their top three strengths. The students applied their strengths in activities and incorporated them into capstone projects. Our pathway schools continued to use the strengths through their focus programs. This enabled students to progress even further with this self-reflection tool. Identifying their strengths helped the school personalize their learning experience. We encouraged students to use whatever program they needed to complete their capstone project and demonstrate knowledge.

In terms of instructional design, the school ran on a year-round calendar that started in July and ended toward the end of June. For example, one year we began on July 21st, with teachers having in-service and workdays until July 26th, and school started with students on July 27th. That year, the last day of school for students was June 22nd, and the staff had in-service and workdays from June 25th to June 28th. It varied slightly from year to year, depending on where dates would land during the work week.

The rest of the calendar year had some mini breaks and included staff time. It ended up being 190 student days, but we gained more time by starting the traditional elementary day earlier. We got an extra hour by starting our days with buses arriving at 7:20 AM and starting school at 8:00 AM. On Mondays and Fridays, we got out at 3:30 PM, which allowed approximately two Mondays a month to be used for staff training. Tuesdays, Wednesdays, and Thursdays would be used for enrichment classes.

An enrichment class would start with a snack at 3:15 PM and a short recess until 3:40 PM. Classes ran until 4:30 PM. The students signed up for classes electronically. Alex Gates--a programmer who had students at our building--created the digital sign-up system. Each enrichment session ran about 8-10 weeks, with students in a different class on Tuesdays, Wednesdays, and Thursdays. Originally, we started with enrichment four days a week and gradually dropped Monday, so we could use it for staff meetings and training. Then we dropped Friday as well due to longer workday exhaustion.

This calendar built in 41 days over the regular district schedule. We ended up having 1,505.25 hours and were well over the state required 1,032. hours. This showed in our student progress. Time matters! Getting the most out of our time was a priority.

Enrichment classes were a prime interest, and one goal was to help students make connections to school as they learn new skills. Being a STEAM school, we created many enrichment courses around this theme. Teachers could choose to teach courses which strengthened these areas. We also brought in professionals to teach classes that families would normally pay for outside of school. We used extra pay as an incentive for staff members to work beyond their regular duty hours. They had the option to be creative with courses and teach something that was a hobby or strength area.

We built this extra pay into our grant, and figured out the amount needed each year to sustain a solid enrichment program. We also used this enrichment time to strategically steer some students toward tutoring support in math, reading, and science. At one point, we had a writing course when there was still a state writing test as part of our standardized testing.

Other examples of enrichment classes offered included Coding, Minecraft, Chess Club, Tech Monsters, Raspberry Pi, Garden Club, Magic Man Math, Magic School Bus Reading, ROAR (Read Often and Relax), Vex Robotics, Dance, Cheerleading, Soccer, Playground Pals, Kicking Tigers Tae Kwon Do, Yoga, Walking Club, Photography, Empowerment, Etiquette, and Sketch Up. The school continuously added fresh courses and changed them every session and year. These enrichment classes for extended learning were a major strength of the focus school.

An instructional facilitator ran the enrichment, which was a part of the focus program. As we were developing partners, we all ended up teaching these enrichment classes at one point or another. At the first focus school, I ended up teaching a drawing course and a leadership class about public speaking. I didn't really have the time to do it, but we needed teachers, and it ended up being fun, while keeping me connected. It took a while to grow our partners and develop classes.

I also noticed that paying the instructional facilitator extra hours was expensive for us as a school. They were part of the leadership team and easily worked over 40 hours a week. We paid anything over the regular hours through extra pay. I decided a great way to cut costs and have more of a stable budget was to make the position an assistant principal instead of an instructional facilitator. It could then be a steppingstone for a potential administrator and could help train future leaders. It, of course, made a more stable salary and actually saved the district money. I presented this idea to our superintendent at the time, and he agreed it was a good idea. At Wilson Focus, we could make this a reality for most of my time there.

My first facilitator was from another district, Deb Gernandt, and she was with me a year, then became a principal and facilitator in her home district. My second facilitator was Jean LaGrone, from a different district as well. She had a diverse curriculum background and excellent experience and knowledge. Curriculum design was one of her strengths. She retired from the focus school as we were moving the building and changing names.

Christine Moats was my instructional facilitator at the Wilson Focus Site before becoming assistant principal. She fit the bill well since the unique programming of our school kept both of us constantly busy. She was skilled at finding partners and organizing activities, while also being an assistant principal.

Our enrichment classes were an intensive extended program structure. We intentionally did not call it after school programming and worked to keep the feeling that it is just a longer school day. It makes a difference in how the students view the program. If they see it as after school, students think it is not as important and treat it as separate.

The day I knew it was really working was when we took a group of our students to a special dinner at the Metro Culinary Arts Center, through Susan Adams' Empower Class. This dinner was with different schools present, and what the students said made me proud. I heard other students ask our students what time they got out. They quickly said 3:30 PM on Mondays and Fridays, and 4:30 PM on Tuesdays, Wednesdays, and Thursdays. That was it! They said our regular school day ended with enrichment at 4:30 PM and they did not call it after school anything. This was a change in our student mindset. Enrichment was a priority! I carefully managed the budget and wrote for a grant to The Sherwood Foundation to cover all the expenses for a successful enrichment program.

Our staff actively used technology to enhance instruction and project-based learning. High engagement was a priority, as were our student-friendly learning targets. Teachers used a gradual release of instruction framework for modeled, shared, guided, and independent learning

(Schmoker, 2006). Our teaching approach included checking understanding, giving feedback, and adjusting the lesson as needed. The instruction was solid. The students engaged in interactive learning experiences which encouraged problem-solving and creative thinking.

The environment was highly collaborative. There were weekly professional learning team meetings and larger staff meetings. We shared and looked at practices that were working. We used Positive Behavioral Interventions and Supports with a focus on relationships. I did the weekly "Look Fors" identifying and encouraging the positives taking place in the building.

The staff used various digital resources such as Garage Band, iPhoto, iMovie, Keynote, Pages, PowerPoint, Excel, Word, Office 365, Sway, Class Flow, Go Noodle, BrainPOP, Anamationish, Bloxels, and Code.org. We also had Lion Links that were approved learning sites on our website. We continued to use programs and websites to enhance our instructional practices.

Our school was a Blended Ed pilot with the state, and we had classroom observations to view our use of technology. Barb Jizba, our original library and media specialist, designed a flexible schedule for collaborating with classrooms, and integrating lessons into project-based learning. She was excellent at sharing technology at in-services and supporting our diverse curriculum needs. She also ran our morning news and assisted me with the delivery and coordination of student teams. The teachers could coordinate more time as needed within the flexible library and media schedule.

All students created presentations using the resources needed to complete them. They concentrated on public speaking. There was a teacher-designed rubric around Leadership, Technology, and

Communication. These were our extra value standards and largely based on our capstone projects. The students took ownership of their learning and could share this through their capstone projects.

We used HeartMath with the emWave as a tool to teach proper breathing, to help students learn to control anger, test anxiety, and their stress (bio feedback). It was a part of our wellness. We accomplished this through the program, with finger or ear sensors attached to the MacBook. We looked for ways to enhance our curriculum. I also incorporated this into interventions for students within our PBIS efforts.

Our needs inspired staff to vary the curriculum. The staff members helped select the actual curriculum we used, as well as created various rubrics around the theme. We used true standards-based grading. The teachers collected evidence using different methods to assess understanding and meet standards. We were looking for evidence of successful learning. The district was using a variation of standards-based grading that was more of a regular grading system.

There were capstone projects at each grade level. The students worked all year on different programs and skills, which were then compiled into their grade-level capstone projects. These skills culminated in the demonstration of their learning through capstone presentations. Each third-grade student created a brochure or Keynote presentation, comparing their strengths with a leader they had chosen from history. Each fourth-grade student did a book presentation with a comparison and contrast of their strengths with characters in their book. Each fifth-grade student did a wax museum character, essentially becoming the leader they were studying. The iMovie character in the Keynote presentation asked themselves questions and discussed strengths. Each sixth-grader student completed a capstone science project around a hypothesis. There was a science fair for the entire school to attend. Every student completed a project-based learning capstone to demonstrate their knowledge.

We worked at maintaining our individuality as a progressive, innovative school and, as a building, we pushed technology. Besides Schoology, we were using Lib Guides, and students could log into the system. I could also send out positive messages and reminders through this platform. The students could open assignments, send emails, and post comments. We were a model for the district and continued to try different resources.

The Lion Pledge started our day right. It helped our students develop pride and ownership of the school. We used Jon Gordon's *Energy Bus for Kids* (2012) school-wide to reinforce our behavior supports. We worked hard at creating a supportive place with a common language around positivity.

We connected our professional development and instructional design to our building mission and vision. Our goals encompassed reading, math, science, behavior, leadership, technology, communication, and community involvement. We had a School Improvement Plan that followed our district format, and we were an AdvancED (nationally) Accredited school.

Our library media specialist, Barb Jizba, did tech updates at staff and team meetings. Our teachers took the Apple Teacher training online through Apple. Twelve classroom teachers had completed all the training to be an Apple Teacher. Ms. Jizba devised a system where we were having the staff build areas within Lib Guides which were for professional development.

In Lib Guides, staff could earn badges from completing an area of professional development. This was a good supplement to our actual instructional work. Ms. Jizba built an area for teachers to use with students. There were constructive learning activities for students when they were done with other assignments. The areas were: science, technology, engineering, arts, math, leadership, communication, and wellness. This was an ongoing process to build and improve this resource base for students.

The assistant principal and I visited classrooms weekly to observe instruction and give feedback using a template. Our action plan guide stressed the importance of checking understanding, offering feedback, and making learning adjustments. We shared the data on a dashboard that showed everything from frequency of visits to strategies we are seeing, and areas of our gradual release teaching framework. This and our behavior dashboard ended up guiding productive discussions in our strategic planning work.

Our data drove our work and assisted our collaboration within our professional learning community. The teachers created rubrics and identified what was working, and we adjusted instruction as needed. This sometimes involved hard, honest conversations. Self-reflection was a large part of making this work successful in improving our teaching and learning.

The students were learning to take ownership of their learning targets and meet them using rubrics. Teachers could experiment and adapt the curriculum. We used district resources too, but our staff selected and implemented a sizable portion of our curriculum. We used EnVision math, which uses many technology pieces. Discussions for Learning uses artwork to teach Marzano's six-step vocabulary process. We used History Alive for social studies, which is full of resources. We also used a reading series with guided reading as a supplement which included literacy stations. We used other resources as needed after being guided by our results. Most of our training was through our staff, with the addition of some district training that matched up with our curriculum.

The teachers excelled in moving beyond regular resources and thinking forward. We treated them as professionals. They had fun at meetings, worked hard, and really focused on what is best for students. The collaboration was a part of the culture of this productive model.

The teachers used our capstone projects to help students find experiences that will help them learn and be more creative. There was immense pride in the unique qualities of our school. Our teachers and staff also looked for opportunities to continue to develop their own skills. Two were Microsoft Innovative Educators and one was going through training to become one, which was a good addition to our Apple Teacher training.

Our year always started with a review of our mission and vision. I presented engaging in-services to set our goals for the year, which included reviewing our data for past progress and building strategies for improvement in the coming year. The second day of training emphasized Positive Behavioral Interventions and Supports and building relationships with students. This kick-off was extremely important to the tone of the year!

We concentrated on getting our students to make connections to school, and what we could do to increase engagement and interest. One of our goals was getting students ready for careers, and to get them to think of things they could do in the future. The rest of the year, we planned professional development around what skills we needed to improve as a staff, and what we needed for our students. It was an ongoing needs assessment.

It was always important the environment enhanced the learning needing to take place and the type of culture we wanted. After the other two districts pulled out, we moved the school from Underwood to Wilson and made several renovations. By my last year, our carpenters upgraded the front office by retrofitting a large L-shaped desk from the library, which opened flexible space there.

Our school worked hard to develop school pride and promote a positive environment. The atmosphere was warm and inviting. When people entered Wilson Focus, Ms. Carole greeted them warmly and expressed her excitement about the latest school happenings. The Emerson quote on the front office wall illuminated what we were about. The mascot of Wilson Focus was a lion, and we had placed statues of lions throughout the building. There were mission and vision statements framed with the staff-created beliefs. Character banners promoted social skills. There were mementos with celebrations of achievement, success, and learning. The school made academics a priority by displaying learning goals and targets.

One sixth grade classroom was set up in a cafe style, with all kinds of student workspaces. This teacher had read some research on the environment while taking classes and wanted to try a more relaxed environment. It worked well after she set guidelines for seat selection and procedures. Many classrooms had lamps, couches, soft chairs, exercise balls, and beanbags. Instead of the usual rows of desks, we wanted collaborative and creative workspaces, so we designed rooms with team tables--rectangular or round. We set our board room up so that a whole classroom could fit around the table, but we could move the tables for working on projects or presenting capstones. On any day, you would see our students working in a variety of ways.

There was no computer lab to confine our technology instruction to a certain time of the day. We were at a ratio of 1:1 student-to-computer and could teach technology anywhere in the building. We also added two large picnic tables to the side of the playground to accommodate two full classes. These became outdoor learning spaces, as well as a delightful spot of shade, under the trees on the property. Classes could also use four large benches out front if they wanted to work outdoors.

We upgraded the playground with rubber surface around the equipment, and we had a field for soccer and other games. There were also 13 large eight-by-ten-foot raised garden beds we had built. Each classroom plants and takes care of their box as part of our green initiative learning in outdoor classrooms. As described earlier in the book, our high school partners assisted our students in caring for the garden and landscaping. There was a compost station and the ability to turn one large box into a greenhouse.

We added more plantings to our grounds, and it was important to the feel of the building to keep them aesthetically pleasing. I added attractive banners to the four poles in the parking lot--each with our lion logo and "Welcome" in large letters. The exterior painting promoted our high-tech stance, and better displayed the building (originally it was only white). We had it painted taupe with a wide brown horizontal band at the top, resting on a thinner navy stripe (thanks to Ingra for the design work).

The schedule aimed to be flexible and help us maximize our day. From the earlier start to the day, coupled with the grab-and-go breakfast in the classrooms, we were getting extra instructional time in. We scheduled team meetings and collaboration during specials (Art, Music, Physical Education, etc.). Classrooms could integrate the curriculum during library and media flex time.

Upgrades to the building infrastructure and the addition of more wireless access points improved our system's performance. This was even more of an improvement over our old Cisco system, which was one gigabyte and high speed. In 2014, we had to upgrade many of our computers with Mac Book Pros, after we had used the white MacBook's for five years. These things seemed indestructible! Then we continued to add 60 Air Books each year. I would squeeze about five more at the start of the year, and five more at the end, depending on the budget. It was a challenge to keep the technology up, but if you ordered replacements every year, it could be done.

As a leader, it is important to plan, constantly look ahead, and establish the future you want for your building. We also became adept at using old machines for parts, buying, and adding more memory, and replacing hard drives. It helped to have good techs, and I had enough tech knowledge to order or scrounge for what we needed. Resourcefulness pays for itself!

The gym had a wireless sound system used for assemblies, plays, presentations, etc. We upgraded it from the existing system which did not work well, and, as a result, we enhanced the sound system in the gym. We also added small Bose speakers in the boardroom, library, and a media cart, which could be used for PE or other activities. We set up the boardroom with light-up microscopes, Raspberry Pi's, old keyboards, and monitors for enrichment classes.

Students ran the news studio, and—as mentioned earlier—we upgraded it at one point, so we could run up to two cameras. When the district upgraded their systems, we had to really work to keep our system running within the current parameters. We turned the entire room into a green screen with painted walls. Ms. Jizba found a special paint that matched the color for a typical green screen. A new MacBook Pro ran the Wirecast program for streaming into classrooms each morning. To meet our requirements, we expanded hardware and memory. We had a building tech two days a week who helped re-image computers and run updates, while keeping our tech functioning. We were constantly looking for ways to improve our system.

I have long been a believer in the importance of social media and using positive posts to promote our school. Our teachers were often posting what was happening in our classrooms. It was a good way to promote our building, and now, social media is a staple for all organizations.

By prioritizing leadership, technology and communication, our school achieved continuous academic growth. The increased opportunities, integration of technology, and project-based learning made a significant impact. Our school made progress in challenging subgroups--even though 65 percent of our population fell into the free-and-reduced lunch category. This is exactly what others looked to do.

In the Nebraska State Accountability (NeSA) Test, our reading moved from 71 percent meets/exceeds (2011-2012) to 80 percent meets or exceeds (2015-2016). Our Math went from 65 percent meets or exceeds (2011-2012) to 76 percent meets or exceeds (2015-2016). Our science moved from 50 percent meets or exceeds (2011-2012) to 79 percent meets or exceeds (2015-2016). Writing started high at 86 percent (2011-2012) and then had a slight drop to 77 percent meets or exceeds (2015-2016). This was most likely due to a change in the writing review process.

After 2016, writing was no longer in the state required assessments, but they added a writing component to the NeSA Reading. The state called this new component a Text Dependent Analysis (TDA). We received a School Excellence Award and Silver Recognition for Excellence in Improvement for 2016-2017 from the district.

We were still getting decent scores when I retired in 2019, and most of the scores for reading and math were above the district and state. In fact, the science scores, which are measured in fifth grade, moved from 76.7 percent to 83.6 percent of students having meets or exceeds—among the highest science scores in the district! The fifth-grade team deserved big kudos, as did the prior grade levels for building the prerequisite knowledge and background. This was extremely high for the 65 percent free-and-reduced lunch population--beating the odds and raising scores in tough areas!

I was so proud of our African American population, who showed a steady increase in growth every year for five years straight. In their sixth year, they maintained--still getting 75 percent meets or exceeds. This was a group traditionally not scoring the highest in science in our district. This showed that, when given the right program, resources, and opportunities, there are no limits to what students can achieve.

Of the tools available to prepare for NeSA, we used a district predictive computer test called Acuity. Students took this two times a year, with Acuity A and C. It provided us with information to reteach concepts and better adjust learning. In 2017, we moved to the Measures of Academic Progress (MAP) test which demonstrated how much the students knew in each area. Students were taking the MAP three times a year, on their Air Books and MacBook Pros. These formative tests provided us with solid growth data for each student in the areas of math, reading and science, and helped us improve instruction.

The state then moved to a new test called the Nebraska Student-Centered Assessment System (NSCAS) as the formal state evaluation. It now measures student performance against Nebraska content area standards, such as English Language Arts (ELA) and math for grades third through eighth and science for grades fifth and eighth. The state also used the Accountability for a Quality Education System, Today and Tomorrow (AQuESTT), which classified schools throughout the state. Evidence was evaluated in various areas, including partnerships, student success, transitions, education, readiness for college and career, assessment, and educator effectiveness.

Our school received an excellent AQuESTT rating because of our academic scores and received 89 out of 90 for evidence-based supports for students in 2015. The following year, we received a *Great* status (one below *Excellent*) after the state changed the rules for AQuESTT. Evidence had to be submitted and reviewed to substantiate your placement. We submitted over 400 pieces of evidence, but remained at *Great* without knowing what exactly they needed to upgrade our status. This assessment game changes often--shooting at a moving target without all the parameters clearly defined—it is a challenge!

In my last year, 2018-2019, I went through the review of questions and again submitted that the school met the requirements for being *Excellent* (my inner achiever would not let this go!). We were first initially given the *Great* rating. The new principal and staff received an invitation to submit additional evidence to support the *Excellent* claim or status. They could provide evidence of the status, and the focus school was able to come back again to *Excellent*.

While I was the leader, we chose to be AdvancED nationally accredited, so we could adhere to more rigorous standards and compete with any school or district--particularly those around us with this accreditation. In 2010-2011, we were highly functional in all areas: vision, leadership, teaching, using results, resources, communication, and continuous improvement.

In February 2015, we again had our AdvancED visit, and we had an excellent review. We scored above worldwide schools who were AdvancED accredited. In a scoring rubric where 400 is the best, our overall was 341.27 while the average was 274.14. Our leadership capacity was 369.70 while the average was 296.08. Our resource utilization was 328.57, while the average was 286.32. The areas that we were to adjust were building our leadership, technology, and communication rubric more to represent student goals. We did this while tracking the success rate of students within this rubric. We adjusted this during the 2016-2017 school year, and we updated the rubrics. The school was getting close to a 100 percent completion rate of capstone projects which correlated with our theme.

We also did an annual district climate survey, sent to staff, students, and parents, and we had some growth there as well. The scale goes up to five--with five being the highest--meaning strong agreement. In the student survey, School Climate went up from 3.30 in 2015-2016 to 4.05 in 2018-2019. In that same timeframe, School Safety went from 3.79 to 4.17; Equity and Respect for Diversity went from 3.73 to 4.07; and Discipline went from 3.68 to 3.94. These gains are significant since typically, the students are the hardest to please, and staff and parent scores are generally higher.

In the parent survey over that same timeframe, School Climate went from 4.68 to 4.86; School Safety went from 4.62 to 4.60; Equity and

Respect for Diversity went from 4.68 to 4.71; and Discipline went from 4.50 to 4.55.

In the staff survey over that same timeframe, School Climate went from 4.56 to 4.28; School Safety went from 4.72 to 4.41; Equity and Respect for Diversity went from 4.86 to 4.68; and Discipline went from 4.43 to 4.18. This tool was excellent for monitoring/adjusting.

The best rating was by parents on the statement: "The atmosphere of this school is positive". We went from 4.77 in 2017-2018 to 5.0 in 2018-2019. They also rated us high in communication, encouragement and how accessible the staff is. Our climate survey data showed the success of the supports set up for our families, students, and staff.

We have also been successful in continuing to move forward with innovation and creativity within technology. Our school has received an award as an Apple Distinguished Program twice, 2012-2013, 2013-2015, and became an Apple Distinguished School twice for 2015-2017 and 2017-2019. We wanted to continue to be a model school for our district and continue to be a national model. This, of course, will depend upon the staff and new leadership in the future.

We encouraged our teachers to write for grant funds. Our district has a strong education foundation. As I write this, the Omaha Public Schools Foundation (OPSF) is under the leadership of Toba Cohen Dunning, who is the executive director. She has been very supportive of our school and the program. Foundation support can be powerful. Toba and her colleagues have worked with the Sherwood Foundation and other funders to bring philanthropic support to our district.

They awarded two of our teachers an *Invest in Success* Grant while I was there. One was for alternative seating and the other was for science. The science grant enabled students to work in small groups to research dogfish sharks within the fifth grade science curriculum. *Invest In Success* is a smaller OPSF grant opportunity for which more teachers should apply, in my opinion. Urban districts have access to foundations and grant supporters, which can be great resources.

It is important to find partners interested in seeing students gain opportunities, grow, and build a future for success. These are resources which can assist any school or program. Other Omaha Public School Initiatives have incorporated characteristics from Wilson Focus School. Our success has been a jump-off point for school improvement. Before I retired, two buildings had looked at us and crafted a longer schedule, extended time, enrichment, and the use of technology.

The model has so much potential, but I am not sure if someone will ever replicate it to the extent it could. We were changing the status quo, and many people dislike change. I was on the Empowerment Network Advisory Cradle-to-Career group looking at ways to improve high-poverty schools in the North Omaha area. Our model inspired them to look at transforming eight schools into Village Focus Schools. The concepts that have made us successful could be implemented in many schools. Will they ever become a reality? It is hard to say. There are a lot of dynamics at work, including the challenge of keeping consistent leadership.

One Nation Indivisible, a group from Harvard University, visited us in 2013 and created a story entitled *Upstream People: Can Nebraska Show a Separate, Unequal Nation a Better Way?* Susan Eaton wrote it, with photographs by Gina Chirichigno. It highlighted Wilson Focus School as a successful example of a way to create diverse innovative schools. One Nation also visited the Empowerment Network to see the progress made in creating a diverse community in our city. Both

Omaha groups were pleased to be recognized as national models of success!

In 2016, Nebraska Loves Public Schools (a group that has since been rebranded as I Love Public Schools) created a documentary about the focus school entitled *Choosing Wilson: Challenging Norms to Achieve Student Success*. The organization is funded through the Sherwood Foundation. This film can be viewed at iloveps.org catalogued as *Challenging Norms to Achieve Student Success*. The stories are all about the amazing success and programming taking place in our public schools. They have wonderful promotional apparel showing the I Love Public Schools logo (with a heart in place of the word love).

STEM and technology were important to the development of the school. At one time, we had four to six VEX Robotics teams, who continually did well, with teams even going to nationals. We also hosted a VEX Robotics Tournament at our school in 2017, and it filled up with the maximum number of teams. It was an excellent event, and we heard many positive comments about how it was run. It was a good STEM experience for our staff and students.

The feedback we were receiving on the focus school continued to reinforce the success we were having as a school. I took the following comments directly from a 2016-2017 survey of parents:

"Mr. Anderson has always been enthusiastic about the accomplishments of the school and the students within it every time I see him. This is my son's first year at Wilson Focus, but my husband and I are very impressed with the environment and curriculum of the school. I see growth in my son and his abilities in areas to which we normally would not be exposed (ex. Spanish, Computer Literacy, Technology). He comes home excited about sharing ideas with me he learned that day. Mr. Anderson is leader of the school, and I must give credit to his leadership of the teachers and staff to account for this enthusiasm."

Another comment was: "The focus program is the best education in OPS a child can get. My child started the program, and the program continued until they were part of the first graduating class from focus. They awarded my child the Susie Buffett scholarship and several others. The program develops children to be greater than they could ever imagine. I believe if the focus program were in place throughout OPS, the need for magnet schools wouldn't be there. The teacher that I know is retired and is terrified of the program. Could it be they need to put effort and imagination forth instead of the same old thoughts?"

Wilson was heading in the right direction before I left. Will it be able to withstand those who want to bring it back to the status quo? Will opportunities, creativity and innovation be a factor in its success? Will teachers still maintain the ability to try new things without it counting against them? Only time will tell. These forces are powerful, and it is easier to go with the standard curriculum and be like everyone else.

As a leadership consultant, I will continue to promote the qualities that made us successful and encourage districts to move out of the shadows and into relevancy--developing more socially and academically rounded students who hold our future in their hands!

"It's never enough to just tell people about some new insight. Rather, you have to get them to experience it in a way that evokes its power and possibility. Instead of pouring knowledge into people's heads, you need to help them grind a new set of eyeglasses, so they can see the world in a new way."

— *John Seely Brown*

Chapter 20:
The Big Three - Relationships, Opportunities and Freedom

When Nebraska Loves Public Schools came to learn about our success and how we encourage innovation, the team created a film about a day in the lives of our third through sixth graders. The previous chapter described the short documentary called *Choosing Wilson: Challenging Norms to Achieve Student Success*, which the team created. Again, it can be viewed at the iloveps.org website, along with many other success stories within public schools. The organization has now transitioned into I Love Public Schools and is still promoting the positives!

While visiting our school, they asked me a simple yet complex question: "What makes Wilson Focus School successful and why are the students doing so well?" I told them it was no magic program, but a number of variables that--when working together--made a big difference. They made me narrow it down to three. I included these in this chapter since I think they are key to making a school successful.

These variables became the Big Three. The first is relationships because, without them, nothing can happen with staff, students, or families. The second is opportunities as all students need chances to grow and make their own choices for success. The third is freedom—giving teachers the ability to use their strengths and try new things without it counting against them. This freedom is also ownership of the curriculum and personal investment in what is working--true staff ownership of their class's success.

The Big Three were some of the key factors which helped in the successes of the buildings I led. They are also attributes I believe can help any school or organization. The interesting unseen factor is the element that pulls all of this together, and that is leadership. Without effective leadership, these three things will not happen. Let's take a deeper look at each one individually.

Relationships

I have discussed this topic, and it continues to be a common thread in all the research on working with adults and children. While I had an earlier chapter highlighting the importance of relationships, it is so important and falls under the Big Three, so it is well worth reiterating. It all boils down to positive relationships and the ability to work with all kinds of people. When teachers can develop positive relationships, they are already over the first hurdle. Children know if you are being sincere, and they know if you are telling the truth, or just feeding them information to manipulate.

Over my 31+ years in education, the best teachers have always been the ones who relate well with children. It doesn't matter how much they know, or whether they earned their teaching degree from an Ivy League or local university. Their ability to relate to others and develop a strong rapport is extremely important. Even if they're experts--without the ability to relate, they lose a significant part of the battle.

They will have a tough time getting students motivated and interested in learning. Building positive relationships is crucial for successful learning and achievement, regardless of individual differences.

Strong educators can attract kids into their circle of learning, develop interest, and make strong connections. One letter I received from a parent at the focus school said: "I am so grateful [name of student] is at your school, because really, every person in your building--starting with you--has always been there to help in whatever she has a need in, without even hesitating, and that's a huge part in any child's academic and personal development. It's amazing the caring staff you have assembled in this school." It was amazing for the parent to even take the time to write the letter. It was obvious she was grateful for the work being done. I had another parent say his kids actually thanked him for putting them in our school. I think every parent would love that response about their child's school!

The leader must pull people together and relate well with staff, students, and the community. Success is a result of the leader's ability to work with everyone and model this behavior for all. Respecting all people is a step in the right direction. Ingra came up with an excellent quote and said, "Leadership is about inspiring people to be the best version of themselves." I totally agree. Effective leaders allow people to be who they really are, to use their individual wiring as a strength, and to empower them to move mountains! Relationships and caring guidance can make a difference in the culture.

Opportunities

I have a firm belief in giving students as many opportunities as possible. I have been very vocal about this and have shared my view in different committees and groups. There is a widespread belief that we need to increase the number of minorities in Advanced Placement (AP) classes, especially in math and science. Educators consistently complain about the lack of diversity in important fields.

My stance is: we must stop acting as guards and give more choices to all students. What is our number one indicator of placement by the time students reach High School? It is test scores and assessments which qualify them for these classes. If children do not fit into gifted programs or perform well on tests, they miss these opportunities, beginning in elementary school. This is because we are gatekeepers and really are the ones who decide who gets to advance. If we open opportunities in their younger years, we will see more of our diverse population represented in upper-level classes. Not all students test well. One way around this is to give a variety of class offerings to all.

At the focus school, we were strength-based and provided a wide range of opportunities for students to succeed and develop. Our enrichment classes for extended learning had courses all students could take. These courses helped them increase their knowledge and achievement. A few good examples of this were the coding courses which used computers, Raspberry Pi, and games (such as Mine Craft), all the while were still teaching math. If done right, these kinds of courses can increase a student's math abilities and help them gain needed experiences. Most often, only *Gifted and Talented Education* (GATE) students get these opportunities, yet they could enhance the performance of all students. Robotics was an offering we had for all students, and, at one point, we had eight robotics teams with four to five students each.

I invited our GATE teacher to be open to working with all students, and not just those who met the score requirement. Another enrichment we had was Monster Tech, which was a wonderful course. College students--who reminded me of characters in The Big Bang television series--led it. They taught Raspberry Pi, where students made their own computer and learned to program. They also had students grow ecosystems with pond water and review the life forms under microscopes. These are experiences that help all students grow and learn, and are great examples of providing unique opportunities! This helps explain why our science scores were off the charts and better than state and district scores for all student groups.

These opportunities gave students the ability to grow and move beyond regular learning. How fast they advanced was shown in the data and opened doors for many of them to get into higher-level classes as secondary students. It is so important to not limit your students. The same goes for staff. Give them opportunities for growth. Staff had choices in curriculum, curriculum design, and all processes of the school. This created ownership, empowerment, and excitement that carried through the culture. Leadership can provide intentional opportunities that will make a difference for all.

Freedom

This concept is quite simple, yet I rarely see it played out across educational systems. As stated, giving teachers the freedom to try new things without it counting against them, and the ability to use their strengths, benefits everyone. This element is important and really does belong in the Big Three. School systems don't always treat teachers like professionals. Think of all the research out there on empowering your teams and staff. There is an abundance of information about this throughout effective leadership and team building. Training programs often use curriculum and materials to achieve educational enlightenment. Educational trends come and go, and new initiatives constantly reboot old ideas with alternative names, while the forefront keeps changing. Having too many initiatives can overwhelm your staff. Instead, focus on solid instructional practices and following the data.

Teachers are often experts in many areas, and I have found they have amazing ideas, can pull from best practice materials, and develop powerful lessons. Giving this freedom allows a creative wealth of knowledge to come forward. If you collaborate with your staff within a professional learning community, remarkable things can happen and then watch out, improvement will come!

The experts and their innovative ideas are often right in front of you, in your own building. In the buildings I've led, the district curriculum has been a guideline for me, but not the end all. I have always gone back to "Is it working?" I have continued to say that it is okay to try something different, but let's monitor it carefully and ensure it gets successful results. If we cannot show it is making an impact, then we need to move in another direction. What is the data showing and what evidence of success do we have? The trick is not trying too many new things at once, or it is hard to follow the data and see what is working.

Results do matter and, if we continue to use the same practices with no change, then we need to look at alternatives. Education is notorious for doing something a certain way because it has always been done that way. It may not even consistently provide results or improvement, but we blame it on the fact that it is our students and not us. This continues to be a pet peeve of mine.

We showed this concept of freedom in the documentary film created about our school by Nebraska Loves Public Schools. Since becoming a consultant, I've visited other buildings, and some of the restrictions leaders impose on their staff have surprised me. I have seen some pockets of success, but it doesn't always seem to be the norm.

If you want to get the best out of people, let them spread their wings. I know it sounds like a phrase you might read on a greeting card, but it is true. As a leader, you must allow this freedom to exist within your culture. One of the most successful things you can do as a leader is empower your staff! As I firmly believe, we should let them try new things without it counting against them. Ignite their passion and allow freedom. This will unlock possibilities and help develop a culture of creativity. If you do this, you will watch your scores grow, and see your students succeed in ways you never thought possible.

"The harder I work, the more luck I seem to have."

— Thomas Jefferson

Chapter 21:
Challenging Leadership

As a leader, it is important to manage what comes your way, and some situations may challenge your leadership. Everyone who was alive and old enough to remember September 11th, 2001, probably knows what they were doing exactly at the time the 9/11 tragedies began. That morning, terrorists hijacked four planes and at 8:46 AM Eastern Standard Time (EST), Flight 11 crashed into the north face of the North Tower of the World Trade Center in New York City, NY. This began the unfolding of many historical events in the United States, and the world would never be the same.

This was a Tuesday morning, and I was in my fourth year at Indian Hill Elementary School--my third year as principal. It started out as a normal day. It was 7:46 AM Central Standard Time (CST) in Omaha, where we were. Some of our students were in Kids Club, and others were lining up at the front and the back of the building--waiting to be let in for breakfast. Staff members were in their normal routines, assisting with supervision and connecting with students. My security guard stepped in and asked if I saw what had happened on the news. He had the TV on in the library and was getting the latest news cast.

I went in and watched for a minute, amazed at what was happening. At 9:03 AM EST, Flight 175 crashed into the south face of the South Tower. It was 8:03 AM our time, as we continued to line students up for breakfast. I told them we need to leave the TV off as students go to class, and that we don't need them in a panic, since they were safe at school at that point. We knew at this point that we were under some type of attack, but we didn't know the extent. I remember going into my office restroom, looking in the mirror, and reminding myself I was the leader and needed to remain calm.

I was only in there briefly when my phone rang. It was Ingra asking if I had heard the news. During her meeting with a business owner in downtown Bellevue, she witnessed airplanes taking off and landing at Offutt Air Force Base. I was hearing these planes overhead as well. My school was in South Omaha, which borders Bellevue, where Offutt, the home of the U.S. Strategic Command (Stratcom) is located. I talked with Ingra for a minute, we said we loved each other, and she said she was heading home and checking in with family.

I kept my composure, monitored the situation, and sent out an email to staff members about keeping school business going as usual. At this point, I asked them to leave their televisions off, and I would update them as I could. Then we continued to hear more details, and the fact that this was an act of terrorism. All morning, things kept unfolding. At 9:37 AM EST, Flight 77 crashed into the western side of the Pentagon. At 10:03 AM EST, Flight 93 crashed in Somerset County, PA, after the passengers had heroically overpowered the hijackers.

At 9:03 AM our time, this incident took place, leaving the news media confused. We were unsure if there would be any additional occurrences at this stage. I started getting district responses from public information, as well as updates. By early afternoon, we realized this was the extent of the attack. The damage was extensive, especially in New York. I remember preparing a letter for families and students. It explained we would do everything to help students understand and to reinforce their feelings of being safe at school.

School leadership has also been a challenge with the growing number of school shootings that have taken place over the years. Leaders have had to rework and rethink school safety. This has caused the reorganization of educational buildings. Many schools have moved office areas close to the entrance. The goal is having clear views of the surroundings and the ability to remain secure—only allowing people in through electronic means. Securing doors has become the norm. School safety has become even higher in importance, with drills and action plans to ensure student safety and building security.

The 2020 pandemic has also made leadership in schools especially challenging, as buildings try to address attendance and create new learning models. Plans had to be created for how to get students back in school safely and to protect them from COVID-19. Many districts worked out remote learning plans. This became the era of increased technological help. Most districts produced hybrid models to get students back into instruction. This has taken its toll on all staff and students. If this is not challenging to leadership, I don't know what is. Finding a model that everyone in the community agrees on has been a challenge because of differing views on the pandemic.

Another challenge at the time of this writing is finding teachers and keeping a pipeline of teachers coming into the profession. At this time, we are in a national teacher shortage of 300,000. Benefits and incentives are being looked at by districts as ways of keeping current staff and bringing in new teachers. There are pay incentives being added for student teaching and benefits to bring people into certain areas. The main area that needs to be addressed is effective leadership. We all know people leave leaders. If we increase the number of positive, collaborative leaders, there is no doubt to me how many teachers would stay in the profession. Create a positive culture that supports all. Allow everyone to be the professionals they are and create powerful learning communities. We must recognize the importance of effective leadership and cultivate it within our districts.

As a principal and friend, I had staff and community funerals to attend while supporting our school family. As a principal, you may have to be a leader at some of the saddest times for your staff. When I had my neighborhood community president, Belinda Malone, pass from a disease, it was very difficult. She was not only a member of our school community, she was also a friend. We were close and working hard to improve the community. She was an example of strength, who never complained. We had her children and worked to get them through the situation. Ingra and I created and dedicated a school garden to Belinda and added a memorial plaque in her honor.

Death is painful and especially when it affects your school community. I also had a third-grade teacher, Nancy Bossemeyer, who was having a health difficulty and some minor memory issues. She left for our school break and never came back. She had something that attacked her brain and she soon passed. These were harsh circumstances as, after the break, I was addressing the needs of her students and looking for a new teacher. She was an excellent teacher and her students loved her. We dedicated some books and added a plaque outside the library, since she had a love of reading.

As a principal, losing a student is tough. The hardest service I ever attended was that of Chang, one of our resource students. One evening during the week, a car struck and killed him as he was crossing a busy street near the school. We attended the funeral service for him with his teachers. He was a Sudanese student, and they did not prepare me for the cultural traditions that followed. It was a normal service, but especially sad with it being for a child. The hardest part was when his mother and the other females started wailing for him in the service.

There is nothing more gut wrenching than hearing a mother wail in deep grief after losing her child. This was an extremely emotional practice for letting out the pain, and one I will never forget.

Increased needs of students and families when it comes to mental health is an ever-growing area which challenges leadership. There is more need for support within schools and with families--adults and children. Mental health does not differentiate between cultures and income. It is true you may find more mental health needs in higher poverty populations, but poverty does not define parameters for mental health. Increased cases of suicide have led to heightened awareness and a greater focus on mental health. It is still somewhat of a taboo and carries a label most people do not want to get into. Help your staff to identify red flags, and they may be the connection a student or staff member needs for support at the right time. There is also now the National Suicide and Crisis Prevention Lifeline, with a direct phone number of 988.

The area of trauma informed teaching has developed as we learn that, as humans, all of us have been in varying degrees of trauma throughout our lives. Many of us fall within the defined eight areas of Adverse Childhood Experiences (ACEs) and could easily have some attributes. The importance of understanding students has grown even more. Social Emotional Learning (SEL) has become a priority. Trauma informed teaching is a new requirement of the profession. Schools are increasingly reorganizing and adjusting to meet the current needs of students and staff. Leadership continues to be challenging and will continue to be so in the future. We will need to continue to develop effective, resilient leaders who can adapt and lead through any circumstances.

"Success is not final; failure is not fatal: it is
the courage to continue that counts."

— *Winston Churchill*

Chapter 22:
Sharing Lessons Learned

There are many things I have compiled from what I have read,
experienced, and developed. Hopefully, you will find some words of
wisdom, or tips that can help you develop your leadership. The
following is a brief synopsis of most of the leadership contents of this
book, in no particular order.

In an effort to share insights from having served as a principal and
effective leader for more than 20 years, here is a list of lessons I have
learned:

Relationships are the key to everything--yes, everything.

Develop a collaborative vision and use it as a driver to motivate and
encourage.

Develop trust, mean what you say, be reliable, keep your integrity
(trust comes with time, be patient).

Leadership positions are only titles; real leadership is earned.

Leaders can take on any task and are not afraid to tackle any job to
ensure things get done!

Lead by example. Your actions must match your words.

Servant leaders are best. Provide resources and assist your staff.

Study leadership. You are never there. Keep the learning going. Read, study, and continue to grow.

Self-reflect. Be honest with yourself.

Build community, get families and businesses involved, the extra effort is worth it, stay involved!

Loyal friends are hard to find and when the chips are down, you will know who your loyal friends are.

Keeping "Is this best for children" top of mind is the goal, not just doing what is convenient for the district, teachers, etc.

Develop a professional learning community, with teams that look at what is really working and what needs improvement.

Praise, encourage, and praise more—real, authentic, genuine praise!

A positive culture matters, and your culture can make a significant difference in success!

Aesthetics matter! Keep the environment pleasing!

Use social media to promote your school. Social Media platforms are an effective way to promote and market.

Lesson Plans do not determine an excellent lesson. Observing instructional prowess and the ability to teach and inspire is a better measure.

Do a weekly *Friday Focus* or weekly recap created in your style and designed for your needs.

A weekly calendar, digital or otherwise, is a must.

Figure out ways to stay organized and develop efficiencies--especially as a leader.

Assemble a team that has strong relationship skills and can collaborate and interact well. Assess these traits during interviews, as you can always teach the curriculum.

Give staff the ability to be creative and try new things without it counting against them. This is extremely important!

Build an effective leadership team that supplements strengths you need and provides a well-rounded approach to increase effectiveness.

Allow people to work within their strengths and use their talents. They will be happiest and do more toward the vision.

A solid, excellent teacher with relationship skills can make a significant difference, no matter what materials or programs they are using.

Talk *with* kids, not *at* them (same with adults).

Set Goals.

Clear learning targets matter. Every teacher should post the learning target of a lesson.

Use checks for understanding with clear feedback and adjust instruction for better learning.

Coaching best practices and teaching strategies matters.

Mentoring matters. Developing leaders only makes you better.

Balance your life and find ways of recharging yourself. This is a must!

Have outlets for stress: exercise, weight training, yoga, etc.

Have a spiritual component in your life: meditate, pray, stay grounded.

Be Grateful! Be Grateful! Be Grateful! Especially when everything seems to go wrong. There is always something for which to be grateful.

Stay positive. You will always find what you are looking for—whether it be negative or positive!

Smile and laugh more, keep a good sense of humor, and use it. Often, a well-placed comment can diffuse a tough situation.

Be prepared for anything, crisis etc.

Always keep your cool.

Have an open door and be a good listener.

First impressions matter.

Always be on the lookout for more effective ways of doing things.

Use your data as your guide (assessments, climate, student, etc.).

Be available for parent visits--even unannounced stop-ins. It shows they are a priority.

As a leader, your opinions matter. Guide with care.

Take care of your staff: give birthday cards, give Emergen-C when they're feeling ill, give compliments, invest time, and remember that little things matter.

All children benefit from opportunities. Open them to everyone.

Consistency matters.

Actions must match words--especially to build trust!

Family matters! You only have so much time with them, so make the most of it!

Enjoy the little things.

Take your vacation days--all of them.

Try new things. Innovate.

Laugh and maintain a sense of humor, always!

Develop positive habits.

Promote your school or business with social media, an elevator speech, newsletters, etc.

Don't underestimate the power of your words in every situation. Careful choices can build your culture for the better.

Speak well of others.

Pass compliments along and send positive news articles to people you know who are in those stories.

Encourage others every day!

Develop partnerships and collaborations.

Set children up for success, provide schedule planners, water bottles with a school logo, etc. Develop school pride!

In creating the right environment, always be on the lookout for mascot-related décor.

Culture building is always at the forefront as a positive culture is important to success.

Limit staff meetings. Ensure they are effective and collaborative.

The principal must run opening meetings to set the tone and priorities for the year.

Time is crucial--you cannot get it back.

Stay resilient. Our students are amazingly resilient!

Students need connections to be successful at school.

All districts and organizations have politics. Enough said. Stay focused!

Teach your staff to be culturally responsive.

Illuminate your school demographics and teach cultural understanding.

Stand your ground, especially if it is in the best interest of students.

Push the status quo--not just for change, but to truly make a difference.

Achievement can change.

As Eric Jenson's research has shown, we can change the learning patterns of students in poverty.

When reteaching, make sure students know you dislike the behavior, not the student.

Genuinely dislike the behavior, not the student.

As Ruby Payne and Eric Jensen say, "Don't expect students to know what they don't know."

Gear professional development around the genuine needs of your building.

The two Ts--*tone* and *tact*—matter and can de-escalate a situation.

Be intentional. Intentional leadership matters!

Know your building, organization, and community demographics.

Create a fact sheet about your school or organization.

Collaborate and build teams and people.

There is nothing better than experience. Build your experience base.

Continue to learn about people and what makes them tick. Leaders need emotional intelligence.

Leadership is helping people be the best version of themselves.

Thank the staff for just being present.

Empower and stand back!

"Strive not to be a success, but to be of value."

— *Albert Einstein*

Chapter 23:
Unfolding Successes

When I look back on what successes we had as buildings, here is what I discovered. As a leader, the more we plugged away, the more we developed relationships, collaborated, and worked, the more successes we had. The more the staff worked with me, we developed as a team. The opportunities came by, and we took them. I continually got involved in educational initiatives. These were areas in which I had a strong passion, and this built, promoted, and propelled the school. Success then followed! I love the quote by Dhirubhai Ambani, who said, "If you don't build your dream, someone else will hire you to help them build theirs."

I need to share a story that I just wasn't comfortable sharing in the past. In fact, I rarely shared this with anyone and have not shared this until introducing this book. My birthday is August 29th. This means the beginning of the school year came early for me. The decision had to be made whether to start me in school after my birthday or wait to give me growth time. I started Kindergarten on September 3rd, after having just turned five.

This was not ideal since other students would have a longer time to mature. Sure enough, since my progress was not what was normal, my parents eventually had to decide to retain me. My grades were fine, but they decided, based on my developmental progress, to have me repeat second grade, so I would be more mature and catch up with my peers. What may have added extra challenges was the first year I was in second grade, they bussed me from the neighborhood school to another school across town due to overcrowding. I would walk to my home school and board a bus to the other school. As a result, I ended up being in a different elementary school each year, from first through fourth grade: first, Betz Elementary, then Wake Robin Elementary (due to a house move), then bused from Wake Robin to Birchcrest Elementary for a year (due to overcrowding), then back to Wake Robin.

They retained me when I went back to my home school the following year. I don't really remember much of it. As a child, I didn't really have input. I was just told what was going to happen. I guess it was good I went through two different schools at that point. It made it easier for me not to attend the same school. To this day, I am not big on retention. Imagine that! This sensitive background may have been what ignited my desire to achieve and continue the ongoing growth mindset I maintain today.

This school situation--compiled with my parents getting divorced shortly thereafter--made an impact and pushed me into a continual wave of proving myself. I remember, as a kid, looking out the window, watching my father leave, and wondering if it was for good. I remember consoling my crying mother when she found herself alone. My brother and I were not aware of the decisions being made about what would happen in the future. My brother was four years older, so he could easily leave and be with friends. As a child, I saw my world falling apart. As an educator, I could always relate well with students going through family life changes, and this also assisted me as a principal in counseling students.

There are many factors which set forth your life trajectory, and with experiences that cause growth. My Grandma Edna played a significant role in raising me with her daughter--my mother--Wanda. Grandma was a widow by that time and was always there to lend a hand with any kind of task. She would come over to our house and help with laundry, cleaning, and cooking, while my mom went back into the workforce. Grandma loved this sense of purpose in helping to raise us. She had an excellent work ethic. I watched and learned. Her modeling came through and affected me. She was never afraid to complete any task. She was a hard worker.

My mother was resourceful. She refreshed her typing and office skills and jumped back into the job market. She worked her way up to helping run admissions at Metropolitan Community College. This eventually became a blessing as she was able to retire with an annuity.

My dad--Dr. Fred Anderson--was with the Omaha Public Schools from 1960 to 1993. He was a science teacher, an assistant principal at a middle school and, for many years, the District Coordinator of Media, from which he eventually retired. He started the West Maple Instructional Media Center (IMC) which became the Media Technology Center (MTC). The MTC was a resource center for teachers, and he was also the first to get computers out into the schools. He had his PHD, and he influenced me to get into education, for which I am eternally grateful. I still saw my father on weekends, and both my parents eventually married other people and had long, happy second marriages.

As stated earlier, one of my main strengths is *achiever*, and it has been clear throughout my life. I have always had an inner drive to do more! I even had a period as a child where I dealt with self-esteem issues and was bullied in junior high school. This definitely affected me, and how I wanted to provide the best for students in the schools I led.

This may be why I eventually became part of a committee of educators that helped draft the bullying definition for the state of Nebraska. As a principal, I would walk students all the way home to their door in the projects if needed. Everyone deserved the right to be safe. I took measures to protect them. I also wrote a section on bullying for the Respect 2 drama group's booklet of guidelines to address bullying. They are an excellent live drama group that helps teach students empathy and how to handle bullying. I used them for many years to reinforce our philosophy.

To further address this issue, my partnership with the Anti-Defamation League (ADL) increased. I was interested in becoming a "No Place for Hate" school, to help students develop an acceptance and understanding of each other. The ADL added me to a panel of experts at the local screening of the movie *Bullying*. I still strongly dislike bullying and want students to be more accepting of each other. It helps to have gone through some of the same issues--although I would not wish such things on others.

I was a skinny kid growing up, and that led to my ordering the old Charles Atlas Bodybuilding Course when I was in junior high school. I still have this and sometimes use it in my presentations when guest speaking. If you're not familiar with that advertisement, it was in about every comic book I ever saw early on. Comic books were about heroes, and that is another reason they had a mass appeal for children-- especially for any children going through life changes, like I had been. It depicted the heroes as facing challenges, defying the odds, and performing acts of kindness. These publications were a wonderful escape and still are for many children--although not as popular as in the past. They provided hope. Graphic novels have become popular as an alternative, and computer gaming has taken over. Also, the franchise of superhero movies has expanded and developed a whole other world of entertainment options.

Back to the Atlas ad. If you ever saw it, you may remember it depicts a skinny kid getting sand kicked in his face, then he builds some muscle, and gets fit. I purchased it in 1978. I was only five-feet-two-inches and 92 pounds at the time. I started Charles Atlas's iso-tension muscle control and exercises. I tried to increase my calories and saw changes. This is not something I shared with others. I did this quietly. The prospect of getting in shape excited me.

Later, while looking at a magazine stand, I soon stumbled upon a Muscle Builder Magazine, and I was hooked! These guys looked like Reg Park, Steve Reeves, and the muscle guys in the old Hercules movies of which I would see reruns on TV. I admired the physique and success of Frank Zane, who also was an educator and a three-time Mr. Olympia. They were comic heroes come to life, and they looked confident, strong, healthy, and fit--the way I wanted to be.

I started lifting and gaining muscle weight. Early on, I really just needed to gain weight! By the time I started high school, I had built up to about 150 pounds. By the time I graduated, I was 184 pounds and had also grown to a height of six-feet-one-inch. I was a drummer in the marching band and had found a place to belong (school connections make a difference). Lifting and bodybuilding became my passion, and I found a positive outlet. The gym was my escape and sanctuary. I was at peace working out and lifting. I still find this in the gym.

I was soon in the 190-200 lb. range. It was noticeable, and my body started changing. This is when I entered a teen Mr. Nebraska bodybuilding contest, came in third, and continued to compete through my early undergraduate college years. I competed mainly in pairs bodybuilding competitions with a former girlfriend. I left competing when I didn't want to make the move into pharmaceuticals and steroids. I used supplements, but I opted for better health, longevity, and lifelong strength.

It is funny, when I started college, everyone I ran into assumed I had played football or was into sports more than I was. To this day, I still love lifting weights, bodybuilding, fitness, and yoga. I am into nutrition and keeping my body healthy. That early Charles Atlas course was a driver for me in developing more confidence. Experiences help create mold and shape you. The bullying, parents divorcing, grade retention, and self-esteem challenges were all attributes that created a deep desire in me to improve and excel. Again, this is probably where the seed of my achiever mindset grew.

Most of the things in this chapter I have not shared with anyone outside the family. It is private and often kept to myself. I guess, with the writing of this book, I wanted people to know more of my background, and some of my *why*. As Brene Brown would encourage, I am showing my vulnerability.

Most people do not like sharing experiences from their past, especially if they contain any hurt or harsh feelings. However, this is all a part of self-reflection which can be helpful in knowing why we are the way we are. I find, for example, my life experiences have developed my perspective and interest in leadership.

When I was a teacher, I was also pushing to be better and making achievements along the way. I wanted to do more and leave more of a mark. When I became a principal, we used everyone's strengths and talents. Indian Hill Elementary had many successes and became a model of what a high poverty building can accomplish. The focus school at Underwood Hills and Wilson became a model of what could be done with innovation and technology while promoting a diverse culture.

The following is a list of the successes I have had in my educational career. These are not just mine, of course, they belong to everyone who worked in the teams I led. Many thanks to all the staff members for the great collaboration which helped make these things happen:

Recipient of Sherwood Foundation School Grants to support focus program (2008-2021)

Honored with a one-year Focus School Scholarship in my name to assist a graduating senior who has completed at least three years within the Focus School (2019)

Recipient of an Empowerment Champion Award from the Empowerment Network (2019)

Recipient of the First ADL Plains States Commitment to Fighting Hate for Good Award (2019)

Recipient of an Apple Distinguished School Award (2017-2019)

Recognition as a Common-Sense Media School/Certified Digital Citizenship School (2017-2018)

Honored with Having Five Alice Buffett Outstanding Teacher Award Winners: Maggie Douglas (2019), Tom Gamble (2016), Therese McGee (2015), Jay Beyer (2014), Gail May (2007)

Honored to publish the iBook: *Wilson Focus: Celebrating a New Dawn in Leadership, Technology and Communication* (2017)

Recipient of Champion for Excellence and Equity Award. From the North Omaha Cradle-to-Career Collaborative for Wilson Focus, demonstrating 10 years of Innovation and Excellence (2017)

Honored to have Wilson Focus Recognized in a documentary film by Nebraska Loves Public Schools (ilovesps.org): *Choosing Wilson: Challenging Norms to Achieve Student Success* (2017)

Recipient of an Apple Distinguished School Award (2015-2017)

Honored with Excellent School Rating Through the State in AQuESTT. Getting 89 out of 90 in evidence-based supports for students (2015)

Recipient of AdvancED School Accreditation, Receiving 341.27 out of 400 overall in rubric (2015)

Recognized as an author and consultant in Respect 2's Staging Conversations–Resource Guide featured in the segment on Bullying in the Primary Grades (2015)

Recipient of the Green Ribbon Award by U.S. Department of Education (2014)

Recipient of an Apple Outstanding Program Award (2013-2015)

Recipient of an Apple Outstanding Program Award (2012-2013)

Honored to be Recognized in One Nation Indivisible Publication from Harvard University, which listed Wilson Focus School as a possible national model for moving diversity (2013)

Recipient of the Gold Award for Wilson Focus, recognizing an over five percent increase in three academic areas

Recipient of AdvancED School Accreditation, Receiving Exemplary in All Seven Areas (2011)

Honored to be a Panel Expert for the Anti-Defamation League at Aksarben Cinema's Premiere of the Movie: *Bullying* (2011)

Honored to have a Milken Educator Award Winner: Garret Higginbotham (2010)

Recipient of an Outstanding Educational Leadership Award from Phi Delta Kappa (2009)

Honored to have established the first Innovative Leadership Focus School in Nebraska (2008)

Honored to be invited as a Presenter on *Indian Hill Elementary's Successful Use of Positive Behavioral Interventions and Supports* at the Special Education Conference in Washington, D.C. (2004). On

Recipient of the Lorraine Giles Award for School Safety, Greater Omaha Safety and Health Council (2002)

Recipient of the MVP Award: Most Valuable Principal for Outstanding Commitment to the Indian Hill Community, from the South Omaha Neighborhood Association (2001)

Honored with Special Recognition for Indian Hill Elementary through the Nebraska Department of Education as one of Five Model Safe, Secure and Disciplined Schools in OPS (2000-2008)

Recipient of Several School Assistance Grants (2000-2017)

Recipient of an Outstanding Service Award from University of Nebraska at Omaha, for completing a 12-by-200-foot mural representing UNO at Offutt Air Force Base (Joint Project with Ingra Anderson, 1996)

Honored with opportunity to design a 14-foot Sculpture for King Science Center (1990)

Success as a principal does not just happen. It comes from hard work, perseverance, and a firm belief you are making a difference. Staff must work together with shared leadership and empowerment to drive positive change. It takes everyone to make the organization work and, I mean, everyone at all levels. Not every leader wants to put in the extra effort to be more than ordinary.

If you put in 100 percent and go the extra mile, success happens. Opportunities increase and positive outcomes are sure to follow. Many of the staff I had worked with moved on and became leaders themselves. Success is contagious! They are out in the world making changes, mentoring, and making a difference!

Everyone occasionally has doubts, but you cannot let these thoughts get the best of you. It is important to take risks and move beyond the norm. Everyone has heard that the busiest people get things done. That is true! They are skilled at organizing and managing many tasks, while making continuous progress. Don't just settle. These leaders persevere and don't give up, despite the obstacles. They are movers and shakers and can make things happen. Plan on being one of those outliers who makes things happen and success will follow!

"The key is not to prioritize what's on your schedule,
but to schedule your priorities."

— Stephen Covey

Chapter 24:
Balancing Your Life

Being in any leadership role is hard and can take its toll. Being a principal is a tough job and no one can understand it until they are in that role. No book on being an effective leader is complete without talking about balancing all aspects of your life. It is important to balance your life and work. This can be challenging but is crucial for managing your stress.

What is balance and what does it really mean? I think the mode of operation is different for all people, but it is basically a way of shifting from work to family, and doing the things that re-energize you. This is easier said than done. When I first started as a principal, it was hard not to put in many extra hours--especially at a high needs building, where we were working on a turnaround scenario. It takes time and extra work. Then at the next building I was starting from scratch, and it was a new concept, also equaling a great deal of time--including evening commitments.

Once you get established in your role, you fall into a rhythm. This is easier to do in education, since everything is around a schedule. In my case, for example, as the years went on, I became better at managing my time. I also developed efficiencies to get things done. This means I needed less time for tasks that were previously more demanding. Experience helps teach ways of working more efficiently, although it can often be from learning the hard way. Leadership roles of all types require more time, and the secret is learning to balance it by prioritizing tasks.

It is important to make family events and special occasions. You can't get back time, so it is crucial to use it well. I have many regrets of missing certain events and life moments that I cannot get back. Consider these life events and the importance to you and your family. At this stage in my life, I really value time and scheduling the way I need to around my family work and consulting.

Time is one of the most precious commodities. You never know how much time you actually have on this earth. I truly believe in developing the mind, body, and spirit. I am spiritual, consider myself a Christian and have a strong faith. Follow whatever you believe and use this to help you focus on maintaining yourself and balancing your life. Everyone needs a center--a way to connect and re-focus.

My career started with 10 years as a teacher. Then I became a leader and spent 10 years in a high poverty, acute needs building. Then I moved on to build and lead a high-profile building for 11 years. These were all ongoing stressors with no break in between. For example, I moved from serving as a summer school principal with a tutoring program at one building to immediately entering a 12-month contract to start the focus school. These were all pushing the boundaries of a regular work schedule, which is often how many of us work. I was ready for a break!

I have read it takes a good two weeks to fully recharge. How many of us get that kind of break from work or from only a hectic pace? Often these days, we remain tied to technology, so it's not a totally disconnected break. Many employees in the United States do not fully use their vacation days every year, leading to the loss of many days.

There is research, of course, recommending taking the break for your own health. There was a commercial awhile back that had children talking about the importance of a vacation. They encouraged taking them somewhere, getting away, and just spending time with family. It was pretty effective--especially coming from a child's perspective.

As the Focus School developed, it became highly successful. Situations like this can be a problem for a leader. Since then, you are working at staying at that high level while continuing to move forward. This can cause stress and pressure--as leading any organization can— which can also lead to burnout. Having positive outlets can help you combat this and effectively cope.

The research on happiness is interesting. More money doesn't make you happy. It is more about doing something for which you have a passion. It is like we have all heard: if you love your work, it isn't work. Finding the work that makes you happy, and finding a purpose you believe in, is a powerful driver. Having purpose and knowing your *why* is important. What drives you at your core? If you are working within your zone--using your talents and strengths--you will be happy. I have a passion for leadership and my work but enjoy many other activities as well. These are excellent breaks to help me stay recharged.

Stress is an interesting factor that can have all kinds of influences on your body. When I was at Indian Hill for 10 years, I used Heart Math (biofeedback) and an online stress-monitoring system. We also used this with students, as I explained earlier. Brent Kahn, an expert from Clarkson Hospital, trained me in executive stress management. He also worked with the staff on stress and test anxiety in students. I had a portable monitor and was using an online tracking system daily to gauge where I was and guess what? There were three color areas: red, blue and green. The goal was to be operating more in the blue and ideally the green level, which meant you were calm and not in a stressed state. At this high poverty school--with things happening all the time--managing crisis and even trying to be as proactive as possible, I was operating in the red (stressed) state most of the time. I sometimes read in the blue, which was better, but still in the middle. Green was the best (calmest) state to be in. I rarely saw this while I was addressing issues and working to be pro-active.

This stressed state was where I was functioning most of the time. Mr. Kahn said this is something a person cannot maintain over the long haul. Stress is something that catches up with you. If you do not figure out a way to control it, it can creep up and cause all kinds of mental and physical problems. How many leaders function close to the edge? How many end up with stress-related ailments? I would imagine many do with all the things we are juggling at the same time. We need to maintain our own health and wellness, so we can effectively lead others.

It is important to self-reflect and be able to tell where you are mentally and physically. To monitor stress levels, I used a quick system that checked heart rate and breathing. The goal was to use breathing techniques to help relax when the body feels stressed. I did not even know I was operating in this manner. Later, I learned the power of Yoga box breathing, and Navy Seal tactical breathing, to refocus your body and mind. I recently heard a quote from somewhere that said it is important to be "calmly contagious" as a leader. This totally makes sense, since the leader sets the tone for the organization.

There will be many stressful times as a leader. Before leaving for the focus school, they asked me to recommend leaders that could jump right in after me at Indian Hill. I made three recommendations, and they followed none. The district ended up picking a first-year assistant principal and moved her up to the principal position of this extra-challenging school. I tried to assist her and give help in the transition, but there was too much to learn. This really wasn't a good fit for a new first year principal. It was one of the toughest buildings in the district. She lasted a year and left for another school system in another state. As I write this, the school is on its fifth principal since I left. It is a highly stressful position.

Here is a story about my stress. Originally, while the district was trying to pick a leader to follow me, I was running Indian Hill while also starting the new focus school from scratch. I was still in charge at Indian Hill and was going back and forth between buildings for months. I ordered supplies and planned construction at the other building, preparing for the creation of the focus school. The Educare construction was back on at the Indian Hill campus, and there were plans underway for the addition of classrooms. This was a stressful time leading two busy buildings. I had a new assistant principal, Jennifer Schlapia (who is now a principal), so that helped take some of the strain off, but everything is still under the principal. That is where the buck stops, and I was ready for a break!

I was leading both for about three months, and it was taking its toll on me. Then, on July 2, 2008, I had just mowed our lawn and was getting ready for our big July 3rd bash (our pre-4th celebration). While moving, I had a call from the superintendent needing me to complete an award recommendation for an outstanding teacher of mine. I cranked the letter out that night and went to bed exhausted.

Then, early the next morning, our Shiba Inu had a seizure. I jumped up out of bed to help calm him. He was coming out of his seizure and, as I laid back down, I told Ingra I wasn't feeling well and, before I knew it, Ingra says my eyes turned black and I passed out cold. I awakened, with her having called for an ambulance, and paramedics at the door to take me to the hospital.

They gave me a saline drip to rehydrate me and did full heart and body checks. I ended up being okay. It was a vasovagal syncope, probably due to exhaustion and dehydration. I was also gearing up for the opening of this new focus school and we were starting August 1st. Ingra saw my eyes turn black and said I was out with my eyes open. This freaked her out and as she said, she didn't want to see black-eyed Bret ever again! This shows how high stress with no relief will eventually catch up with you.

Even though I took this as a sign to slow down and watch it, that wouldn't be the only time. It happened again in 2015, when we were out to eat with Ingra's folks, Larry and Claudia. While at the restaurant, I wasn't feeling well and got up to go to the restroom. When I started walking back to the table and just before I was about to sit down— whoosh--it happened again. I passed out. One of the servers--a girl who knew someone with a similar condition--had been watching my actions and saw I was about to collapse. She caught my head before it connected with the concrete floor. I was thankful for her quick response!

Then shortly after, I woke up surrounded by paramedics, and fainted again! They took me to the hospital, and I checked out fine. I was re-hydrated and released. This timeframe was at the start of school, with many things going on. Stress will do weird things to you. I now drink plenty of water, Gatorade Zero, Powerade Zero, Propel water (my liquids of choice), and electrolytes as needed. This still would not be the last time my body chose to re-boot when the shadow of stress showed up.

Don't overlook the significance of staying hydrated and getting electrolytes, especially if you're always on the go. It also helps to slow down. It is important to have positive outlets for your stress, and to re-energize. I have always worked out and continue to lift weights, walk, practice yoga, take supplements and work at staying healthy. This has been one of the positive outlets for me and a must in high-stress jobs. Exercise helps release endorphins (the feel-good hormones). As a leader, you must have a way to de-stress.

I also have many interests and hobbies, which are good ways to rejuvenate and take mental breaks from what I normally do. I enjoy working out, motorcycling, bicycling, building things, landscaping, spending time with our pets, and creating artwork. When I first started this book, we had two Pommeranians (Toby and Mojo) and a Shiba Inu (Bushido) who passed during the writing. We also had a cat (Tula) who has passed, three birds, an aquarium and a pond full of fish. We call it The Anderson Zoo. As I was completing this book, we added a Kolu Husky named Kiki to our mix and she adds a lot of energy to our pack. Animals can be wonderful de-stressors. Our dogs always bring us joy with their unconditional love and that is hard to beat!

Ingra and I are avid landscapers and Do-It-Yourselfers, (DIYers). Over the years, we have added a Koi Pond with a waterfall, a pool, a small bridge, a gazebo, a *boatzebo* we designed and built, and many walking paths throughout our landscaping. We even added a gazebo one year. Our constant activities include planting, weeding, moving items, trimming vines, and working outside. We have bird-feeding stations throughout and enjoy a wide variety. It is a great stress relief. Once, a counselor and friend from Indian Hill, James Cunningham, came over to get some plants. I showed him the backyard and said this was our stress relief. He made me laugh because his comment was, "You must have a hell of a lot of stress!" It is our calm, peaceful getaway--an escape. It is our outlet. Everyone needs somewhere to unwind.

My nephew's wife is a heart surgeon nurse practitioner and her comment after hearing about my episodes was that she sees yoga in my future. It is true I can maintain my cool at work and under most situations, and I have had some incredibly serious ones, but that level of stress cannot be maintained. Everyone must have a way to get stress out and balance their lives while re-grouping when necessary. I started doing yoga in 2017 and have added that practice to the end of all my workouts. It is a wonderful mix of stretching, while relaxing the body and mind. The moves are challenging and keep the body working, then the cool down provides escape and refreshes the mind and body.

Ingra and I were raised Presbyterian Christians and have a strong faith. This is something personal for everyone, but research has shown that faith can increase a person's well-being. Being spiritual can help bring peace and a feeling of being connected. "Get the spiritual experience that really changes things, the in-depth type that brings you alive and keeps you alive every day all the way" (Peale, 1976).

In May 2015, doctors diagnosed my mother with pulmonary fibrosis, despite her never having smoked and not having any apparent reason to have contracted this disease. Her strain was called Idiopathic Pulmonary Fibrosis (IPF) and they are not sure what caused it. IPF is considered a terminal illness, and they usually say three-to-five years is the average lifespan following diagnosis. She was on portable oxygen and was still very positive. She could do most things, including playing a few holes of golf. This disease slowed her down some, but she had a great attitude. Mom lived her best life as the IPF took its course. We had been increasing our visits to see her in Arkansas and staying longer. I loved our getaways to see Mom and it was also a great break from our regular stressors.

Then it happened again, Black-Eyed Bret--as Ingra calls it--returned. It was 2017, and we were visiting Mom at her home in Arkansas. Ingra and I stopped for a quick lunch, and it didn't sit well with me. I started feeling nauseated and, for many miles, said I wasn't feeling well. Right before we were ready to get on the interstate, I pulled over, put the car in park, and immediately, I passed out. Here we go again!

As I was waking up in that "Where am I" state, Ingra informed me what had happened. In her quick thinking, she had jumped out of the car, ran around to the driver's side, opened the door and lifted my feet up to get the blood running back to my brain. This was something she had learned from a paramedic in one of my earlier bouts. He had likened it to a computer crash and compared getting blood back to the brain as a system reboot. It worked and I woke up. We both later laughed at the show we had just put on for the nursing home who had the whole scene in view.

I thought it might be poisoning, and we stopped to get me something for my stomach. Ingra drove the rest of the way to my mom's house, and I took it easy. I did all right on our visit, was careful what I ate, and tried to rest.

When I got back, I made an appointment with my doctor, and they started running tests. He said I was having this vasovagal syncope effect, which causes passing out, but why? What is the reason my body was having this reaction? My heart checked out fine. The stress test checked out fine. In fact, they said to keep working out--my heart and circulation looked healthy. While I was on the treadmill, they wanted to see how high I could go, so they really pushed me, and said I did extremely well. I was thinking I was done with tests and that I was okay, but apparently there was more in store for me.

The last test they wanted to do was a Gastrointestinal (GI) endoscopy. It didn't sound like fun, and I was ready to give up on the tests, thinking, "Who knows what causes this condition I have?"

Ingra said I might as well follow through with the last test and see what it tells us. Dr. Taylor (my general practice doctor) said they still needed to find out what was causing the pain I would get below my heart, and the stomach discomfort I was having. This in-turn caused other stuff to happen within my body, so they sent me to a GI doctor who ended up doing an endoscopy.

During the test, they put me under anesthesia, and they used a scope to examine my throat and determine the cause of my condition. They ended up taking pictures, but I am sure they knew at the time what they were seeing. They put me on a timed-release prescription antacid two times a day at a high dose. When they called me at work a few days later, they said the test came back negative for my stomach and intestines, but they found something with my throat.

Apparently, I had an ulcer in my throat, and it had turned into what they call Barrett's Esophagus. The medical professionals classify this as pre-cancerous because the cells in my throat are damaged and can become more prone to cancer. If I continue to watch what I eat and take the prescription medication, as well as getting it checked every three years, they said I should be fine.

This also meant I needed to lower and manage stress better. My first thought was, "I am a principal and I deal with stress and pressure all the time." Now you can't tell me stress hasn't played a part in the upset stomach and ulcer that developed. In fact, most likely it was a big part, and it was causing these other reactions my body was having. It is so important to pay attention to your body. I am pretty in tune with my body and can tell when something is wrong, especially now.

No job is worth your health and wellness, so it is important to find stress-relieving outlets. As Ingra learned from that paramedic, the passing out was like a computer rebooting, hinting I needed to slow down and start over. It resulted from many things going on. Now that I am controlling the stomach acid and throat more, I have had no incidents. I am now on a lower dose of a prescription once a day. I have gotten to where I can feel if it is going to happen and can control it through breathing, etc.

The doctor's assistant called me and said I was to be put on Pantoprazole for the rest of my life. I had read on the internet that you shouldn't stay on Pantoprazole for a prolonged period due to side effects. Her response was you can either be on this prescription the rest of your life or get throat cancer. What do you say to that? Now, I have gone down to a time-released 40 mg a day. It took a while to get this figured out and under control, but I am glad we finally found the culprit.

If you are having difficulties in health as a leader, it is worth it to find out the cause before your body decides to progress into something life-threatening. Stress can have powerful effects. I didn't even share this much with many people, since I didn't want them to see this as a weakness. I still do all kinds of activities, but I am managing my stress better. I talked to a colleague of mine who was an assistant superintendent, and she said the minute she retired and left her position; it was baffling the change her body had taken. She no longer needed the medications she was on and the doctor asked what she was doing differently. She said she had retired and was doing more things she loved. Her body responded positively to the improved circumstances. This is more proof it is important to control your stress levels. Many times, the stress is even self-imposed because of all that you want to do--the pressure of success. The body is an amazing organism, and it will tell you when it needs to regroup, or it will force you to do so under negative circumstances. Make it your choice to slow down and control the stress. Find your positive outlets and ways to cope that enable you to regroup and re-energize for another day. While writing this book, my mother, Wanda Stuck, passed away September 19th, 2018, from complications with pulmonary fibrosis. I miss her and miss our conversations. I would call her weekly and share things happening with my career and our lives. It is important to cherish the time we have with family and friends. We always think we will have plenty of time later. Many say this same thing, but often forget it while in the *rat race* of life or climbing the proverbial ladder.

Ingra and I had a busy number of years prior to this with her father, Dr. Larry Winkler, passing away from a sudden heart attack on August 16th, 2016. He was a retired United States Air Force Lieutenant Colonel and then retired from a second career as Dean Emeritus of the College of Continuing Studies at the University of Nebraska at Omaha. Then two months later, on October 11th, 2016, my stepfather, Ralph Stuck, passed away from cancer. He was retired and living in Arkansas with my mother. On April 2nd, 2017, Joyce Eikenbary, my aunt, passed away. She was an excellent educator and English as a Second Language Teacher for Westside and Omaha Public Schools. My stepmother, Mary Anderson, passed on July 17th, 2022. She was in education and a media specialist. My dad, Dr. Fred Anderson, also suffered from pulmonary fibrosis (the same illness from which my biological mother passed), and he passed January 25th, 2023. He was the district coordinator of media for Omaha Public Schools. He was an advocate for education and encouraged me to finish this book.

The point I am making is you really don't know how much time you have in this life, and what time you have with family. Cherish those moments and enjoy every one of them. You need to use your time wisely, and if you want to make an impact, don't wait for your dreams to come to you. You need to go after them. Time and how I spend it is more precious to me now more than ever. I set priorities, work at doing what makes me happy, and direct my energies to where I want to affect the world.

I control my stress more. Working out and staying healthy are priorities for me. I spend time with family, our zoo, my goals and hobbies. These many outlets help keep me focused and positive. I feel lucky to still be working in education, and in a job where I can make a difference. Non-profits are the same way. You are doing more than just making a living. It is important to have a purpose.

I am organized, a planner, an achiever, and I develop routines to get things done effectively, but as a leader, I have learned no one can do it all in one day. Set and juggle priorities. You also can't do everything yourself. This is where shared leadership comes in. Develop the people around you--a strong leadership team can successfully collaborate and help move goals forward. Use your time well and make a difference in the lives of others. Stay positive and kind. The people around you matter.

Effective leadership is not a simple task, and we need more effective principals and leaders who can get meaningful results. If you have found one nugget of wisdom that is useful to you as a leader, I will feel I have done my task. This may not be your usual educational leadership book, but it is based upon experience and things that have worked for me. The concepts are sound, and the principles could apply to any school building.

Becoming an effective leader requires work. There are many styles of leadership: servant leadership, transformational leadership, relational leadership, and transitional leadership. The best principals can move as needed to adjust to the environment and become courageous leaders. People need to be better at supporting, encouraging and developing others. I cannot stress this point enough. It is so important to support and develop your staff. Much of the work must be intentional and modeled. We are all in this together and it works against us to be so competitive that we can't learn from and support each other.

We can help by forming relationships, maintaining a positive attitude, and valuing one another. Everyone can be an important piece in the puzzle that makes an organization excellent. We each have a part to play. I need to say to all the principals and leaders out there: move the status quo, make things better, keep learning, collaborate, empower others, stay positive, and keep the faith!

"Be the change you wish to see, even when you feel like the only one who can see it."

— *Jennifer Milews*

Chapter 25:
Making Meaningful Changes

Wilson Focus School, and the concepts to create such an innovative school, demonstrate success. The social and academic growth cannot be overlooked, given the powerful trend data we gathered. We were beating the odds with a diverse, free-and-reduced lunch population. Students need opportunities and they will rise to the occasion! Schools and education are at a crossroads. Building the right culture, positivity and developing staff capacity to work with students, can change society. We have spent many years doing things the same ways and schools need to change with the students. Despite the success of the focus school and other innovative models, most states and districts will stick to their usual practices.

There are so many pockets of success, from classroom teachers, to principals, buildings and districts. Many do not wish to rock the boat and will remain in a district-driven status quo, even if they see areas which could be improved. Outside of education, creativity and innovation are increasing more than ever, and future companies are going to have jobs that have never existed before. The technology will continue to grow and change the face of society--like it or not. We must prepare students for a new frontier!

Our students have many interests and can multi-task better than most adults. They are growing up with access to many things those of us in previous generations never had and will someday have access to things we never had in our lifetime. The world is fast-paced and developing. We need to open those doors of accessibility. There is a need to develop the strengths and talents of our students while promoting opportunities for all. We need to develop powerful leaders with passion, and the drive to be successful and effective. We can only do this if we continue to mentor, build, develop, and cultivate a stream of people with positive effective leadership skills.

Effective principals can help change the educational landscape of our country. Principals with the collaboration of teachers and all staff can create teams to push forward positively. Let's get back to making schools exciting for kids. I will never forget a letter I received from a parent about the focus school. It said, "My daughter has been telling me about school and the things she is doing. She is excited–she has never done this before." My question would be why not? What needs to be done to improve schools. If you are an educator, do some self-reflecting and asking yourself, "Would I want to attend this school?"

Earlier in this book, I said I don't even remember my elementary, junior high or high school principals. Why is that? When I became a principal, I made a commitment that I would not be that kind of leader. I wanted to make connections, really be a part of the school community, and truly make a difference. I wanted my students to know me. If you are a leader of an organization that is just trudging along, what could you do to excite and connect people? Is your organization an exciting, dynamic place to work, and does it touch the lives of those it serves? If not, how can it be improved? The same applies to schools.

I know I am getting preachy, but policy makers, states, federal laws and mandates need to get back to focusing on what is best for students. In fact, we need to get back to true collaboration, lighten up, roll up our sleeves, and get the job done. Schools can be better, can increase achievement, and can make a difference. Policy makers need to quit adding roadblocks to our path, and let educators do that for which we have a passion: educating children.

As an educator, principal or other type of leader, you never really know the impact you are having. Once, as a principal at a new teacher induction, I was getting ready to introduce my new staff to the district for the year. This induction took place at a high school auditorium and was with all the district's schools. While there, someone brought me a note from a new teacher. It said she was in my middle school PAWS (Preparing All Wildcat students) home room group when I was a teacher. She said I had supported her and provided money for her to attend our middle school dance. She hadn't forgotten this kind gesture and is now being inducted as a teacher. I would have loved to have talked with her, but with it being so busy with the induction of so many people, we weren't able to. I was proud she chose the profession of being an educator. I am sure I wasn't her only influence, but I was able to encourage her like many of you are doing every day. You just don't know the impact you are having.

It surprised me many years into my career when, out of the blue, I received an email that read: "Mr. Anderson, I cannot say that I would be surprised if you did not remember me, but I was one of your students when you taught art and weight training at King Science Center back in 1996-97. I have looked fondly upon the time that I spent at King, and you in particular stand out. I'm not sure what you did differently. I had not thought of the old school for many years until one day, a few years back, I saw you on the morning news as I was getting ready for work. It took me a second to place you, but then I just smiled and remembered that you had always wanted to become a principal. I can only imagine that you are a great principal, and the students are very lucky to have you. For some reason, I have been feeling rather nostalgic, and it prompted me to perform some research to find the school that you now manage and write you. Congratulations on all of your accomplishments, and I'm glad to see that you developed your goal and strived to make it a reality. You have been and still are an inspiration." Signed Chris T.

It is rare you get this kind of a letter. I came across it again while compiling this book and going through old documents.In your role as a leader, you never know who you will inspire or know the impact you are making every day and every year. If you are in education, you have been a life changer. Despite the normal rhetoric, it happens all the time. You change lives. Let's make it for the better!

As the Wallace Foundation discovered in its extensive study titled *How Principals Affect Students and Schools: A Systematic Synthesis of Two Decades of Research,* the principal has the largest impact on a culture and the success of a school. It states that:

"Effective principals are at least as important for student achievement as previous reports have concluded—and in fact, their importance may not have been stated strongly enough. Replacing a below-average principal (at the 25th percentile) with an above-average one (at the 75th percentile) would increase the typical student's learning by nearly three months in both math and reading annually. But this is just an average effect across students in a school, meaning a principal's effects are felt by potentially hundreds of students in a school year." (Grissom, Egalite, Lindsay, 2021)

You are a part of the driving force to break that status quo and move all students and staff forward. Teach people to be culturally responsive and understand differing points of view. Value and empower people. Treat all people well and stay positive. Leave a legacy. Let's be part of a meaningful change. What are you waiting for? Go for your dreams, and better yet, become a principal!

"Ideas without action are worthless."

-- *Harvey Mackay*

Afterword

As I was getting this book wrapped up, we were recovering from COVID-19. In 2020, It happened, we had a worldwide reboot and COVID-19 became a global pandemic. This caused schools and all organizations to come to a complete halt, and reconsider ways of doing business. As I have referred to in this book, the worldwide pandemic forced a change in the status quo. Federal and state mandates shut many services down, as we encouraged people to shelter in place, and work from home to "flatten the curve" during the COVID-19 outbreak.

It forced school districts to close schools, and teachers suddenly had to teach from home. We have had an emergency plan for everything else, but no one had really planned for a major shutdown like this. It forced school boards and superintendents into suddenly being more creative than ever. Teachers were having to teach from home and were doing so through all kinds of technology. Remote learning became a regular thing. Our students are very resilient and are in the process of bouncing back from this--probably easier than we will.

Organizations scrambled to provide food for our student families during the pandemic. This not only hit our high poverty families hard, but many lost jobs and were out of work for prolonged periods. There were so many wonderful examples of teachers reaching out to students through technology and social media. Schools and neighborhoods found creative ways to connect, and families developed more respect for the role of educators.

Heroic efforts were being maintained by front line responders and many people within the medical field. There was an unprecedented collaboration to work on a cure, and many nations were working together to develop the vaccines. People can be amazing!

I had been retired when the pandemic began, but later experienced it firsthand when I served as a substitute principal for a couple months. My first concern with the pandemic was the needs of our high poverty students and families. I knew, even with teachers providing lessons online and teaching through technology, that many did not have equal access to these services. There was not always a computer for every child, a phone for every child, or equal access to technology in every home. This was especially true with the internet and Wi-Fi. I have worked with many children who are often on their own, and yet, are very resourceful. They do not have the same access as middle-class families. This was not a fair situation for most families, and I wondered how we could narrow the learning gap.

The pandemic caused us to look closer at this divide, and the equity of resources for families. Federal dollars were given to states and school educational systems, and many of the districts in our area used the funds to create more of a 1:1 technology environment for our students. Our largest district purchased iPads for every student. Each came with cellular access paid for by the grant funds. School districts were closing early, and now had the ability for students to work from home.

Summer school looked different--if it happened at all. During this time, they cancelled many activities and events, such as sports, academic competitions, proms, and more. Some districts found creative ways to host virtual versions of these events. The pandemic caused the year 2020 to see virtual graduation ceremonies throughout the country. Many people came up with creative ways of still making memories. The traditional transitions for students moving from elementary to middle and middle to high school happened in a non-traditional way. Districts looked at alternatives to opening in the fall. Essentially, the machine had stopped, and it forced us to look at the way schools work. Standardized testing and many of the different state accountability systems were on hold. Students were still learning, but it forced districts to look at effective ways to meet student needs and inequities. When we had no voice in changing the status quo, it forced us to look at things differently. We had to identify solutions to problems that existed even before the change. This pandemic has shed light on several aspects of the current inequity within education.

Then, in the middle of the pandemic, we had a surge of worldwide protests surrounding race. Young people of all cultures and backgrounds started coming together in unity. I can't remember a time in history that this happened with such fervor. This sparked a cultural evolution, with our young people coming together to challenge, to collaborate, and to create a better world.

When educators came back, our students required more Social Emotional Learning (SEL) and Trauma-Informed Education (TIE) strategies. Many schools and staff did this through PBIS. If you are not familiar with SEL, it is the process where children and adults learn to understand and manage emotions. They set and achieve constructive goals. They cultivate empathy and build positive relationships. In addition, they learn to make responsible decisions.

As TIE strategies increased, we found more students having trauma experiences coming out of the pandemic. In fact, many adults fell into this area of concern and needed support as well. The number of people with Adverse Childhood Experiences (ACEs) has increased. More support and training are needed. It will be interesting to see if schools can continue to look toward better ways of delivering instruction. After addressing some of the old paradigms and creating a fresh path, education has been forever changed—mostly for the better.

From my experience, most people are resistant to change. Change for the sake of change is bad but change for the better is excellent! Let's use this push in a new direction to make sure we are moving ahead with all students in mind. I am looking forward to assisting in this effort to develop more effective schools, principals, and leaders. Education is at a turning point. Let's choose our path wisely!

References / Favorite Resources

Some of the following authors and experts are referenced in this book. I love studying leadership and have quite a collection of educational and leadership-oriented books. This is a sampling of some useful resources. I have included full author names to assist in locating resources in case of interest.

Achor, Shawn (2018). *Big Potential: How Transforming the Pursuit of Success Raises Our Achievement, Happiness and Well Being.* New York, NY: Crown Publishing Group, A Division of Penguin Random House, LLC.

Achor, Shawn (2010). *The Happiness Advantage: The Seven Principles of Psychology That Fuel Success and Performance at Work.* New York, NY: Crown Publishing Group, A Division of Random House, Inc.

Anderson, Bret and Focus Innovation Team (2017). *Wilson Focus School: Celebrating A New Dawn in Leadership, Technology and Communication.* Omaha, NE: Apple iBook.

Bennis, Warren (1999). *Managing People Is Like Herding Cats: Warren Bennis on Leadership.* Provo, UT: Executive Excellence Publishing.

Blankstein, Alan M. and Noguera, Pedro (2015). *Excellence Through Equity.* Thousand Oaks, CA: Corwin, Sage Publications Ltd.

Boyatzis, Richard and McKee, Annie (2005). *Resonant Leadership.* Boston, MA: Harvard Business School Press.

Brown, Brene' (2018). *Dare to Lead.* New York, NY: Random House, A Division of Penguin Random House, LLC.

Buckingham, Marcus (2007). *Go Put Your Strengths to Work: 6 Powerful Steps to Achieve Outstanding Performance.* New York, NY: Free Press, Simon & Schuster Press, Inc.

Buckingham, Marcus (2005). *The One Thing You Need to Know: About Great Managing, Great Leading, and Sustained Individual Success.* New York, NY: One Thing Productions, Inc. Free Press a Division of Simon & Schuster, Inc.

Buckingham, Marcus and Clifton, Donald O., Ph.D. (2001). *Now, Discover Your Strengths.* The Gallup Organization. New York, NY: The Free Press, A Division of Simon & Schuster Inc.

Buckingham, Marcus and Coffman, Curt (1999). *First, Break All the Rules: What the World's Greatest Managers Do Differently.* Gallup Press, 1st Edition. New York, NY: Simon & Schuster Inc.

Chappuis, Jan (2009). *Seven Strategies for Assessment for Learning.* Boston, MA: Pearson.

Chism, Dwayne (2022). *Leading Your School Toward Equity: A Practical Framework for Walking the Talk.* Arlington, VA: ASCD.

Colors, Barbara (2003). *The Bully, the Bullied, and the Bystander: From Preschool to High School--How Parents and Teachers Can Help Break the Cycle of Violence.* New York, NY: Harper Collins Publishers Inc.

Collins, Jim (2001). *Good To Great: Why Some Companies Make the Leap...and Others Don't.* New York, NY: Harper Collins Publishers Inc.

Covey, Stephen R. (1991). *Principle-Centered Leadership.* New York, NY: Simon & Schuster Inc.

Curwin, Richard L. and Mendler, Allen N. and Mendler, Brian D. (2018). *Discipline With Dignity: How to Build Responsibility, Relationships, and Respect in Your Classroom, 4th Edition.* Alexandria, VA: ASCD.

Davis, Bonnie M. (2012). *How to Teach Students Who Don't Look Like You: Culturally Relevant Teaching Strategies.* Thousand Oaks, CA: Corwin, Sage Publications Ltd.

Davis, Bonnie M. (2008). *How to Coach Teachers Who Don't Think Like You: Using Literacy Strategies to Coach Across Content Area.* Thousand Oaks, CA: Corwin, Sage Publications Ltd.

Dearborn, Grace and Sturgeon, Scott and Forward by Whittaker, Todd (2019*). Yeah, But What About This Kid? Tier 3 Behavior Interventions That Work.* Fairfax, CA: Conscious Teaching, LLC.

Drucker, Peter F. (1996). *The Executive in Action: Managing for Results, Innovation and Entrepreneurship, The Effective Executive.* New York, NY: Harper Collins Publishers, Inc.

DuFour, Richard and DuFour, Rebecca and Eaker, Robert (2008). *Revisiting Professional Learning Communities at Work: New Insights for Improving Schools.* Bloomington, IN: Solution Tree.

DuFour, Richard and DuFour, Rebecca and Eaker, Robert and Karhanek, Gayle (2006). *Whatever It Takes: How Professional Learning Communities Respond When Kids Don't Learn.* Bloomington, IN: Solution Tree.

Eaton, Susan and Chiricuigno, Gina (2013). *Upstream People, Can We Show a Separate Unequal Nation a Better Way,* January Edition. Boston, MA: Harvard Law School's *One Nation Indivisible* publication.

Fay, Jim and Funk, David (1994). *Teaching with Love & Logic: Taking Control of the Classroom,* 1st Edition. *USA:* Love and Logic Press.

Ferris, Tim (2017). *Tools Of Titans: The Tactics, Routines, and Habits of Billionaires, Icons and World-Class Performers.* New York, NY: Houghton Mifflin Harcourt Publishing Company.

Ferris, Tim (2017). *Tribe Of Mentors: Short Advice from The Best In The World.* New York, NY: Houghton Mifflin Harcourt Publishing Company.

Fisher, Douglas and Frey, Nancy (2010) *Enhancing RTI: How to Ensure Success with Effective Classroom Instruction & Intervention.* Alexandria, VA: ASCD.

Fullan, Michael (2019). *Nuance: Why Some Leaders Succeed and Others Fail.* Thousand Oaks, CA: Sage Publications Ltd. Corwin.

Fullan, Michael (2014). *The Principal: Three Keys to Maximizing Impact.* San Fransisco, CA: John Wiley and Sons, Inc.

Gladwell, Malcolm (2008). *Outliers: The Story of Success,* 1st Edition. New York, NY: Little, Brown and Company.

Gladwell, Malcolm (2002). *The Tipping Point: How Little Things Can Make a Big Difference.* New York, NY: Back Bay Books.

Goleman, Daniel and Boyatzis, Richard and McKee, Annie (2013). *Primal Leadership: Unleashing The Power of Emotional Intelligence.* Boston, MA: Harvard Business Review Press.

Coleman, Daniel (2006). *Emotional Intelligence: Why It Can Matter More Than IQ--10th Anniversary Edition.* New York, NY: Bantam Dell A Division of Random House, Inc.

Gordon, Jon (2018). *The Power of The Positive Team: Proven Principles and Practices That Make Great Teams Great.* Hoboken, NJ: John Wiley & Sons, Inc.

Gordon, Jon (2017). *The Power of Positive Leadership: How and Why Positive Leaders Transform Teams and Organizations and Change the World.* Hoboken, NJ: John Wiley & Sons, Inc.

Gordon, Jon, Illustrated by Korey Scott (2012). *The Energy Bus for Kids: A Story About Staying Positive and Overcoming Challenges.* Hoboken, NJ: John Wiley & Sons, Inc.

Gordon, Jon (2008). *The No Complaining Rule: Positive Ways to Deal with Negativity at Work.* Hoboken, NJ: John Wiley & Sons, Inc.

Gordon, Jon (2007). *The Energy Bus.* Hoboken, NJ: John Wiley & Sons, Inc.

Grissom, Jason A., Anna J. Egalite, and Constance A. Lindsay. 2021. "How Principals Affect Students and Schools: A Systematic Synthesis of Two Decades of Research." New York: The Wallace Foundation. Available at www.wallacefoundation.org/principalsynthesis.

Gruenert, Steve and Whitaker, Todd (2015). *School Culture Rewired: How to Define, Assess and Transform It.* Alexandria, VA: ASCD.

Harari, Oren (2002). *The Leadership Secrets of Colin Powell.* New York, NY: McGraw-Hill Books.

Hattie, John (2008). *Visible Learning: A Synthesis of Over 800 Meta-Analyses Relating to Achievement.* Philadelphia, PA: Routledge Press.

I Love Public Schools, formerly Nebraska Loves Public Schools (2016). *Choosing Wilson: Challenging Norms to Achieve Student Success,* now listed under STEM titled: *Challenging Norms to Achieve Student Success.* Omaha, NE: Film Documentary, Sherwood Foundation https://:iloveps.org

Jensen, Eric (2017). *Poor Students Richer Teaching: Mindsets That Raise Student Achievement.* Bloomington, IN: Solution Tree Press.

Jensen, Eric (2009). *Teaching With Poverty in Mind: What Being Poor Does to Kid's Brains and What Schools Can Do About It.* Alexandria, VA: ASCD.

Jenson, William R. Ph.D. and Rhode, Ginger Ph.D. and Reavis, H. Kenton Ed.D. (1994). *The Tough Kid Toolbox.* Longmont, CO: Sopris West.

Knight, Jim (2022), *The Definitive Guide to Instructional Coaching: Seven factors For Success.* Alexandria, VA: ASCD.

Knight, Jim and forward by Fullan, Michael (2011). *Unmistakable Impact: A Partnership Approach for Dramatically Improving Instruction.* Thousand Oaks, CA: Corwin, a Sage Company.

Kouzes, James M. and Posner, Barry Z., (2002). *The Leadership Challenge Third Edition.* San Fransisco, CA: John Wiley & Sons, Inc.

Kozol, Jonathan. (2005). *The Shame of The Nation: The Restoration of Apartheid Schooling in America.* New York, NY: Crown Publishing Group, A Division of Random House, Inc.

Lemov, Doug (2010). *Teach Like a Champion: 49 Techniques That Put Students on the Path to College.* San Fransisco, CA: John Wiley & Sons, Inc.

Maxwell, John (2019). *Leader Shift: The 11 Essential Changes Every Leader Must Embrace.* Nashville, TN: Harper Collins Leadership.

Maxwell, John (2017). *No Limits: Blow the Cap Off Your Capacity.* New York, NY: Hachette Book Group, Inc.

Maxwell, John (2008*). Leadership Gold: Lessons I've Learned from a Lifetime of Leading.* Nashville, TN: Thomas Nelson, Inc.

Maxwell, John (2004). *Winning With People: Discover The People Principles That Work for You Every Time.* Nashville, TN: Thomas Nelson, Inc.

Maxwell, John (2001). *The 17 Indisputable Laws of Teamwork: Embrace Them and Empower Your Team.* Nashville, TN: Maxwell Motivation, Inc., A Georgia Corporation.

Maxwell, John (1998). *The 21 Irrefutable Laws of Leadership: Follow Them and People Will Follow You.* Nashville, TN: Maxwell Motivation, Inc., A Georgia Corporation.

Maynard, Nathan and Weinstein, Brad (2019). *Hacking School Discipline: 9 Ways to Create a Culture of Empathy & Relationship.* Highland Heights, OH: Times 10 Publications.

Marzano, Robert J. and Pickering, Debran J. and Pollack, Jane E. (2001) *Classroom Instruction That Works: Research-Based Strategies for Increasing Achievement.* Alexandria, VA: ASCD.

Mooney, Nancy J. and Mausbach, Ann T. (2008). *Align the Design: A Blueprint for School Improvement.* Alexandria, VA: ASCD.

Nelson, Ron J. and Carr, Beth Ann (2004). *The Think Time Strategy for Schools.* Longmont, CO: Sopris West Educational Services.

Parrett, William H. and Budge, Kathleen M. (2020). *Turning High-Poverty Schools into High Performing Schools: 2nd Edition.* Alexandira, VA: ASCD.

Peale, Norman Vincent (1990). *The Power of Positive Living.* New York, NY: Ballentine Publishing Group, A Division of Random House Inc.

Peale, Norman Vincent (1976). *The Positive Principle Today.* Englewood, NJ: Prentice-Hall.

Peale, Norman Vincent (1967). *Enthusiasm Makes the Difference.* Englewood, NJ: Prentice-Hall.

Peale, Norman Vincent (1952). *The Power of Positive Thinking.* Englewood, NJ: Prentice-Hall, Inc.

Payne, Ruby K. Ph.D. (2018). *A Framework For Understanding Poverty: A Cognitive Approach, 6th Edition.* Highlands, TX: Aha! Process, Inc.

Rath, Tom and Conchie, Barry (2008). *Strengths Based Leadership: Great Leaders, Teams, and Why People Follow*. New York, NY: Gallup Press.

Rath, Tom (2007). *StrengthsFinder 2.0*. New York, NY: Gallup Press.

Rath, Tom and Clifton, Donald O. (2010). *How Full is Your Bucket, Educator's Edition*. New York, NY: Gallup Press.

Reeves, Douglas B., (2009). *Leading Change in Your School: How to Conquer Myths, Build Commitment, and Get Results*. Alexandria, VA: ASCD.

Sanfelippo, Joe and Sinai, Tony (2016). *Hacking Leadership: 10 Ways Great Leaders Inspire Learning That Teachers, Students, and Parents Love*. Cleveland, OH: Times 10 Publications.

Schmoker, Mike (2018). *Focus: Elevating The Essentials to Radically Improve Student Learning, 2nd Edition*. Alexandria, VA: ASCD.

Schmoker, Mike (2016). *Leading With Focus: Elevating the Essentials for School and District Improvement*. Alexandria, VA: ASCD.

Schmoker, Mike (2006). *Results Now*. Alexandria, VA: ASCD.

Search Institute (1997). *40 Developmental Assets*, Minneapolis, MN.

Sinek, Simon (2017). *Leaders Eat Last: Why Some Teams Pull Together and Others Don't*. New York, NY: Penguin Random House LLC.

Singleton, Glenn E. and Linton, Curtis (2006). *Courageous Conversations About Race*. Thousand Oaks, CA: Corwin, Sage Publications Ltd.

Smith, Dominique and Fisher, Douglas and Frey, Nancy (2015). *Better Than Carrots or Sticks: Restorative Practices for Positive Classroom Management*. Alexandria, VA: ASCD.

Smith, Rick (2004). *Conscious Classroom Management: Unlocking the Secrets of Great Teaching*. Fairfax, CA: Conscious Teaching Publications.

Souers, Kristin and Hall, Pete (2016). *Fostering Resilient Learners*. Alexandria, VA: ASCD.

Sprague, Jeff R. and Golly, Annemieke (2005). *Best Behavior: Building Positive Behavior Supports in Schools, 2nd Edition*. Longmont, CO: Sopris West Educational Services.

Sprick, Randy and Wise, B.J. and Marcum, Kim and Haykin, Mike and McLaughlin, Bob and Hays, Suzanne (2016). *Leadership In Behavior Support*. Eugene, OR: Pacific Northwest Publishing, Inc.

Stiggins, Rick J. and Arter, Judith and Chappuis, Jan and Chappuis, Steve (2006). *Classroom Assessment for Learning*. Boston, MA: Pearson.

Stockman, Angela and Gray, Ellen Feig (2018). *Hacking School Culture: Designing Compassionate Classrooms*. Highland Heights, OH: Times 10 Publications.

Whitaker, Todd and Breaux, Annette (2013). *The Ten-Minute Inservice: 40 Quick Training Sessions that Build Teacher Effectiveness*. San Fransisco, CA: John Wiley & Sons, Inc.

Whitaker, Todd and Breaux, Annette (2010). *50 Ways to Improve Student Behavior: Simple Solutions to Complex Challenges.* Larchmont, NY: Eye on Education, Inc.

Whitaker, Todd and Whitaker, Beth and Lumpa, Dale (2000). *Motivating & Inspiring Teachers: The Educational Leader's Guide for Building Morale.* Larchmont, NY: Eye on Education, Inc.

Wong, Harry K. and Wong, Rosemary T. (2009). *The First Days of School: How to Be an Effective Teacher.* Mountain View, CA: Harry K. Wong Publications, Inc.

Wooden, John and Jamison, Steve (2007). *The Essential Wooden: A Lifetime of Lessons on Leaders and Leadership.* New York, NY: McGraw-Hill Books.

About The Author

Bret Anderson is presently a leadership consultant, speaker, trainer, coach, and motivator. His career included 20 years as a principal, one year as an assistant principal and 10 years as a teacher. His background includes successfully turning around a high poverty building, and launching an innovative new year-round school concept. In 2019, he founded Bret Anderson Consulting LLC to support schools and districts, and to cultivate better leaders. He has supervised and coached student teachers for Iowa State University and the University of Nebraska--Lincoln. In addition, he has filled in for principals and conducted staff training. His expertise lies in leadership, building a positive culture, behavior intervention, and staff capacity-building for student engagement. He mentors leaders and delivers the weekly podcast *Urban Principal: Leadership Lessons.*

Anderson has a bachelor's degree in education, a bachelor's in fine arts with a K-12 endorsement, and a master's degree in administration and supervision with a K-12 endorsement from the University of Nebraska at Omaha. He and wife Ingra received an Outstanding Service Award from the same university. They have also earned certifications as behavior consultants in the DISC Assessment System to aid in leadership development. He has received many awards, including the Outstanding Educational Leadership Award by Phi Delta Kappa.

Bret Anderson Consulting

Urban Principal: Leadership Lessons Podcast

A Word of Thanks

Hello fellow principals and leaders! I just wanted to thank everyone for liking and sharing my weekly podcast over the years. We have listeners from many countries and the podcast has become popular because of people like you! I started it on January 21st, 2020, after having retired following 31 years in a large urban district. In my 21 years as a principal, I worked to turn around a high poverty, 90% free-and-reduced lunch building for 10 years. We became a model safe school and changed achievement. I then started a one-of-a-kind innovative public school to encourage opportunities and diversity. You name it, I've probably experienced it or something close to it. Join me as I share stories, review research, and provide effective leadership practices--all with the goal of helping principals and other leaders create a positive culture.

After I retired, I started Bret Anderson Consulting LLC to assist developing leaders and train staff. The best school consultants have experienced life as a principal, have practiced leadership in schools, and have met the *10 Years--10,000 Hours Rule* (Gladwell, 2008) defining an expert in the field. I also became a certified behavior consultant to fully develop leaders. I have mentored and coached many principals and teachers. I have filled in as principal for Nebraska's largest district--including assisting the lowest ranked building in the state (in terms of state testing). My goal at this point is to promote effective leadership wherever I am able. Find out more online at BretAndersonConsulting.com!

Printed in the USA
CPSIA information can be obtained
at www.ICGtesting.com
LVHW050050180524
780611LV00001B/80